WAR OR PEACE

THE MACMILLAN COMPANY
NEW YORK · BOSTON · CHICAGO
DALLAS · ATLANTA · SAN FRANCISCO

MACMILLAN AND CO., LIMITED
LONDON · BOMBAY · CALCUTTA
MADRAS · MELBOURNE

THE MACMILLAN COMPANY
OF CANADA, LIMITED
TORONTO

WAR OR PEACE

JOHN FOSTER DULLES

THE MACMILLAN COMPANY : NEW YORK   1950

CONTENTS

PART I: *The Problem*

PART III: *The Measure of Our Foreign Policies*

PART IV: *What Needs to Be Done*

WAR OR PEACE

WARS OR PEACE

PART I

THE PROBLEM

CHAPTER ONE

THE DANGER

War is probable—unless by positive and well-directed efforts we fend it off.

War is not inevitable, and I do not think that it is imminent. Something can be done about it. If I did not think so, I would not be writing this book.

There is hope:

Provided our people see the danger clearly, as it is, so that we are not decoyed into false moves;

Provided we understand the many present policies that are good, so that we get behind them unitedly and resolutely;

Provided we see the inadequacy of present policies, so that we round them out to a global whole;

Provided we develop the spiritual power without which no policy can be more than a makeshift.

If we look about the world, we see warning signals that in the past forecast reliably the coming of war.

There exists a great power—Russia—under the control of a despotic group fanatical in their acceptance of a creed that teaches world domination and that would deny those personal freedoms which constitute our most cherished political and religious heritage.

Already Soviet Communism has extended its control over more than 700,000,000 people, or about one-third of the human race. This has happened in thirty-three years. Never before have so few gained so much so fast. Such great successes usually make men lose their heads and go on more recklessly.

The Soviet leaders have great military power. They control the world's greatest pool of dependable man power, and they now have atomic weapons.

Over against the Soviet Union stand other great powers, amongst them the United States. We, too, are maintaining a great military establishment and are intensively pushing the accumulation of atom bombs. We have decided to go ahead with the manufacture of hydrogen bombs.

An armament race is in full swing, and United Nations efforts to check that race have so far proved fruitless.

Communists have always assumed that Communism and Capitalism would become locked in a death struggle. Many people in the United States are today making that same assumption. That in turn makes war more likely and impels political leaders more and more to be guided by military judgments about winning a future war rather than by political judgments about winning peace. All of that makes for increasing tension and ultimate explosion.

If history is any guide, war will come out of this situation.

There should be no illusion about the reality of the danger. It is immense.

Future generations will look back with amazement if war is averted. It will be an achievement without precedent. Yet that is our task.

It is a task that requires an effort like the one required to win a great war.

Why should we not make that effort? Neither voice nor pen can portray the awful horror of World War III. Why should we not, for the averting of war, develop and use the qualities that would be evoked in the effort to win war?

Mankind will never win lasting peace so long as men use their full resources only in tasks of war.

While we are yet at peace, let us mobilize the potentialities, particularly the moral and spiritual potentialities, which we usually reserve for war. That is perhaps asking a good deal. But is it asking too much? I do not think so, and I believe that the American people would not think so.

Political leaders—and that goes for all, irrespective of party—tend to underestimate the people. They think that people want to be carried through life on flowery beds of ease. They usually seem zealous to provide the good things, the more abundant material life, that they think the people want.

The political leaders of the so-called "democratic" nations, who depend on popular choice, seldom try to develop moral power and a sacrificial spirit until war is upon them and when the task is no longer one of averting war but one of winning it.

If this time we wait that long, we shall have waited too long. No one will be able to "win" the next war.

I have confidence that the people of the United States are ready to make a sustained effort for peace if this is called for by leaders, official and unofficial, whom they trust, in accordance with a program which they understand and believe in. This quest for peace can be an enthralling adventure to those who recognize the danger, see the goals, and follow the moves and countermoves.

The arena is vast. It embraces the whole world, and all political, military, economic, and spiritual forces within it. The agencies are many, national and international. The scene is constantly shifting. There is no simple formula for peace, and no single act that will assure peace. Any who preach that are dangerously deluded. Only the combined result of many efforts at different levels, and at many places, will assure peace. In these efforts, everyone has a part to play.

The stakes are the greatest for which men have ever played.

I recall, as a boy, reading Robert Louis Stevenson's story "The Suicide Club." The club members were dealt cards every Saturday night and the one who drew the ace of clubs had to kill within twenty-four hours the one who drew the ace of spades. I read and re-read that story with bated breath. Today we are all, in a sense, members of a suicide club with the difference that for us it is not just a game of luck: we have the opportunity to prevent the suicide of humanity.

CHAPTER TWO

"KNOW YOUR ENEMY"

The advice to "know your enemy" has always proved good.

If we do not know who is treating us as an enemy, if we do not know what kind of person he is and how his mind works, then we cannot defend ourselves intelligently. We may find that we are building defenses against an imagined peril while exposing ourselves to the real peril.

In football there is an old trick play that still works, called the "Statue of Liberty" play. One member of the team that is on the offensive stands conspicuously poised as if to throw a forward pass. The defenders rush him, leaving a fatal gap through which the real ball carrier penetrates.

The United States must not be victimized by a "Statue of Liberty" play in which public opinion gets excited about a phantom peril, leaving the nation exposed to the real peril.

First, it is necessary to know who generates the enmity that poisons the atmosphere in which we live. There is no enmity in the hearts of the Russian people at large. No one has a quarrel with them, and they have no quarrel with us. The Russians as a nation have repeatedly shown fine qualities of loyalty, courage, and discipline. Many millions of them died in the most cruel large-scale land operation of the war, the invasion by Germany. The Russians want peace at least as much as do any other people. They are not our enemies.

The "enemy"—the self-proclaimed enemy—is the relatively small, fanatical Soviet Communist Party. Stalin is its leader, and the Politburo is the principal source of the decisions which command the blind obedience of the hard core of loyal Communist Party members everywhere in the world.

These party members have despotic political power in Russia and elsewhere. They believe that it is their duty to extend that power to all the world. They believe it right to use fraud, terrorism, and violence, and any other means that will promote their ends. They treat as enemies all who oppose their will.

Four years ago, in 1946, I wrote a study entitled "Soviet Foreign Policy, and What to Do About It." [1] What I then said has been confirmed by what has happened. Also, it has won me Communist attack and defamation ever since.

Mr. Vishinsky, in the United Nations, has attacked me as a "warmonger." He has stated, publicly, that I should be "thrown into chains." Secretary Marshall and I were portrayed in a float in the 1947 Moscow May Day Parade as chopping down the Tree of Peace, and Mr. Churchill and I have been caricatured as two torpedoes launched from a pirate submarine to sink the Ship of Peace.

Such "smear" by Communists implies no personal animus. In conferences and at social occasions we get along quite normally, and with every show of respect.

Stalin, Molotov, and Vishinsky have often tried to throw dust in our eyes by "peace offensives" which portray Western leaders as "warmongers" while Soviet leaders profess, for foreign consumption, that Soviet Communism wants to live peacefully side by side with capitalism.

The actual purposes of Soviet Communism are to be judged in the light of its official creed that is taught to the millions of Communists who make up the Party in Russia and in other countries. That creed is a far more reliable guide than the words that are occasionally uttered for our confusion.

It is not easy to understand the doctrines of Soviet Communism. They are complicated and involve rather difficult mental gymnastics. But they have a powerful grip on millions of people throughout the world. If others can understand them, they are certainly not beyond the intelligence of Americans.

[1] *Life*, June 3 and 10, 1946.

The official *History of the Communist Party of the Soviet Union* says (p. 355) that "only a party which has mastered the Marxist-Leninist theory can confidently advance and lead the working class forward."

It is equally true that only those who have mastered that theory can anticipate and thwart the moves of those who use it as a "guide to action" (p. 356).

The mechanism of a time fuse may be complicated. But if such a fuse is attached to an explosive that may blow us into eternity, it is worth while to devote a little study to the mechanism which, so long as it ticks, is ticking off the minutes that we have left to live.

The authoritative exposition of present-day Communist theory is that of Stalin. The works of Marx, Engels, and Lenin have historical interest; but their views are no longer a "guide to action" except as they are reaffirmed by Stalin.

Stalin's views are set out most authentically in the volume *Problems of Leninism*. The most recent edition, and the one currently in use, is the eleventh Russian edition published in Moscow in 1940.

The official 1940 Index of U.S.S.R. Publications, *Knijnaya Palata,* states that there were printed 13,774,000 copies of the earlier editions. There have been three printings of the 1940 edition, and the last page of the 1947 printing states that the total printing, until then, of the eleventh edition was 4,000,000 copies. That makes a total printing, to 1947, of nearly 18,000,000 copies. It has been translated into thirty-five languages.

This work of Stalin's has become to the Communist Party what Hitler's *Mein Kampf* was to the Nazi Party. It spells out the creed and purposes of Soviet Communism and its plans and methods for achieving world domination. The world neglected Hitler's book until it was too late for anything but regret. We should not make the same mistake regarding Stalin's *Problems of Leninism*.

It is not exactly amusing to read about "dialectical materialism." But, once the Soviet Communist creed is understood, it makes clear many things that are happening in the world.

Soviet Communism starts with an atheistic, Godless premise. Everything else flows from that premise.

If there is no God, there is no moral or natural law and "the material world is primary." [2] While Soviet Communism recognizes that there are spiritual things such as thought and ideas, these are merely "a reflection" of man's material environment. Therefore, according to Stalin, the principal task is "development of the material life of society" (p. 602), and particularly of the group called "the masses" or "the proletariat," who operate the mechanical tools of production.

In order to promote this material development and to "end the exploitation of man by man," all the tools of production are vested in the State, to be operated by it in accordance with the policies determined by the Party leaders.

This, it should be noted, is State socialism, *not* communism. The Soviet Union is run by a Communist Party but it does not purport to practice communism. "For the U.S.S.R. Socialism is something already achieved and won. But Soviet society has not yet reached the higher phase of Communism." (P. 569.)

The political leadership has absolute power. The dictatorship of the proletariat means "unlimited power, based on force and not on law" (p. 129). That is because only through such power can the struggle on behalf of the "masses" be won.

"Law" is not an effort to establish "right" or "justice." Since there is no moral law, there is no such thing as abstract right or justice. Laws are the means, the decrees, by which the dictatorship of the proletariat enforces its will "for suppressing the resistance of its class enemies" (p. 32).

Also, since there is no God, individuals have no God-given rights, and the individual personality has no sacredness. What is important is the material welfare of the social group. So any individuals who may have desires or beliefs that cut across the welfare of the group should be removed.

"Peace," internal and international, is looked upon as a con-

---

[2] Stalin, *Problems of Leninism*, 11th Russian ed., English text, Moscow, 1940, p. 601. The page references for later quotations from Stalin are, unless otherwise indicated, to this title and edition.

dition where everyone agrees with everyone else, where there is no disharmony, and where the productive machine is running smoothly under the direction of the political leaders acting as master mechanics. Any who do not conform are like grit in the wheels of the machine and have to be cleaned out. That explains why the population of Russian concentration camps keeps constant at around 15,000,000, despite the very high rate of mortality.

There is a duty to extend this system to all the world. It is not a "moral" duty, for of course there is no moral law. It is explained as a matter of expediency, for, it is believed and taught, the "dictatorship of the proletariat" cannot exist safely if it operates in only a few countries. There will be safety only "*if* we assume that Socialism is already victorious in all countries, or in the majority of countries, that a Socialist encirclement exists instead of a capitalist encirclement" (p. 658).

Soviet Communism teaches that the capitalist system of the so-called "imperialist" nations depends upon recurrent war. "It includes as an inevitable element imperialist wars" (p. 3), and there is in these "imperialist" countries such a hatred of Communism that their leaders are bound to try to destroy the Communist system if they can. "The bourgeois states and their organs . . . send spies, assassins and wreckers into our country and are waiting for a favorable opportunity to attack it by armed force" (p. 657).

Ever since 1917 the United States has been classified as one of the "imperialist" states (p. 34).

Since the "imperialists" will inevitably seek to destroy Communism by war, the Communist Party, it is taught, must, as a matter of defense, take the offensive and overthrow the non-Communist governments, first taking over the weaker countries, perhaps those which have been the colonial dependencies of the Western imperialists (p. 52). In that way there will be a gradual extension of "Socialism" which will, more and more, encircle the stronger "imperialist" nations.

When such encirclement has been completed or nearly completed, the moment may come for the final assault which will "smash entirely the bourgeois state machine and its old army" (p. 660) and bring about the "single state union" (p. 37) which is the international goal of Communism. Then all people, everywhere in the world, will be compelled to think alike and act in harmony in order to assure the world peace to which Soviet Communists profess to be dedicated.

The following quotations from Stalin's volume are worth pondering:

Up to a certain period the development of the productive forces and the changes in the realm of the relations of production proceed spontaneously, independently of the will of men. But that is so only up to a certain moment, until the new and developing productive forces have reached a proper state of maturity. After the new productive forces have matured, the existing relations of production and their upholders —the ruling classes—become that "insuperable" obstacle which can only be removed by the conscious action of the new classes, by the forcible acts of these classes, by revolution. (P. 617.)

To think that such a revolution can be carried out peacefully within the framework of bourgeois democracy, which is adapted to the rule of the bourgeoisie, means that one has either gone out of one's mind and lost normal human understanding, or has grossly and openly repudiated the proletarian revolution. (P. 126.)

"We are living," says Lenin, "not merely in a state, but in *a system of states,* and the existence of the Soviet Republic side by side with imperialist states for a long time is unthinkable. One or the other must triumph in the end. And before that end supervenes a series of frightful collisions between the Soviet Republic and the bourgeois states will be inevitable. That means that if the ruling class, the proletariat, wants to hold sway, it must prove its capacity to do so by military organization also." (P. 156.)

So much for theory, for creed. Turning to matters of organization, we find that the organization of the Soviet Union follows an aggressive pattern. The Communist Party and its leaders are described as the "General Staff" which the Party must have "for the successful seizure of power" (p. 79). The Soviet proletariat is considered as "the shock brigade of the world proletariat" (p. 538). The Party itself operates under "iron discipline." "The achievement and maintenance of the dictatorship of the proletariat is impossible without a party which is strong by reason of its solidarity and iron discipline . . . the parties of the Communist International, which base their activities on the task of achieving and consolidating the dictatorship of the proletariat, cannot afford to be 'liberal' or to permit freedom of factions. The Party represents unity of will, which precludes all factionalism and division of authority in the Party." (Pp. 80, 81, 82.) This internal unity is achieved by periodic purges, in the course of which it is necessary "to handle some of these comrades roughly. But that cannot be helped." (P. 542.)

The Soviet State is one of the tools of the Party. "The Party exercises the dictatorship of the proletariat. . . . not a single important political or organizational question is decided by our Soviet . . . without guiding directions from the Party." (Pp. 134–135.)

The State, in turn, under such guiding direction from the Party, is a militant organization. "The state is a machine in the hands of the ruling class for suppressing the resistance of its class enemies. . . . The dictatorship of the proletariat is the rule —unrestricted by law and based on force—of the proletariat over the bourgeoisie . . ." (Pp. 32–33.)

Under this rule, individuality is suppressed. In politics, and even in literature, science, and the arts, there is coercion to think and act along uniform Party lines, and there is forcible elimination of any elements that might be discordant.

In its foreign policy, the Soviet Union shows its adherence to the theory that the ends which it seeks can only be achieved by violent means.

For colonial areas it claims that political independence cannot come through peaceful evolution but only through revolution (p. 52).

In non-colonial areas there is penetration, secret and open, designed to bring into key positions those who accept the iron discipline of the Party and, as conditions seem opportune, resort is had to such methods as political strikes, sabotage, terrorism, guerrilla warfare and civil war.

The Party doctrines to which we have referred are intensively taught to all Party members and are fanatically accepted by many. As we shall see, there is ample evidence that Soviet policy in fact reflects those doctrines—notably, the concept that the desired changes cannot be brought about peacefully and "a 'peaceful' path of development" is possible only "in the remote future, if the proletariat is victorious in the most important capitalist countries" (p. 35).

Since the formation of the Soviet Union there has been a constant effort to portray the Union as surrounded by vicious and rapacious enemies. "We must remember that we are surrounded by people, classes and governments who openly express their intense hatred for us. We must remember that we are at all times but a hair's breadth from every manner of invasion." (P. 157.) There has been constant effort to arouse hatred toward "bourgeois" or "imperialist" peoples, and notably the British and Americans. "Let not our hatred of our foes grow cold" (*Pravda*, January, 1948). There is constant abuse and vilification of leading persons in non-Communist countries as "fascists." Normal social intercourse is looked upon as partaking of treason; intermarriage is forbidden.

It is, however, significant that *class* war, rather than *national* war, is taught as the preferred method of achieving Soviet Communist encirclement. That explains why Stalin can say, as he not infrequently does, that the Soviet Union and the United States, as nations, can coexist peacefully, i.e., without national war.

The Soviet State maintains a very powerful military establishment and devotes to it a large percentage of the national income. The existence, in the background, of this military power strengthens the hand of the Communist parties elsewhere. But, so far, there has been little to suggest that the Soviet Union intends now to use the Red Army as an actually attacking force.

The Soviet Communist Party has consistently taught that the military establishment of the State is primarily an instrument of *defense,* and that offense is primarily the task of the Party, to be carried out by its methods of class war, civil war, penetration, terrorism, and propaganda.

The distinction is important. Many feel that because Soviet Communist leaders treat us as "enemies," and because their nation has a great military establishment, it necessarily follows that the Soviet Union will fight a national war against us, and that we should concentrate on military things. Whether Soviet leaders do plan a fighting war, we shall consider more fully later on; but it is by no means *certain,* and if we treat it as certain and make our dispositions accordingly, we may fall victim to a fatal trick play.

The Party stirs up class war, civil war, or guerrilla war wherever conditions seem propitious. This technique has been successful in China, and it is now being followed in Indo-China. It was used in Greece.

The Party introduces its agents into key positions in labor unions and political parties, with a view to bringing about strikes, sabotage, and parliamentary confusion that will weaken free institutions and lay the foundation for civil unrest. This method has been used conspicuously in France and in Italy.

By intensive radio and press propaganda, it stirs up discontent wherever it can. It pictures its own system as one that will give all the unsatisfied all that they want.

By ruthlessly suppressing all opponents who fall within their power, Communist leaders terrorize many opponents still beyond it, so that they become mute lest they, too, incur a like fate if Communist power be extended to their country.

Soviet Communist tactics are the more formidable because they include the "tactics of retreat." The strategic planner, Stalin points out, always remembers that there are periods for offensive tactics and other periods for retreat; it is not necessary constantly to be on the offensive everywhere, and it is just as important to learn "how to retreat properly" as it is to learn "how to attack." It is vitally important not to be premature, and "the moment for the decisive blow" must be carefully timed (p. 64).

In this respect Soviet Communism is far more formidable than Hitler's Nazism, which seemed to believe that it was necessary always to be on the offensive and demanded victory on a short-time schedule. Speaking on August 22, 1939, Hitler said: "Essentially it [the success of the Nazi program] depends on me, my existence . . . There will probably never again be a man in the future with more authority than I have. My existence is therefore a factor of great value." [3]

Soviet Communism thinks in terms of longer time periods not measured by the life of any one man. Stalin says that "the transition from capitalism to Communism must not be regarded as a fleeting period . . . but as an entire historical era" (pp. 30, 31).

In the foregoing paragraphs I have presented as fairly as I can the doctrine of Soviet Communism and its methods as taught by Stalin. There are, I know, recurrent efforts to say that this is "old stuff" and "obsolete"; that Soviet Communism has changed; that it no longer seeks world conquest and no longer uses methods of fraud, secret penetration, and civil violence. That, in my opinion, represents wishful thinking.

I hope and believe that some day some future Russian government will declare "obsolete" much of Stalin's doctrine, just as Stalin has declared obsolete much of what Marx and Engels said. That could happen, for there have been major doctrinal changes in the past. Trotsky and Bukharin taught a very different brand of communism from Stalin's. So, too, does Tito, the "heretic." But we should never let ourselves believe that Soviet Communism has really changed from the creed above described so long as the Soviet Communists and their affiliates treat Stalin's book as their Bible and preach it and teach it to Communists and would-be Communists everywhere. Nor should we believe that Soviet Communism has changed its methods so long as we can see those methods actually applied throughout the world.

I recall a discussion that I had in the winter of 1947 in London with a leading official of a Communist country. He told me

[3] See *Nazi Conspiracy and Aggression* (published by the Office of Chief of Counsel for Prosecution of Axis Criminality), Vol. III, p. 582.

that the Communists were quite willing to lie down like lambs
with the capitalists and to give up methods of class violence.

I asked him to explain the violent political strikes then going
on in France, strikes which had been called by Thorez, the head
of the French Communist Party, when he was in Moscow. "Why,"
he said, "that is only being done because it is a necessary reply
to the Marshall Plan." I had with me a copy of Stalin's *Problems
of Leninism,* and took it from the shelf and read to him this
passage from page 597:

> ... the transition from capitalism to Socialism and the liberation of
> the working class from the yoke of capitalism cannot be effected by
> slow changes, by reforms, but only by a qualitative change of the
> capitalist system, by revolution.
>
> Hence, in order not to err in policy, one must be a revolutionary,
> not a reformist.

And I read to him from page 12 a teaching on the use of "the
political general strike."

That, I said, had been written long before there was a Marshall
Plan. So how could the Marshall Plan explain it?

We are up against something that is formidable. It is, for
the time being, immutable, though its tactics are flexible and unpredictable. The Soviet Union is not ruled by an individual
despot, like Hitler, who can act erratically, according to his own
whim and fancy. When our government negotiates with the government of the Soviet Union, it is not dealing with individuals;
it is not even dealing just with heads of State; it is dealing with
those who, in addition to being heads of State, are heads of a
Party which has a clearly enunciated creed and a membership
which adheres to that creed with almost religious fervor. There
is, in Russia, a dictatorship; but it is the dictatorship of a
party, not of an individual (p. 80).

Russians, socially, can be amiable and likable, but as officials
they are members of the Party—indeed, they are prisoners of
the Party and its creed. In Russia no Party leader can publicly
deviate from the Party line without signing his death warrant.

That applies to everyone, no matter how highly placed. It could apply even to Stalin himself.

In important negotiations with the Soviet Union, no foreigner ever deals face to face with those who make the final decision. The final decision is made by the Politburo, the top Party committee, meeting in secret.

There is no illusion greater or more dangerous than that Soviet intentions can be deflected by persuasion.

No important concessions are made except with the approval of the Politburo as a matter of expediency, "to buy off a powerful enemy and gain a respite" (p. 62).

Mark well that word "powerful."

Power is the key to success in dealing with the Soviet leadership. Power, of course, includes not merely military power, but economic power and the intangibles, such as moral judgment and world opinion, which determine what men do and the intensity with which they do it.

The Soviet Communist leaders themselves possess and exercise tremendous power; they recognize and respect power in others; but they have only contempt for pleading that stems from weakness or fear.

That is the nature of our self-styled "enemy."

CHAPTER THREE

THE GOAL

If we are going to embark upon the great task of waging peace, we should know what we mean by "peace."

Some people have a conception of peace so strange and distorted that to seek it really means war.

For example, some Americans think of peace as a condition in which our nation is isolated from all external forces and lives its own solitary life. To accept this idea is to invite war and defeat.

The Soviet program is to encircle us and to isolate us. They want this, not in order that we may go on living our own lives in peaceful isolation, but in order that they may finish us off in quick order.

I can think of nothing that would make war, and defeat, more certain for the United States than for the American people to view what is going on about them with indifference, and to sit idly by while Soviet Communism takes over country after country and completes the encirclement which it has planned in order to isolate us, to weaken us, and eventually to strangle us.

A second American misconception of peace is that it means a world dominated by the United States.

It is nothing new for peoples to identify peace with their possession of power over others. Thucydides tells us that the Corinthians, seeking to organize the Peloponnesians for war against Athens, urged them: "Vote for war; and be not afraid of the immediate danger, but fix your thoughts on the durable peace which will follow."

In 1939, a few weeks before the Second World War broke out, I was in Geneva attending an international conference. Some Germans there attempted to explain the Nazi theory, as follows: The world was like a garden which should bloom with beautiful flowers of all varieties; but only the Germans were qualified by nature and by God to be the gardeners. Therefore, if the Germans were accepted as world gardeners, everyone would be happy and bloom; the world would be a beautiful place, and Hitler would then have his "Thousand Years of Peace."

There are some Americans who rather naïvely, and to some extent unconsciously, assume that a world at peace will conform to *our* ideals and *our* wishes. There are perhaps a few who would like to assure American supremacy by what they call a "preventive war" to suppress the only apparent major obstacle to an "American peace." A few others think that peace can be achieved by so organizing the United Nations that it will always do what is "right"—by American standards.

The world has known periods when a single nation was politically dominant—in a position to compel others to conform to its views. There have been a Pax Romana and a Pax Britannica. But both were won by war. That kind of peace can be won only by war; and under modern conditions there can never be a successful "war to end war."

A third misconception is that in a world at peace everything stands still and remains as it is. This is the idea of those who are satisfied.

A frequent cause of war has been the effort of satisfied peoples to identify peace as a perpetuation of the *status quo.*

Change is the law of life, of international life as well as national and personal life. If we set up barriers to all change, we make it certain that there will be violent and explosive change.

Victors in war usually try to carve up the world to suit themselves. Then they say that "peace" means keeping it that way forever.

That is both immoral and impractical.

If you want to test that assertion, go to a public library and get out an old atlas of the world, preferably an "historical atlas."

Look at the political arrangement of the world fifty years ago, a hundred years ago, or a thousand years ago, and ask yourselves if you would like it if the world was that way today. Would it have been right or practicable to keep millions of people under the dead hand of a decaying and rotting empire?

One great weakness of the League of Nations was its attempt to preserve the *status quo*.

Peace must be a condition where international changes can be made peacefully.

So, as we strive for peace, let us not see peace as isolation, or as world domination by the United States, or as stagnation.

Peace is a condition of community, of diversity, and of change.

Americans know this, because it is the nature of our own peaceful society.

We have community, having broken down the barriers to the interstate movement of goods, people, and ideas.

We have diversity, because it is basic under our Constitution that there shall be freedom of thought and freedom of belief, and that every man shall have the right to try to persuade others to agree with him.

We have peaceful change. Our laws are made and changed by representative processes, and social and economic changes have been immense.

In the pattern of our own national life we can find the pattern for world peace.

A peaceful world will be a world in which there is intercommunication. It does not need to be a world of free trade and free emigration and immigration. But it does need to be a world in which national boundaries are not Iron Curtains.

A peaceful world is a world in which differences are tolerated, and are not eliminated by violence.

How are we to achieve the goal of a peaceful world in which governments and parties will have given up the use of fraud, terrorism, and violence?

Some people have such high moral standards that they voluntarily refrain from using bad methods to get what they want; they believe that even good and desired ends do not justify evil means. But atheists can hardly be expected to conform to an ideal so high. The only test that they can be expected to apply is the test of expediency: Does it work? Certainly, so far, Soviet Communist methods have brought amazing success.

A little band of fanatical revolutionaries, who at the beginning of the year 1917 controlled nothing, have within a generation won political control over more than 700,000,000 people representing what were twelve independent nations. They also exert a tremendous influence in the rest of the world. There is not a country in which they do not have great power through labor unions and political parties. There is scarcely a country that could not be plunged into economic disorder by political strikes called from Moscow.

How can we rid the world of evil methods if those methods can achieve such spectacular success for the users?

The answer lies in making the world such that those who use such evil methods will not, in fact, achieve great success. That means inventing policies which will cause evil methods to fail.

There is little doubt that the Communist methods of fraud, terrorism, and violence are repugnant to most people. That is agreed by the representatives of the countries who meet in the General Assembly of the United Nations.

But the repugnance is still largely in an emotional stage. It has not yet given birth to concrete policies, with power behind them, capable of so frustrating the evil methods of Soviet Communism that these will be abandoned as inexpedient.

The United States has developed a military establishment so formidable that Soviet leaders may think it inexpedient to use direct and open military aggression where it would provoke war with us. In this respect, our military policy may be good; but it does not solve the whole problem.

There is bound to be deep anxiety so long as a large part of the man power and the natural resources of the world is despotically controlled by a group who have no scruples against war as a means of getting what they want, who act in secrecy, and who could strike without warning.

Furthermore, the fact that the United States has a strong

military establishment does not check the use of fraud, terrorism, and violence as methods of indirect aggression. By these evil methods Soviet Communism has won its great postwar successes. Since the close of World War II, the Soviet Union has not actually used the Red Army for invasion in direct aggression. Therefore, a policy which, at best, merely counters direct aggression is bound to be inadequate.

We shall consider in Part II what postwar policies for peace our nation has so far evolved. In Part III, we shall appraise these policies for what we can expect from them and what are their limitations. In Part IV, we shall go on to consider what further needs to be done in order that our policies, while always peaceful, may be adequate to end the present menace.

PART II

THE POLICIES WE HAVE

CHAPTER FOUR

"NO APPEASEMENT"

The word "appease," although defined in the dictionary as, "to bring to a state of peace; to pacify," has had a bad reputation ever since the Munich deal of September 29, 1938.

At Munich, Chamberlain, Daladier, and Mussolini agreed with Hitler that Germany might annex part of Czechoslovakia. Hitler promised, in exchange, that Germany would seek no more territory. That deal was supposed to bring "peace in our time"; and for a few days it was joyously hailed by some who had felt the hot breath of imminent war.

However, it turned out otherwise. Giving Hitler part of Czechoslovakia merely whetted his appetite. On March 15, 1939, he occupied additional Czech territory. On March 20, he took Memel from Lithuania; and then he started to make passes at Poland.

The British government thereupon changed its policy. It said on March 24, 1939, that it would guarantee the integrity of Poland. Nevertheless, Hitler attacked Poland on September 1; and then, on September 3, England, with France joining, declared war on Germany and the Second World War began.

Stalin gave a vivid portrayal of this period of "appeasement." On March 10, 1939, he taunted what he called "the non-aggressive states, primarily England, France and the U.S.A.," for

making concession after concession to the aggressors. . . . Thus we are witnessing an open redivision of the world and spheres of influence at the expense of the non-aggressive states.

The chief reason is that the majority of the non-aggressive countries, particularly England and France, have rejected the policy of collective security, the policy of collective resistance to the aggressors, and have taken up a position of non-intervention, a position of "neutrality" (p. 625).

The conclusion generally drawn from the happenings of this 1938–1939 period is that Stalin was right. Strong nations which want peace cannot buy it by throwing bits of weaker nations into the jaws of ambitious despots. That only makes them more rapacious.

However, when both Russia and the United States were drawn into the Second World War and became military allies, Stalin took a different view. Then he demanded, notably at Yalta in February, 1945, that the Soviet Union should be appeased by England and the United States agreeing to the expansion of Soviet power in China and in Poland and other Central European areas.

Whether or not that appeasement was justified as a war measure will, no doubt, always remain controversial.

Our concern here is with the influence of wartime appeasements upon United States postwar policies for peace.

The Soviet thesis was that future peace required agreement between the United States and the Soviet Union. If these two great powers *did* agree, they argued, then peace was assured. If they fell out, then war was probable. Therefore, the argument went on, the United States, in the interest of peace, must do whatever the Soviet Union demanded as the price of agreement. If the United States did not, those who represented it would be "warmongers."

The United States had to face that issue at the first major postwar conference. That was the initial meeting of the Council of Foreign Ministers. It was held in London in September and October, 1945. Mr. Byrnes was there as the United States Secretary of State; and I, as a Republican, was with him as adviser.

The Council, as provided by the Potsdam Agreement, was made up of the foreign ministers of China, France, the United Kingdom, the Soviet Union, and the United States. The five began to discuss the Italian, Balkan, and Finnish peace treaties. We made quite good progress and, in fact, agreed to what became the essential elements of these peace treaties as finally signed on February 10, 1947. But after about ten days Mr. Molotov, to the amazement of all of us, stated that he had just come to realize that our procedure was faulty. The Chinese foreign minister, he said, had had no right to be in the room during discussions relating to the Italian peace treaty, and the foreign ministers of France and China had had no right to be in the room when the Balkan and Finnish peace treaties were discussed, because their nations were not parties to the "surrender terms." Accordingly, the French and Chinese foreign ministers should be compelled to withdraw, and the decisions already taken in their presence would have to be rescinded because they were tainted with illegality.

On its face, the question seemed procedural; but it had plenty of substance. The demand was, in essence, that England and the United States should join the Soviet Union in publicly humiliating the governments of France and China.

If the United States had given in to that demand, we would have destroyed the chance, which we then still had, of keeping in China a government that was friendly to us. We would have destroyed the chance of keeping in France a government friendly to us.

In both China and France there were at that time very powerful Communist parties seeking control. They surely would have gained it quickly if the United States had consented to humiliate publicly the non-Communist leaders of these countries at the demand of the Soviet leaders. That, however, was the price tag that Molotov put on Soviet agreement. President Truman tried to alter the demand by a personal message to Marshal Stalin. But Stalin sent back a flat rejection.

The Soviet demand raised clearly the broad issue of whether, now that the war was over, the United States would go on sacrificing the interests of friendly, but weaker, governments in order to preserve the outward appearance of agreement with the Soviet

Union. Was *war* appeasement to be continued in the form of *peace* appeasement?

During these days of the 1945 London Council of Foreign Ministers, Mr. Molotov conducted himself with an adroitness which has been seldom equaled in diplomacy. The Council gatherings were small—the foreign ministers, each with four advisers, gathered around a large round table. It is in groups of such a size that Mr. Molotov, a skillful fencer, performs to best advantage. Large gatherings are more effectively addressed by Mr. Vishinsky, the great prosecutor. His words, even when uttered in a language that is not understood, strike with the force of bullets from a machine gun.

Mr. Molotov at London in 1945 was at his best.

Circumstances favored him. He himself had had long international experience, having been foreign minister since 1939. His four colleagues were attending their first important conference as foreign ministers, except that Mr. Bevin had been at Potsdam for the last five days of that conference.

Mr. Molotov had sized up with consummate skill possibilities through which, by artful exploitation, he might advance his ends.

Secretary Byrnes spoke freely, and wholly "off the cuff." He had proven ability to talk men into agreement, but he was not always legalistically precise. Molotov sought repeatedly to draw him out, hoping that, since Mr. Byrnes was speaking extemporaneously, he might somewhere in the course of an extended talk utter some words or phrases that could be seized upon as fitting into the Soviet program. After Mr. Byrnes had spoken, Mr. Molotov would frequently say that he was perplexed because Mr. Byrnes had seemed to state his position in slightly different ways. What, precisely, was it that he proposed? Would not Mr. Byrnes be good enough to restate the case so as to clarify it? Mr. Molotov obviously hoped that, by evoking statements and restatements that were extemporaneous, he might bring about a misstatement upon which he could seize.

Mr. Byrnes eluded all dangerous pitfalls. It was a game of wits that was fascinating to observe.

Towards Mr. Bevin, Mr. Molotov adopted a different technique. Mr. Bevin was bluff and hearty, easily angered and quickly repentant of his anger. Mr. Molotov treated him as a banderillero treats a bull, planting darts that would arouse him to an outburst—from which he rapidly reacted in a manner implying a tendency to make concessions. On one occasion he was provoked into saying that Mr. Molotov talked like Hitler. Mr. Molotov jumped to his feet, saying that he had not come to London to be insulted by the British foreign minister. He left his place at the table and stalked to the door. Mr. Bevin, with contrition, hastened to explain away his heated words and, as a mark of his sincerity, indicated that he would concede the point then in dispute.

Mr. Molotov had been careful to open the door very slowly, and he got back long before the translation into Russian had been made. But he gained, he thought, a slight advantage.

Mr. Molotov's objective with Mr. Bidault was to provoke him to leave the conference. To that end, he played upon the sensitiveness which is natural to the French character, and which was particularly marked at that time. For the first time since the surrender of 1940, France was sitting as an equal at the table of the great. French feelings were still raw from the indignity of exclusion from the inner conferences at San Francisco and total exclusion at Potsdam. So, Mr. Molotov tried to outrage French honor by petty slights. He would, for example, ask Mr. Bevin and Mr. Byrnes for a postponement by an hour of the time for meeting and then would not tell Mr. Bidault. Mr. Bidault, appearing punctually at the original hour, would sit with growing impatience as no colleagues appeared; or he would return to his hotel. On occasions, he was on the verge of returning to Paris. But he always stopped short of falling into the trap which Mr. Molotov had set.

Mr. Wang, the Chinese Foreign Minister, was stolid and shrewd. He spoke rarely and could not be provoked. The Molotov technique was to ignore him. When Mr. Wang did speak, Mr. Molotov paid no attention whatever and proceeded as though nothing were being said. He made it clear that China, or at least

Nationalist China, was to him a cipher, and that Mr. Wang's seat might as well have been vacant.

Mr. Molotov put on a remarkable performance. His techniques, different in each case, were carried out with extraordinary skill. I have seen in action all the great international statesmen of this century, beginning with those who met at the Hague Peace Conference of 1907. I have never seen personal diplomatic skill at so high a degree of perfection as Mr. Molotov's at that session.

It did not, however, get the results that Mr. Molotov wanted. The professional artistry of Mr. Molotov had to succumb to the sincerity of his colleagues. In the end, Mr. Molotov had to fall back on a crude ultimatum—the Soviet would not proceed unless France and China withdrew, and unless all decisions contaminated by their presence were deemed null and void and considered anew.

When it appeared that the Soviet position was adamant, the United States delegation had days of great anxiety. It was difficult for Secretary Byrnes. This was his first great conference as Secretary of State and the first meeting of the Council of Foreign Ministers. He had come to his position as Secretary of State partly because he had a great faculty for compromise of political differences, for finding formulas on which opposing interests could agree. It was not pleasant for him to contemplate returning empty-handed.

It was also apparent that failure to reach agreement with the Soviet Union would have grave consequences. There was much truth in the Soviet argument that, if our two nations were unable to agree, peace would be in jeopardy.

On Sunday morning, September 30, 1945, Secretary Byrnes and I talked alone in his bedroom at Claridge's Hotel. We explored together the problem, and the Secretary asked whether I did not feel that there was some basis upon which we could effect a compromise. I told him that I saw none.

We went from the hotel to the Council chamber at Lancaster House. Secretary Byrnes had given me no inkling as to what would be his final decision. It emerged, however, in the course of the day's debate. He rejected the Soviet demand. He would not, for the sake of agreement with the Soviet Union, make a compromise that would sacrifice our country's historic friendship with China and France.

At that moment our postwar policy of "no appeasement" was born; and, on the whole, it has been adhered to ever since. We refused to pay international blackmail.

The policy of "no appeasement" does not, of course, mean a policy of refusing to make genuine compromises. Neither does it mean that we seek disagreement just for disagreement's sake. Compromise is an essential part of every peaceful society. But compromise implies a genuine willingness on the part of each party to give something up, and usually something of its own, not something that belongs to another nation. But it is contrary to the creed of Soviet Communism to give up anything that it is in its *power* to take or keep.

At Yalta, Marshal Stalin may have seemed to agree to some restraining conditions. In fact, the Soviet Union never observed those restraints. Once the Soviet leaders had what they wanted from the United States, they went on to achieve their original objective, using our concessions as a springboard for further aggressive expansion, a further "redivision" of the world in their favor.

Our action at the London meeting has had momentous consequences—as we realized it would have. It marked the end of an epoch, the epoch of Teheran, Yalta, Potsdam. It marked the ending of any pretense by Soviet Communists that they were our "friends." It began the period when their hostility to us was openly proclaimed throughout the world.

That has been an unpleasant business; but it was bound to come. It is better that it came before we had made any further great concessions to the Soviet Union at the expense of our friends. A little more, and we should have been without friends or honor in the world.

On my return to the United States, I said in a radio broadcast on October 6, 1945, that what had happened at London "has not *created* difficulties. It has merely *revealed* difficulties of long standing which war has obscured. It is healthier that we now know the facts."

After nearly five years of undisguised unfriendliness, public opinion in many of the Western countries is showing a natural and proper anxiety to have the strain relieved. That should not, however, mean going back to the pattern of Teheran and Yalta where fine-sounding words gave an appearance of agreement and friendliness.

Soviet leaders are constantly dangling that old bait before us. At all recent meetings of the United Nations Assembly the Soviet leaders have pressed for "agreements" to disarm. They have constantly urged "agreements" to outlaw atomic weapons. They have made it clear, not once but many times, that they want "agreements." But always these "agreements" are agreements:

> Which we would live up to, but which they could evade;
>
> Which would lull us into a sense of false security so that we would cut out the military and economic props that undergird the free world;
>
> Which would give Soviet Communism a basis to claim that we were their moral accomplices in consolidating their positions in the vast areas they had overrun, and in extending those positions so long as they used methods short of war.

Secretary Acheson said on February 8, 1950, that it is possible to have agreements with the Soviet Union "when those agreements register or record an existing situation or fact, but otherwise they are not of much use."

At the meeting of the Council of Foreign Ministers held in Paris during May and June, 1949, where Secretary Acheson represented the United States and I was with him as adviser, we did indeed make some agreements with the Soviet Union. The most significant one provided against reimposing the blockade on Berlin. That agreement recognized the fact that by the airlift we had demonstrated our ability and our resolve to overcome the blockade.

We did not sacrifice either our own position or the interests of our friends to get that agreement. We were not lulled by the agreement into thinking that there is no more danger to our position in Western Berlin. The airlift is kept ready to resume on a moment's notice.

Agreements of limited scope may from time to time be practical and advantageous. But lack of agreement should not so frighten us that we cast reason and experience to the winds and revert to the policy of seeking agreement in words merely in order to have a pretext for relaxing. We dropped that mood at the 1945 London Council of Foreign Ministers, and it was a good riddance.

We should never make concessions or alter our position merely because the Soviet leaders give us promises or merely because we want a façade of agreement, irrespective of whether there is reality behind it.

If we stick to that rule of conduct we shall have one of the good and solid policies needed to support our program for peace. It is a negative policy, and so not of itself sufficient. But it is a sound policy that cannot long be ignored without disaster.

CHAPTER FIVE

UNITED NATIONS

It is often said that the United Nations is the cornerstone of United States foreign policy. That is a good sentiment. However, it is rather vague. In order to judge just what can be accomplished by or through the United Nations, it is important to understand the nature of this world organization. What can it do? And what can it not do? It cannot do everything. It does not automatically guarantee peace. It has great possibilities. But those possibilities are different from what many people think they are.

A little history may be illuminating.

ATLANTIC CHARTER

When President Roosevelt and Prime Minister Churchill met off Newfoundland in August, 1941, and drew up their Atlantic Charter statement of peace aims, no mention was made of an international organization. Mr. Churchill, as we have since learned, had proposed to include this; but President Roosevelt was unwilling. He told Mr. Sumner Welles that he thought "nothing could be more futile than the reconstitution of a body such as the Assembly of the League of Nations." According to Mr. Welles, the President felt a transition period would be necessary, "during which period Great Britain and the United States would undertake the policing of the World." [1]

What happened is instructive. It shows the important part that private leadership and individual effort can play in influencing national policies for peace.

[1] Sumner Welles, *Where Are We Heading?* p. 5.

The churches took a strong lead in favor of international organization. The Federal Council of the Churches of Christ in America already, in December, 1940, had acted to set up a Commission on a Just and Durable Peace, of which I was chairman. Our Commission held its first full meeting in September, 1941, just after the promulgation of the Atlantic Charter. We immediately launched a campaign to educate United States public opinion to the need for world organization. Most of the Protestant churches of the country set up "study groups" on world order. The Commission conducted "national missions on world order" which took leading ministers and laymen to the principal cities of the United States. It issued a "Six Pillars of Peace" statement which set out briefly and cogently the need for world organization and the tasks it should assume. The statement became widely known here and abroad.

In this matter the Protestant churches cooperated closely with Roman Catholic and with Jewish groups. Despite theological differences they could, and did in this matter, seek common goals.

These and other efforts bore early fruit in Congress. During 1943 resolutions favoring world organization were adopted by both the Senate and the House; and on October 7, 1943, Secretary Hull went to Moscow for a conference on this subject with the foreign ministers of the United Kingdom and the Soviet Union. On October 30, 1943, he concluded there with the other two ministers and the Chinese Ambassador a "Four Nation Declaration" for a world organization.

Public opinion had taken the lead, and in two years had transformed the attitude of the government.

DUMBARTON OAKS

The Moscow decision of October 30, 1943, was a major step forward. But it was little more than a decision "in principle." To translate the principle into a concrete program raised difficult and important questions. They were dealt with at the conference of representatives of the Soviet Union, United Kingdom, and United States convened at Dumbarton Oaks on August 21, 1944.

That conference had been very ably prepared by Mr. Leo

Pasvolsky of the State Department and his staff, under the guidance of Secretary Hull and, while he was Under Secretary, Mr. Sumner Welles. The United States was now taking a strong initiative.

But the Dumbarton Oaks Conference operated under certain disadvantages.

It was not an open conference. Often preparatory work is better done in private; but, to get the best final results, public opinion should be made a full partner.

In the second place, only the "Big Three" drew up the Dumbarton Oaks Proposals. They were the principal powers then waging war against Germany and Japan, and perhaps on that account felt that peace depended primarily on the strong nations' using military power to impose their idea of "peace" on the rest of the world.

It was perhaps inevitable that the Dumbarton Oaks Conference, which was of a preliminary nature, should be a private conference, and that it should be confined to the then Big Three. (China was allowed afterward to rubber-stamp what the three had done.) That had certain advantages. Also it had disadvantages, one of which was that there crept into the conclusions the conception that peace was a great-power military policing of the world.

When the Dumbarton Oaks Proposals were published on October 9, 1944, they were accepted with some reservation by those of us who had worked to create a body of public opinion in favor of world organization. Church groups and others set to work again in favor of a revision of the Dumbarton Oaks Proposals at the international conference which was to be called sometime in 1945.

We felt that the Dumbarton Oaks Proposals put excessive dependence upon the postwar unity of the "Big Four." In an address to the Federal Council of the Churches on November 28, 1944, I said that the provisions for the use of military contingents by the Security Council, hedged about by veto power, "presuppose a political unanimity of the great powers which has rarely occurred and which, if it prevails, will itself assure peace."

Since concerted military policies by the "great" powers could not be dependably relied on, there would be need for ways for a world organization to invoke moral power—the power of world opinion. Also, the smaller powers deserved a position of greater influence. Both of these objectives called for putting more reliance upon the proposed General Assembly. It was to be made up of representatives of *all* member nations, and the debates which would take place there would both educate world opinion and reflect the moral judgment of the world.

We also felt that there was need for a Commission on Human Rights and for a mechanism whereby the world organization could express its concern for the colonial peoples and help them to evolve peacefully to self-government.

SAN FRANCISCO CONFERENCE

When the San Francisco Conference was first conceived it was assumed that its task would be merely that of getting the smaller nations to endorse what the Big Three, and then China, had agreed to at Dumbarton Oaks. However, when it actually met its task was recognized to be the much greater one of radically revising the Dumbarton Oaks Proposals so that the world organization could survive and accomplish something even if the Big Four should in the future fall out among themselves.

That task of revision was the more difficult because the United States and the United Kingdom felt committed to stand by the Dumbarton Oaks Proposals unless the Soviet Union were willing to change them. Thus the Soviet Union had in effect a veto power over any change from the Dumbarton Oaks Proposals.

The hardest task at San Francisco was to get the Soviet Union to agree to open up the world organization as a place where world problems would be openly discussed. The Soviet government believes in rule by the strong of the weak. It believed that the ideal procedure was for the Soviet Union and the United States, as the two strongest powers, to agree privately on what needed to be done and then to impose their will upon the other nations of the world. Mr. Molotov and Mr. Gromyko, representing the Soviet Union at San Francisco, were particularly stubborn in their opposition to provisions which would enlarge the right of open discussion within the Security Council and the General Assembly.

The Soviet delegates insisted that the Soviet Union should have the right to prevent, by veto, any discussion in the Security Council which it did not like. They claimed that such discussion, in the absence of unanimous agreement, would publicly disclose differences among the great powers, and that such disclosure would itself be against the interests of peace.

The United States Delegation felt that to carry the veto to this length would largely destroy the usefulness of the Security Council. We insisted that there must be a veto-less right of discussion.

It seemed for a time that the conference would break on this issue. The Soviet delegates were adamant. So were we of the United States Delegation. We had the support of virtually all the other nations represented.

When the deadlock at San Francisco seemed complete, Secretary Stettinius sent to Moscow on June 2, 1945, a forthright and courageous statement of the position of the United States. The purport of it was that the United States would rather abandon world organization than have one which would be as impotent as the organization that the Russians demanded. That, we felt, would be a fraud and would frustrate the great hopes of mankind which we were attempting to realize.

At the time, Harry Hopkins was in Moscow discussing generally the future of Soviet-American relations in view of President Roosevelt's death. He and Ambassador Harriman delivered the message to Marshal Stalin on June 6th. The result was immediate instructions to the Soviet Delegation at San Francisco to concede that no single power should have the right to veto discussion within the Security Council.

The same issue arose again when we came to the matter of discussion in the General Assembly. There again the Soviet Union demanded limitations. It did not want the Assembly to be in a position to discuss matters which the Soviet Union thought might concern itself alone, and which it would want to handle in its own way, free of the possibility of public comment and exposure. Again the issue was joined.

We were now nearing the announced last days of the conference, and the time for signing the Charter had already been fixed. Again Secretary Stettinius took a strong line, with the unanimous backing of his Delegation. On June 19th he notified the Soviet delegates and Ambassador Harriman at Moscow that unless a satisfactory solution was found by noon of the next day the United States would propose that the conference vote its own text, leaving the Soviet Union to withdraw if it wanted. Precisely at twelve o'clock the next day, June 20th, Mr. Gromyko telephoned that he had received instructions from Moscow to concur in a formula that was acceptable to the conference as a whole.

There were many important issues at San Francisco in addition to these two I have described. Some of them will be touched on in later chapters dealing with specific policies. I have reviewed at this point the two episodes concerning the right of discussion in the Security Council and in the General Assembly because they reveal what kind of organization we thought we were creating.

Already, the United States Delegation saw that it was unlikely that the United Nations could be a means for "enforcing peace" by using the military and economic might of the great powers to impose policies upon which they agreed. We saw that the only kind of power that could be counted on at this stage of world development was moral power and the power of world opinion. That is why we attached the utmost importance to provisions for insuring freedom of discussion in the General Assembly and at the Security Council. We wanted the United Nations to become, in Senator Vandenberg's words, the "Town Meeting of the World." We knew that, as such, it could exert an influence for peace. That was the possibility which, above all, we sought to develop in San Francisco, and which we did develop.

That is the possibility in the United Nations which needs to be understood today if United States policy is to make the United Nations its cornerstone.

There are today some critics of what was done at San Fran-

cisco. It is said that we should have made the United Nations
into more of a "world government," with a military establishment
of its own which would carry out the decisions of the Security
Council to be arrived at by some majority, free of veto. Some
think that the United Nations is a futility because it is not that
kind of organization, and that it will continue to be a futility
until it is made into that kind of organization.

No one who was at San Francisco or who has any intimate
knowledge of the international conditions that then prevailed can
believe that it was possible, even if desirable, to make the United
Nations into a "world government." It was necessary to strain
relations with the Soviet Union to the utmost in order to get a
veto-less right of discussion in the Security Council and to get a
right of broad discussion in the General Assembly. To think that
the Soviet Union would have exposed itself to military action at
the direction of a Security Council in which it would obviously
be a minority is to abandon reality and to deal in the realm of
fantasy.

Furthermore, even if the Charter had been written in the way
that some would apparently have preferred, we can be sure that
the added powers would not in fact have been used, because use
of them would have precipitated a third world war.

There is much talk of an international "police force," as though
that, if constituted, would itself assure peace. But it should be
remembered that a true "police force" is effective only against a
few individuals *who are defying the will of their own community*.
A "police force" cannot enforce a law that the community considers has no moral sanction. In that case either the law becomes
a dead letter, like our prohibition law, or else the "police force"
has to be expanded into an army and war results, as when our
northern states attempted to enforce upon the southern states
their interpretation of the Constitution.

The "weakness" of the United Nations is not primarily due to
the fact that the San Francisco Conference wrote into the Charter
the veto power which had been agreed upon at Yalta. It is not due
primarily to the failure of the Charter to carry a sufficient grant
of power. The great weakness is that, on many important mat-

ters, there is not a consensus of moral judgment or the moral judgment does not make itself felt. No form of government can work effectively under these conditions except as a despotic "police state."

Recently I read a newspaper dispatch about attempted assassinations and violence in Detroit. It was headed "Something in Detroit Is Seriously Wrong," and said that, although the Detroit police force was thoroughly sound, "in any city the police are a small minority. They can't do much about preserving order unless they have their community's overwhelming moral support. This moral support has deteriorated in Detroit."

World policemen, in this respect, would be no different from Detroit policemen. They could not do much about preserving order in the world unless they had the "overwhelming moral support" of the world community.

The United Nations represents not a *final* stage in the development of world order, but only a primitive stage. Therefore its primary task is to create the conditions which will make possible a more highly developed organization. That requires developing a consensus of moral judgment and stimulating it into becoming an effective influence in the world community. Then, perhaps, a world police force could work.

The great achievement at San Francisco was a charter that was reasonably related to the actual state of the world. At the time I said:

The present Charter represents a conscientious and successful effort to create the best world organization which the realities permit. Of course, anyone who is free to disregard realities and to act only in the realm of theory can write a "better" Charter. A reasonably intelligent schoolboy could do that. The task of statesmanship, however, is to relate theory to reality. Political institutions ought to come as close to theoretical perfection as is consonant with their vigorous survival in the existing environment. Orchids may be the perfect flower. But it is a waste of time to plant orchids in Iceland. That is what many peace planners would do.[2]

[2] *Foreign Affairs*, Oct., 1945.

It is vitally important to understand what the United Nations is, and what it is not. A great deal of disappointment and disillusionment comes from the fact that many people thought that the Charter as drawn up at San Francisco created "world government." Because it does not work that way, they feel that the United Nations has failed.

Every instrument has its own distinctive possibilities and, in order to get the best results, has to be used with skill. The United Nations is a political instrumentality that has great possibilities for good, if these are understood. The United Nations cannot do everything. Its uses are limited by its nature. It is not a substitute for United States foreign policy, and its activities cannot relieve the United States of major responsibilities of its own. But, as we shall see as we go on to discuss the United Nations in operation, its possibilities are such that the United Nations can be, and should be, a cornerstone of United States foreign policy.

CHAPTER SIX

THE UNITED NATIONS IN OPERATION

There is no room in this book for a history of the manifold activities of the United Nations. It will, however, be useful to take from the actual experience of the United Nations certain examples which illustrate how the United Nations deals with vital political problems. When we examine them we can better judge the extent to which United States policy can support and rely on the United Nations as an agency for peace.

IRAN

The first major political problem that came to the Security Council was the case of Soviet troops in Iran (Persia). The government of Iran wanted the Soviet Union to withdraw them in accordance with an agreement that this would be done after the war was over. Iran took its demand to the Security Council when first the Security Council was organized in London during the January–February, 1946, session of the General Assembly.

The plea of Iran was strongly supported by the United Kingdom, with which it had close political and economic relations. Mr. Bevin, the British Foreign Secretary, sat as the representative of the United Kingdom, and Mr. Vishinsky, then the Soviet Under Secretary for Foreign Affairs, was the representative of the Soviet Union.

As a countermove, the Soviet Union made a request that British troops be withdrawn from Greece and put it on the agenda for February 1, 1946.

Mr. Bevin and Mr. Vishinsky went at each other, hammer and

tongs. It was a frightening beginning for the Security Council. The outcome was that the Soviet troops were withdrawn from Iran on May 21, 1946, and that British troops remained in Greece.

What is the explanation of this result? The Security Council had no legal power of action against the Soviet Union, which possessed, and was prepared to exercise, the right of veto; but, thanks to what we had done at San Francisco, the Soviet Union could not veto discussion. The discussion took place, and world opinion was convinced that the continued presence of Soviet troops in Iran would, in effect, be aggression by a great power against a small power. The Soviet Union did not at that time care to flout that judgment, and moral power prevailed.

In the case of Greece, the discussion in the Security Council made it apparent that the Greek government wanted British troops to stay and help to defend and protect the country against Communist guerrillas who were being spurred on and helped by the three Communist governments to the north—Albania, Bulgaria, and Yugoslavia. The situation was the exact opposite of that in Iran, and world opinion concluded that the British government was not an aggressor against Greece, but a defender of Greece.

Stalin once remarked of the League of Nations that "despite its weakness, the League might nevertheless serve as a place where aggressors can be exposed, and as a certain instrument of peace, however feeble, that might hinder the outbreak of war" (p. 628).

The cases of Iran and Greece show that Stalin's appraisal of the League of Nations is equally applicable to the United Nations. It is, in its own right, weak; but its power to expose gives it influence. If the spotlight is turned on one who is perpetrating a theft, he will often drop his booty. The power to turn on a light so bright that all the world can see is itself an enormous power.

Let us suppose that there had been no veto power in the Security Council, and that it had had a large military establishment at its disposal. Would it have voted to use its military power to expel Soviet armies from Iran? Certainly not. The Soviet government would never have ordered retreat under the threat of any such compulsion; the United Nations would not have had enough power to force retreat, and an attempt to use force could have precipitated World War III.

Soviet withdrawal occurred under an influence far more persuasive than military force; namely, the force of world opinion.

GREECE

The position of Greece has continuously concerned the United Nations. British troops had fought the Germans in Greece during World War II, and, as we have seen, the end of that war found them there. They helped the Greek government to hold in check the guerrilla warfare that was being promoted by the Communist governments to the north. But as the intensity of the Communist threat increased and the burden of resisting it became heavier, the British government came to feel that it alone could no longer carry the cost. Early in 1947 it privately told our government that it felt unable to go on alone in Greece; that, unless the United States was prepared to help out, it would withdraw, with the probable result that Greece would fall, Turkey would be encircled, and the entire Eastern Mediterranean and Near East would fall under Soviet Communist domination.

The stakes were so great that President Truman decided that the United States should step into the breach. On March 12, 1947, in an address to the Congress, he set forth a program for United States aid to Greece and Turkey in recognition of the fact, as he put it, "that totalitarian regimes imposed on free peoples, by direct or indirect aggression, undermine the foundations of international peace and hence the security of the United States." This pronouncement became known as the Truman Doctrine.

However, the United States, while it was disposed to help carry the burden that the United Kingdom felt compelled to lay down, did not want to seem disregardful of the United Nations. The Senate, on the initiative of Senator Vandenberg, wrote provisions into the enabling legislation designed to relate our action to the future wishes of the United Nations.

The Greek government, too, wanted not merely material aid from the United States, but the protection that could come from a United Nations public exposure of the menace of indirect aggression from the Communist governments to the north of Greece.

It seemed clear that the exposure could not be authoritative or command wide public credence unless there was an investigation by a United Nations commission. At first the Security Council attempted to deal with the matter; and with Soviet concurrence it set up a commission of investigation. A majority of the commission reported that Albania, Bulgaria, and Yugoslavia were assisting the Greek guerrillas. But when the Security Council attempted further investigation in the light of the report it was balked by the veto of the Soviet Union. So, on September 15, 1947, the matter was taken off the agenda of the Security Council and transferred to the United Nations Assembly, where there is no veto power.

After long and acrimonious debate, the United Nations Assembly decided, on October 21, 1947, by a vote of 40 to 6 with 11 abstentions, to send a commission to the Balkans. Places on this commission were offered to the Soviet Union and Poland, in order to assure that all viewpoints would be represented. However, they declined to take part.

The commission went to Greece. It was kept out of Albania, Bulgaria, and Yugoslavia, but it continuously observed conditions along the northern border of Greece. The members of the commission were in the thick of the guerrilla operations and, indeed, one of its staff was wounded by a land mine. They saw the extent to which Greek Communist guerrillas based themselves upon the territory of Albania, Bulgaria, and Yugoslavia and received material support from them. The very presence of the commission had a salutary effect. The Communist governments to the north of Greece would have helped Markos, the Greek Communist revolutionary leader, much more had it not been that everything they did would have been observed on the spot by a responsible United Nations Commission and reported to the world in a manner which would leave no doubt as to the truth.

In the fall of 1948 the Assembly voted to continue the Balkan

Commission for another year, and in the fall of 1949 it was continued by a vote of 50 to 6 with 2 abstentions.

During the Assembly debates about this commission the Soviet Union tried to get the United Nations Assembly to call for a termination of United States economic and military aid to Greece. The efforts were defeated by an overwhelming vote that was, in effect, an endorsement of the Truman Doctrine in relation to Greece.

The combined result of Greek courage, United States aid, and United Nations supervision has been that, whereas three years ago it seemed probable that Communism would take over Greece by indirect aggression, now it seems that the indirect aggression has been frustrated, and that the Greek people, at long last, may have enough internal peace to heal the terrible wounds successively inflicted upon them by Fascist Italy, by Nazi Germany, and by Communist-inspired guerrillas.

It must in all honesty be recognized that the favorable turn of events has been aided by the quarrel between Tito and Stalin, which caused the government of Yugoslavia to concentrate upon defending itself against indirect aggression from Soviet Communism. Despite this development, so fortunate for Greece, a great share of the credit must go to the United Nations.

Again it was proved that Stalin was right when he recognized the importance of "a place where aggressors can be exposed."

KOREA

Korea provides another illustration of the power of the United Nations. At Cairo on December 1, 1943, it had been agreed that Japanese-dominated Korea would receive independence "in due course." At Yalta in February, 1945, it was informally agreed that there should be an interim period of trusteeship. At the Moscow Conference held in December, 1945, the foreign ministers of the United States, the United Kingdom, and the U.S.S.R. agreed that the trusteeship should be for five years, administered by four powers—China, the United Kingdom, the Soviet Union, and the United States. However, matters did not work out that way.

Under the Japanese surrender terms, the Japanese in Korea north of the 38th parallel had been instructed to surrender to Soviet armies. Those south of that parallel had been instructed to surrender to the United States armies. The result was a *de facto* division of Korea.

Many months of negotiation demonstrated that it was impossible for the United States and the Soviet Union to agree upon the terms under which these two parts of Korea would be reunited and the Four Power Trusteeship inaugurated.

The United States wanted to withdraw its troops from Southern Korea; but it did not want to do so as a "scuttle and run" operation, which would seem to involve its abandoning a moral responsibility to the people of Korea, whose independence we had pledged.

By the fall of 1947 direct negotiations had totally collapsed, and on September 17th the United States brought the problem to the United Nations Assembly. We proposed that the idea of trusteeship should be scrapped; that Korea should be at once united and given independence under a government of its own, chosen through popular elections to be supervised by a commission of the United Nations.

The Soviet Union violently opposed this proposal. But on November 14th the United Nations Assembly, by an overwhelming vote of 43 to 0 with 6 abstentions, decided to send a commission to Korea to study the situation and to assist in the establishment of a Korean government, provided there could be a fair and free popular election. The United States was not, itself, represented on the commission.

The United Nations commission went to Korea and received full opportunity to conduct its investigations in the South. It was not, however, allowed to set foot in the Soviet zone of North Korea. Since South Korea formed about two-thirds of the country, both in area and in population, and since conditions there permitted a free and fair election, elections were held. A high percentage of the population voted, after a vigorous electoral campaign. The United Nations Assembly found that the resulting government was a "lawful government" and the "only" such government. That verdict was given on December 12, 1948, by a vote of 48 to 6.

The Assembly also recommended that the foreign troops be withdrawn from both portions of Korea. The withdrawal of United States troops was completed on June 29, 1949, and verified by the United Nations commission. The commission was denied access to North Korea to verify the alleged withdrawal of Soviet troops.

Many feared lest the withdrawal of the United States troops would be the signal for an invasion of South Korea from the North, where the Soviet army had created a large, fanatical, well disciplined and well armed Communist force. It was generally believed that it could overcome any resistance that could at that moment be offered by South Korea, which had not developed any important army and constabulary of its own. There have been border raids from the North, but the feared large-scale invasion has not happened in the year and a half since the South Korean government was proclaimed.

By now, the government in South Korea has an armed force of its own. But during most of the last two-year period only one influence has effectively inhibited Communist invasion from the North—the influence of world opinion focused through the United Nations Assembly. It would have been difficult for the Soviet Union to continue to pose as the advocate and lover of peace if Soviet-trained forces from North Korea had promptly moved in to overthrow a South Korean government established under the auspices of the United Nations and under conditions that it certified were free and fair.

It would, of course, be rash to predict that this situation will continue indefinitely. But at least the South Korean government has passed safely the dangerous period of its greatest weakness.

ISRAEL

The establishment of the new nation of Israel is one of history's dramatic happenings. It has been accomplished with pain and anguish. There has been shedding of blood, many thousands of Arabs have become homeless refugees, and much has occurred that seems, to one side or another, to have been unbearably unjust. Nevertheless, Israel exists. It gives realization to the age-old aspirations of the Jewish people to have again their own homeland. Also, it demonstrates spectacularly that world organization can do more than perpetuate the *status quo*—it can promote change.

The United Kingdom had administered Palestine under League of Nations mandate since the end of World War I. After the close of World War II it moved towards relinquishing this responsibility which involved it in the bitter controversy between Jews and Arabs—a controversy which at first revolved primarily around the immigration of Jews into Palestine.

The United Kingdom asked the United States to join it in attempting to find a solution; and on November 13, 1945, the two governments agreed to set up a committee to sift the facts and make recommendations. While the committee was working, on March 22, 1946, the United Kingdom granted independent status to Jordan, the eastern portion of the mandated territory, with only an Arab population. The Joint Anglo-United States Palestine Committee reported on April 30, 1946, and the conclusions met with little favor either from Arabs or from Jews. The problem seemed insoluble, and so on February 14, 1947, Mr. Bevin announced that the United Kingdom had decided to refer the matter to the United Nations—to which, sooner or later, come most of the "insoluble" problems.

A special session of the General Assembly was held in April, 1947. A committee was set up, and it went to work. On August 31st the committee made a majority and a minority report. At the next regular session of the United Nations Assembly, the Assembly recommended the partition of Palestine, with economic unity, along the lines of the majority report and the establishment of Jewish and Arab States. The necessary two-thirds majority was obtained with great difficulty over fierce Arab opposition.

Rumors were current in the corridors at Lake Success that vast Arab armies were to march into Palestine and submerge it by very weight of numbers.

That did not happen. Partly, it did not happen because the Arab people had no great heart for such an adventure. Partly, it did not happen because the Jews in Israel were a tough, vigorous, and well disciplined group who were prepared to fight and die for their country. Also, it did not happen because the United Nations had given its moral sanction to the establishment of the new Jewish State. Sporadic fighting did take place. But the fighting involved more difference of opinion as to where the *boundaries* should be than a challenge to the basic fact that there would be the Nation of Israel.

The Arab nations were still bitterly uncompromising at the time of the United Nations General Assembly in Paris in the fall of 1948. That Assembly met just after the assassination in Jerusalem on September 17th of Count Folke Bernadotte, who had been acting as the United Nations mediator there. His report and recommendations were published on September 20th.

There was an initial effort, participated in by the United States government, to secure the quick adoption of Count Bernadotte's report; but it was strongly opposed by Jews and many others, who felt that its recommendations, if followed, would unduly restrict the boundaries of the proposed new nation and give it little opportunity for growth and the absorption of the Jewish refugees in Europe.

The matter lay pending before the United Nations Assembly for a considerable time and was the subject of much informal discussion between the different member governments and representatives of Israel.

Throughout this period of United Nations action I had withdrawn from active participation. The matter was delicate from the standpoint of United States politics and particularly so during a Presidential campaign. Palestine had never yet been treated as a subject for bipartisan cooperation, and I did not attend the meetings of the United States Delegation when Palestine was discussed.

However, after the Presidential election of November 2, 1948, and particularly after November 18th, when I became acting head of the United States Delegation, the situation changed, and

I shared active responsibility for a solution of the problem, with the backing of the Washington administration.

There was then pending before the Political Committee a joint United States and United Kingdom "Conciliation Resolution" which was designed, in essence, to commit the United Nations to the reality of Israel as an existing nation and to set up a United Nations committee to help work out its problems with its neighbors. The proposed resolution involved features which, in my opinion, reflected unduly the concern of the United Kingdom for its relations with the Arab countries of the Near East; also, they made it unlikely that the resolution would be adopted.

As the matter neared vote in committee, I telephoned to Ambassador Lewis W. Douglas in London, who had kept in close touch with the United States Delegation on all matters relating to the United Kingdom, and told him that I felt the United States would have to act alone in this matter unless the United Kingdom agreed to certain changes. At the time, Ambassador Douglas was laid up with grippe at his home; but he arranged to have members of the Foreign Office come to see him, and we shortly got the Conciliation Resolution into more acceptable form. It passed the Political Committee on December 4, 1948, by a vote of 26 to 21 with 9 abstentions.

In the United Nations the committees act by majority vote. But the Assembly itself acts, in important matters, only by a two-thirds vote. The vote in the Political Committee thus indicated that the Conciliation Resolution would fail of adoption by a considerable margin in the General Assembly itself.

To get the vote necessary for adoption would involve persuading the governments of the Arab nations to "release" a number of delegations which were pledged to vote with them and had voted in committee against the Conciliation Resolution.

I undertook to bring this about, with the help of other members of the United States Delegation.

Shortly before the Assembly vote I spent an evening with the member of the Arab Delegation who had the highest official rank and was in that sense a spokesman for the Arab countries. I emphasized to him in the strongest terms that the nation of Israel *would be,* and that it was foolish and wrong to struggle against it. The United Nations' judgment in the matter had evoked such widespread approval, and had given such strong moral support to the Jewish cause, that the task for the Arab States was to find ways whereby, at peace with Israel, the whole Middle East could be developed and strengthened with the support of all those nations of the world which, like the United States, wished well both to Israel and to the Arab States. I assured him that the United States' position involved no unfriendliness whatever toward the Arab countries, and that the future would demonstrate this.

The result of my effort and that of others was that several Delegations pledged to the Arab cause were released to vote in the Assembly for the Conciliation Resolution. The Arab States themselves voted solidly against it, but it was adopted on December 11th by a vote of 35 to 15 with 8 abstentions.

During this period, Dr. Ralph Bunche had succeeded to the position of Count Bernadotte. He performed a difficult task with outstanding ability and won widespread confidence. Subsequently he negotiated permanent armistices between Israel and its Arab neighbors.

Many matters remained to be settled, notably the "international" status of Jerusalem and the Holy Places and the fate of the Arab refugees. But what had already taken place was an outstanding demonstration of the creative power of the United Nations.

INDONESIA

The establishment of the United States of Indonesia was a work comparable to the establishment of Israel. Israel was born in an environment of unfriendly nations. The United States of Indonesia was born out of colonial status. In both cases there was bloodshed and a risk of large-scale war.

The United Nations would not normally have jurisdiction in a civil war which did not represent "indirect aggression," and which was not yet a threat to world peace. That would be excluded by the "domestic jurisdiction" article of the Charter:

Nothing contained in the present Charter shall authorize the United Nations to intervene in matters which are essentially within the domestic jurisdiction of any state or shall require the Members to submit such matters to settlement under the present Charter; but this principle shall not prejudice the application of enforcement measures under Chapter VII. [Art. 2, Sec. 7.]

However, the Netherlands government, by agreement initialed in November, 1946, and signed on March 25, 1947, had voluntarily accorded a certain autonomous status to the republican regime in Indonesia which was seeking independence. When the implementation of the agreement proved impossible, the Netherlands started to use force to reestablish its sovereignty. In July, 1947, the matter was brought to the United Nations Security Council by India and Australia. The Netherlands government insisted, for the record, that the matter was still essentially within its domestic jurisdiction, and this view had support from France and the United Kingdom. However, recognizing the reality of international concern, the Netherlands, as an act of enlightened statesmanship, refrained from pressing the point and acquiesced in intervention by the Security Council.

The Security Council sent a "Committee of Good Offices" to the spot in an effort to reestablish order and to facilitate the peaceful evolution of the self-government to which all the parties were in principle committed.

The problem was complicated by the fact that there was a large amount of Communist infiltration, and that Communist elements were seeking violent revolution.

The situation was the more difficult because the Dutch people had large investments in Indonesia, and Dutch reconstruction in Europe largely depended upon the receipt of income from these investments.

Many political and economic interests were involved, and there was much distrust on both sides. A heavy burden fell upon the United States as a member of the Good Offices Committee.

Often, during the 1947–1949 period, the members of the Security Council faced the question whether or not to invoke economic sanctions against the Netherlands in order to compel it to comply more promptly and more fully with what the majority in the Security Council at times thought it should do. Here was a situation where the Security Council had indeed *power* to act and to enforce its will. The Netherlands had no veto right in the Security Council to protect itself. The permanent members of the Security Council were often in agreement on proposals that could have been backed by sanctions; and the Netherlands was in such serious economic straits, and so dependent upon the Marshall Plan aid which began to flow from the United States in 1948, that a cutting off of this aid pursuant to Security Council action would have dealt it a serious blow.

Many people became impatient. There arose a popular demand in the United States that economic sanctions be applied. It was felt that in this way a quick solution could be imposed. However, calmer and wiser counsel prevailed. The Security Council resisted the temptation to use coercion, relying on moral pressure, and on December 27, 1949, the Republic of Indonesia was proclaimed.

The United Nations, working with the good will of both the Netherlands government and the Indonesian Republicans, had found the way to give final and full independence to this former colonial group of 76,000,000 people.

There is, of course, no assurance that the new republican government of Indonesia will demonstrate the capacity to rule and to avoid overthrow by Communist elements; but the situation is far better than if there were a prolonged civil war. For that we can thank the United Nations. Its persistence and its moderation and ultimate Dutch cooperation made possible a voluntary, rather than violent, solution in this populous and economically rich area of the world.

BLOCKADE OF BERLIN

When the Germans surrendered, the Allies took over the government of Germany. The country was divided into zones for occupation and administration, and each of the three principal Allies received a zone. The United States and the United Kingdom, pursuant to the Yalta agreement, carved out of their zones a zone for the French. The Soviet zone was the eastern portion of

Germany, including the area within which the city of Berlin is located. The United Kingdom, France, and the United States each had one of three western zones. Because Berlin had been the capital, it was selected to be the place where the representatives of the Big Four would hold their joint meetings for the government of Germany. In order to facilitate this, and to give each of the Big Four a symbol of victory in the German capital, Berlin itself, although it was in the Soviet zone, was divided into four sectors; and one sector was allotted to each of the four occupying powers. The Soviet Union had the eastern sector of Berlin and the United Kingdom, France, and the United States each had one of the western sectors.

The western sectors of Berlin are thus a little island within the eastern (Soviet) zone of Germany. There are about 2,500,000 persons in these three western sectors, and they have their own independent life. They do business largely with the western zones of Germany, and get from the West the food and coal which keep them alive. Traffic between the western sectors of Berlin and the western zones of Germany moves by railroads, highways and canals, which pass through the eastern (Soviet) zone of Germany. Traffic is subject to Soviet control because the Western Allies have no corridor of their own giving them access to Berlin.

In the spring of 1948, the Soviet authorities began to put difficulties of one sort or another in the way of the movement of goods and people between the western sectors of Berlin and the western zones of Germany. They demanded more documents. They required the canal boats to take out new licenses. They claimed that the railroads had to be repaired, and that road traffic had to be suspended until new bridges could be built.

At first no one took this very seriously. But after the complications multiplied, and as all traffic by railroad, road, and canal was gradually slowed to a total stop, the Soviet intention became apparent. The Soviet Union had embarked on a deliberate policy of bringing the Germans of the western sectors of Berlin to a state of starvation and freezing so that they would, in desperation, rebel against the Western authorities and turn to the Soviet authorities for the means of survival.

The Western Allies then had recourse to the airlift. It was conducted by the United States and the United Kingdom, and on June 26, 1948, cargo planes started to carry the food, medicine, and coal required to keep alive the beleaguered population. Also, the Western Allies imposed countermeasures to interrupt East-West trade through Germany.

The Western Allies could not allow the Soviet blockade to continue without protest. It was a use of physical force to gain political ends. It violated the United Nations Charter provisions for settling disputes by "peaceful means" and for refraining from the "use of force." Accordingly, on July 6, 1948, the three Western Allies protested at Moscow. They asserted that as joint victors with agreed responsibilities in Berlin, they had a clearly implied right to take to and from Berlin the food and fuel needed for the life of the people. They couched their protest in strong terms.

The Moscow talks dragged on into August. Then it seemed for a few days, following a talk with Stalin, that agreement had been reached for a lifting of the Berlin blockade on condition that the Soviet mark would be accepted as the currency of western as well as eastern Berlin. Toward the end of August, the detailed negotiations were transferred to Berlin. There they came to naught. The Soviet representatives would not accept any arrangement for implementing the Moscow understanding except such as would, in fact, have given the Soviet authorities complete power over the economic life of the western sectors of Berlin.

That was a critical moment. War may have been near. The prestige of the Western Allies was involved. They could not, without jeopardy to their position in all of Western Europe, accept the rebuff of Moscow as the last word and acquiesce in the Soviet denial of their right to use the railroad, roads and canals to Berlin. The alternative seemed to be to assert these rights by attempting to push armed convoys through from the West.

But there was one other possibility: to refer the matter to the United Nations. That would avoid an immediate crisis and provide a means of settlement involving neither abject surrender nor the use of force against force.

Some, at the time, opposed that step. They felt that it would place on the United Nations a heavier burden than it could carry, and might wreck it.

The dispute did, indeed, have grave implications. Here was a head-on collision between the Big Four, between East and West. Here were four disputants, each of whom had a veto power. It was precisely the kind of situation which, supposedly, made the Security Council totally impotent.

Nevertheless, reference to the Security Council seemed a step worth taking. It was unfortunate that the United Nations, while still immature, had to bear so heavy a burden. But the United Nations was not an end in itself: it was a means to peace. There was no use risking war in order to preserve the United Nations intact as an historical relic. The United Nations, like the Sabbath, was made to serve man, not man to serve it.

So, in Paris, with Secretary Marshall, we decided to take the dispute with the Soviet Union to the Security Council. There was discussion as to whether it could not better go to the Assembly, but that step was reserved for the contingency that the Security Council might prove wholly impotent.

Those were days of great anxiety which brought about day and night discussions and exchange of views in which I participated with Secretary Marshall and a top-level, able State Department group headed by Philip C. Jessup, Charles E. Bohlen, and Dean Rusk. Ambassador Douglas frequently came from London to join us.

On October 5, 1948, the Berlin blockade dispute was put on the agenda of the Security Council as a "threat to the peace." It was at once taken up by the so-called "neutral" members of the Security Council; namely, the members outside the five (France, the United Kingdom, the United States, the Soviet Union, and the Ukraine) which were directly involved in the controversy. The "neutrals" (Argentina, Belgium, Canada, China, Colombia, and Syria), under the chairmanship of Argentina, conducted negotiations and investigated the possibilities of a solution, particularly in terms of implementing the near-agreement that had been arrived at with Stalin in August.

In the meantime, the airlift continued. The Soviet Union did not attempt direct physical interference. It injected the moral hazard of near-by "air maneuvers." But it did not "jam" the radio which was needed for the instrument landings required by the persistent bad weather of the fall. The Western Allies, on their side, did not attempt to get relief to Berlin by armored or convoyed trucks. The situation was stabilized, and the tension began to relax. We no longer thought in terms of imminent war.

The studies by the United Nations Security Council continued throughout the winter of 1948–1949. The "neutrals" found no acceptable solution. But the very fact that they were studying the situation and seeking a solution cushioned the friction between East and West. The small powers were interposed between the great powers. They did not get crushed, as some had feared, and they did prevent a harsh grating which might have produced sparks of war.

The airlift, under the directing energy of General Clay, produced marvels of performance. The total tonnage carried was 1,788,726 metric tons, all for German civilian consumption. The winter was relatively mild. The inhabitants of western Berlin bore hardship with great loyalty and good spirit. As a result, the Western Allies were not driven out of Berlin, and Western prestige mounted throughout Germany to a new high when people saw the resourcefulness and resolution of the free peoples.

During February, 1949, Ambassador Jessup and Mr. Malik, the Soviet delegate on the Security Council, met casually in the Delegates' Lounge at Lake Success. Dr. Jessup mentioned a press interview which had been given by Marshal Stalin, and which suggested that the Berlin dispute might be solvable. Mr. Malik said he would inquire into the matter. After some delay, he reported back that the Soviet government believed that something could be done about lifting the Berlin blockade and removing the counter restrictions on East-West trade that the Western Allies had imposed. These conversations led to an agreement on May 4, 1949, to lift the blockade and to end the retaliatory restrictions. Also, it was agreed to reconvene the Council of Foreign Ministers, which had adjourned *sine die* in December, 1947. The Council was now to discuss the problem of Germany as a whole.

The Berlin blockade was lifted on May 12, 1949, and the Council of Foreign Ministers met again in Paris on May 23, 1949. It was there agreed that the blockade would not be reimposed, and "that the New York Agreement of May 4, 1949, shall be maintained."

The Paris agreement may or may not be lived up to. That is for the future to tell. But the United Nations played well its role. It did act as a buffer between the great powers in a quarrel that could have broken the peace.

No world organization can prevent great powers from fighting if they want to fight. It can help them to avoid fighting when they really do not want to fight but feel that, unless there is some face-saving device, use of force may be the only alternative to a disastrous loss of prestige. World organization provides a lap into which even the great powers may choose to drop their disputes. It provides a third way, as against the alternatives of humiliating surrender and violent defiance.

ITALIAN COLONIES

The problem of what to do with the former Italian colonies gave the great powers many a headache. In the end they had to turn to the United Nations.

There were three of these colonies: Italian Somaliland, Eritrea, and Libya. Libya, in turn, was divided into Cyrenaica, Tripolitania, and the Fezzan, each of which presented special and distinct problems.

Italian Somaliland presented the least complications. It was undeveloped and without strategic value. There was not much competition to get control of Italian Somaliland.

Eritrea was more significant. It was between Ethiopia and the Red Sea, and Ethiopia wanted to annex it in order to have direct access to a good port, Massawa. But only the population of the eastern part is akin, racially and religiously, to the Ethiopians. The peoples of the western part are akin to those of the Anglo-Egyptian Sudan. The two important cities, Massawa and the upland railroad terminal, Asmara, had substantial Italian populations, and there were strong sentimental ties with Italy. There are also radio locations of strategic importance.

Libya was the most important of the colonies. The Fezzan, its interior area under French administration, is without particular significance. Cyrenaica, however, has great strategic importance, and its ports of Tobruk and Bengasi had figured conspicuously in the North African campaign. It had good locations for air fields, and the British looked to it as a new strategic basing point for British power in the Mediterranean to take the place of Palestine and Egypt. The mandate over Palestine was coming to an end, and the Jews there were ill disposed toward them, so that it was no longer suitable as a British base. In Egypt rising nationalism was demanding the withdrawal of British troops. The United States government was inclined to support the British in their estimate of the strategic value of Cyrenaica.

Tripolitania was the area of greatest Italian interest. Tripoli was a good port. There was a substantial Italian population along the coast and agricultural possibilities that suggested that the area might absorb more of the surplus Italian population. Also there was a large native population which had developed some capacity for self-government. In the interior were the Senussi, who had fought valiantly on the British side during the war and had received the promise of the British government that they would never again be put under Italian rule.

Italy had not merely practical interests in her former colonies. For reasons of prestige she sought international recognition of her right and capacity to administer colonies, now that her people had turned against Fascism.

There were also involved historic rivalries between Russia and Great Britain. The British feared for their "life line" to the oil of the Near East and to India and the Far East. They suspected, reasonably, that the Russians wanted to cut it.

The French wanted Tripolitania to go back to Italian colonial administration. The French were particularly fearful of encouraging the inhabitants of Tripolitania in the idea of early independence. They thought it might infect the inhabitants of the adjoining French areas, Tunisia and Algeria, where there was already considerable native unrest, stimulated by Communist propaganda.

The Soviet Union saw the situation as a sea of discord in which it might fish to advantage and perhaps catch a colony in Africa for itself.

The position was, to put it mildly, complicated.

On September 5, 1945, the United States Delegation sailed on the *Queen Elizabeth* for the first session of the Council of Foreign Ministers which was to consider the Italian peace treaty. We discussed the problem on board ship and tentatively concluded that the former Italian colonies should be restored to Italian administration under United Nations trusteeship. However, the Senussi should receive a large measure of autonomy, and Ethiopia should receive an outlet to the sea.

Further reflection in London led us to shift from that *Queen Elizabeth* formula.

One morning I awakened at about two o'clock, disturbed by this Italian colony matter. Our proposed solution was not really in harmony with the new approach to the colonial problem represented in the United Nations Charter. It gave lip service to the principle of trusteeship and self-government but did not really serve the best interest even of the Italians; for it would saddle them with the administration of peoples in Libya and Eritrea who would resist with a fanaticism born out of a hatred of the cruel Fascist rule, a hatred which could not all at once be obliterated.

I thought about the matter the rest of the night and then asked Secretary Byrnes if I might breakfast with him. I did so, and told him of my thoughts. He, too, had been troubled during the night. So we set ourselves to find a different and better solution.

With valuable help from Benjamin V. Cohen, the State Department Counselor, we worked out a new plan. It started with the idea of future independence for all the colonies and, in the interval, administration by the United Nations through a governor general or administrator whom it would appoint.

Secretary Byrnes submitted a formal proposal along those lines. It was promptly endorsed by China and reluctantly by the

United Kingdom, after Mr. Bevin had held a cabinet meeting
on the matter. The French Delegation indicated that they might
agree except for the ten-year independence feature for Libya.
This Mr. Bidault resisted strongly as dangerous to the French
position in Tunisia and Algeria. The Soviet Union rejected the
idea of trusteeship administered by or through the United Nations and demanded the administration of Tripolitania for itself.

Mr. Molotov's demand came as a bombshell. We had known
that the Soviet Union had unrealized Mediterranean ambitions,
but we had assumed that they related only to the Dardanelles
and Turkey. The idea of a Soviet base at Tripoli, in the middle
of the Mediterranean, sent shivers down the spine of Mr. Bevin—
and others.

The entire debate on the matter was fruitless and merely revealed the sharp differences between the great powers, differences
which continued during the succeeding years.

The positions of all the governments shifted, but they never
shifted to bring agreement. The United States and the Soviet
Union reversed positions. The United States abandoned its proposal for direct United Nations trusteeship. After the Soviet representative took his place on the Trusteeship Council, the internal
differences within this Council raised doubt that it could be an
effective administering body. The Soviet Union, however, shifted
its position to favor direct United Nations trusteeship. This was
after it saw that it could never achieve its own ambition to be
the sole administrator of Tripolitania, but still felt that it might
get an influence in North Africa through membership in the
Trusteeship Council if the Council were itself administrator.

When the Italian Peace Treaty was finally signed on February 10, 1947, the future of the former Italian colonies was still
unsettled. By the treaty, Italy surrendered the colonies; but no
recipient was named. Instead, it was provided that if the Big
Four were still unable by September 15, 1948, to agree, the matter would be referred to the United Nations General Assembly
for recommendation—a recommendation which all parties promised in advance to accept.

It is hard to see how there could have been that Italian Peace Treaty without a United Nations.

The General Assembly put the matter on its 1948 agenda, and the delegates discussed it informally at the Paris meeting that began in September, 1948. Many different points of view were explored.

The Italian point of view was strongly backed by the Latin American countries. Their people had close cultural and religious ties with Italy and wanted a solution that would enhance Italian prestige and provide some outlet for the surplus Italian population. Thus a "pro-Italian" proposal could get, to start with, a solid block of nearly twenty votes.

On the other hand, the Arab and the so-called "anti-colonial" nations strongly supported early independence for the colonies. They also provided considerable support for Ethiopia in its claims to Eritrea.

The agenda item had not actually been reached for formal debate on December 12, 1948, when the Paris session adjourned so that the delegates might be at home for Christmas. But because of the importance of this item of unfinished business the General Assembly reconvened at Lake Success in April and debated the matter for several weeks.

A subcommittee prepared a complicated and interlocking over-all proposal, the key to which was a ten-year Italian trusteeship for Tripolitania. However, when the matter came to a vote, paragraph by paragraph, in the General Assembly, this provision failed by a single vote to get the necessary two-thirds majority. The vote was 33 for and 17 against. With that, the entire proposal collapsed, and the matter was put over until the next regular session of the General Assembly.

In the fall session of 1949 good progress was made. By that time the Italian government had come to realize that administration of its former colonies would be a heavy burden, that Italian control would be strongly resented by many elements, and that it would be wiser to cooperate with the native population than to try to rule it. This shift of position was followed by the Latin American states, and opened up new possibilities. It was then decided that Libya should become independent by January 1, 1952. Italian Somaliland was to receive independence in ten years, and meanwhile would be under Italian trusteeship. Decision on Eritrea was reserved. These proposals were approved by a vote of 48 to 1 with 9 abstentions.

The solution found by the United Nations Assembly is not ideal. There is indeed no ideal solution, because of the many conflicting interests. But at least there is a solution. That itself is a very great achievement. Often, in these matters, it is more important to decide than to perpetuate indecision in the search for a perfect decision. Indecision itself breeds serious difficulties and does great wrong to the people involved, since planning, particularly of an economic and monetary nature, is impossible so long as the political future is unsettled.

Here again is a conspicuous demonstration of how the United Nations can advance world order. Seldom has a problem involved as great complications as that of the future of the former Italian colonies. Big-power jealousies, strategic considerations, Italian aspirations, and the aspirations of native peoples for independence are a few of the forces that clashed. The representatives of the four great powers dealt continually with the matter for three years—from September, 1945, to September, 1948. They never approached agreement. The United Nations Assembly broke the back of the problem in a little over a year, in a way which is creditable if not perfect.

Complicated formulas for balancing the political interests of European powers gave way to the broad principle that in case of doubt it is better to give the peoples themselves the chance to work out their own destiny. They may make mistakes, and they probably will; but at least the mistakes will be their own rather than mistakes made for them by others.

Such a principle rarely gets much recognition in the private councils of the great. It does attract strong support in a broadly representative body such as the United Nations General Assembly.

The action of the General Assembly on the Italian colonies has special significance in that it was the first case in which the

Assembly acted with final authority. Normally, it only makes "recommendations"; but in this instance the parties to the Italian treaty had given the General Assembly the right to speak the last word. The example is one which might usefully be followed in other cases.

UNITED NATIONS INTANGIBLES

We have seen some of the accomplishments of the United Nations in the political field—concrete, specific, provable acts. They give an idea of the capacity of the United Nations to deal with international disputes.

If, however, we stopped here, we should have a very inadequate appreciation of the value of the United Nations. There are many activities outside the political field: economic, social, and cultural. The sum total of all these activities makes up a moral and an educational value which promotes world order and international harmony.

The United Nations is not just a *place* where the representatives of governments come together to negotiate. It is not just the sum total of its members. It is something of itself. It changes all who participate in good faith in its activities—it makes them better members of a world society.

This quality is not easy to describe or to prove. However, no one who has worked closely with the United Nations doubts that it has such a quality. The United Nations is much more than the total of resolutions adopted by the requisite majorities. There are intangibles that "weighed not as his work, yet swelled the man's amount."

FELLOWSHIP PRACTICED

The United Nations is the place where, more than anywhere else, genuine fellowship is practiced. The delegates meet freely together, not just in formal meetings but in the lunchrooms, in the lounge halls, and at the dinners and receptions that accompany every regular meeting. They mingle together on a basis of social and intellectual equality, irrespective of nation, race, sex, or creed. Christians, Mohammedans, Hindus, Jews, and agnostics interchange views on a free and friendly basis, as do those whose skins are black, brown, yellow, or white. Men and women meet on a plane of equality, as do the representatives of big states and little states. They discuss any and all topics of common concern.

This fellowship is shared to some extent even by the delegates of the Communist countries. I have had intimate and enlightening talks with many of them. Only the top delegates of the Soviet Union fail to mingle socially. Mr. Molotov and Mr. Vishinsky are seldom to be found in the lounge and lunchrooms of the General Assembly. As soon as the formal proceedings are over, the top Soviet delegates usually retire abruptly, with their bodyguards, to their private residences. Even with them, however, that practice is not invariable. As we have noted, the presence of Soviet Delegate Malik in the delegates' room at Lake Success made it possible to reopen, quite informally, conversations about the Berlin blockade. Mr. Bernard M. Baruch had, at times, cordial social relations with Mr. Gromyko when they were working together on the Atomic Commission.

The United Nations Charter says that one purpose of the United Nations is to be a "center for harmonizing." It helps to fulfill that purpose by developing, informally, fellowship among those whose differences otherwise separate them.

HYPOCRISY EXPOSED

Another intangible asset of the United Nations is its capacity to expose hypocrisy.

It has been well said that hypocrisy is the tribute that vice pays to virtue. I suppose that everyone who comes to the United Nations pretends to be better than he is. That is a good thing. Quite often the pretense becomes perforce a reality. It is often useful to assume that people are as good as they pretend to be.

But there is a degree of hypocrisy that needs exposure, and the United Nations has a great faculty for exposing gross hypocrisy.

One of the most potent Soviet Communist weapons is propaganda that is devised to appeal to the listener without regard to whether it corresponds to the truth. Propaganda is the most important single weapon in the arsenal of Soviet Communism. I suppose that the Soviet government spends more money and effort on propaganda than all the other governments of the world put together.

At the 1947 Moscow Conference, and again in London that year, we had a good opportunity to see at first hand some aspects of the propaganda.

Mr. Molotov would make a long speech of which one part was calculated to please the Poles, another part to please the Germans, a third to please the French, a fourth to please his own public opinion, and still another to promote world Communism.

Many of these parts were utterly inconsistent. Mr. Molotov would, for example, demand for the Russians vast reparation payments from Germany and go on to promise the Germans greatly improved economic conditions. He would promise the Poles large amounts of German territory. He would say that the French should have more coal from the Ruhr, and he would attack the United States, Britain, and France as "imperialist" nations.

After such a speech had been made, sometimes while it was being made, different portions of it would be channeled by radio to the desired recipients. The Germans would not be told about the increased reparation to be exacted from them, or about the territory to be given to Poland, or about the coal to be taken from the Ruhr. These portions were reserved for Russia, for Poland, and for France, respectively. The Germans would only be told about the promised economic improvement. The portions about the "imperialists" would be used generally, particularly in the colonial areas.

At Moscow, the Communist Party agents took advantage of the presence of representatives of many foreign newspapers to try to extend their influence by buying these newspapers or by making loans to owners who would promise pro-Communist news and editorial policies, or by promising the owners pulp paper from Finland, or immunity from strikes. By such methods the

Communist Party attained widespread outlets for its propaganda.

Propaganda is the Communists' first line of attack. By it they soften up the peoples whom they hope to bring under their rule. Aside from specific items of propaganda of the kind that emanated from the Council of Foreign Ministers, Communist propaganda is designed generally to portray Soviet Communism in the most ideal terms, to disparage the opposition and to smear its leaders. It promises that, if only Communist leadership is accepted, there will be a new and better world order which will realize the hopes of all the discontented, the dreams of all the idealists, and the ambitions of all the greedy.

As soon as the United Nations got under way, Soviet Communists used it as a forum for their world propaganda. They knew that sensational speeches made at the United Nations Assembly by their Minister of Foreign Affairs would attract worldwide attention. Indeed, the non-Communist press and radio have always reported very fully the major pronouncements made by Soviet Communist leaders in the United Nations.

During the first year or two of the United Nations, many in non-Communist countries feared that the Soviet leaders were getting too much propaganda advantage through using the United Nations as a sounding board and thought something should be done about it.

Actually, this abuse of United Nations privileges has by now recoiled against the Soviet leaders. The contrast between what they said and what they did was so great that the net result was to create distrust and suspicion.

One of the main Soviet Communist propaganda lines is to portray the Soviet Union as "peace-loving" and the other great powers as "imperialists" plotting war against it.

At the opening of the General Assembly in New York, Mr. Vishinsky made [September 18, 1947] his famous—or infamous—"warmongering" speech in which, among other things, he attacked me personally, although I was sitting as a delegate with him. That was supposed to be sensational, and it was.

It was the opening gun in a "peace offensive" which has been carried on intensively through all the organs of the United Nations with a view to winning the support of all men who love peace. It portrayed the Soviet Union as the nation with a peace-loving government which wanted disarmament. The governments of the United States and the United Kingdom were, according to Mr. Vishinsky, dominated by those who loved war and pursued it.

The boldness of the initial attack was at first startling. It seemed to some who heard Mr. Vishinsky's tirade repeated over the world-wide radio that he would not dare publicly to accuse fellow delegates who sat in the same Assembly with him unless there were at least some truth in the charge. That is a reaction often counted on by people who use "smear" as a weapon. They make charges so bold and extravagant that many who underestimate man's capacity for guile feel that the charges must contain an element of truth.

But the Soviet propaganda line shortly began to fall flat. When delegates, red in the face, violently shouted abuse of their fellows as "warmongers," it was realized that, if such manners were generally adopted, they would be in themselves a disturbance of the peace. The very intemperance of the words and the manner of the Soviet delegates made a striking contrast with the sober and calm attitude of the delegates who were alleged to be lovers of violence. It was felt that peace was not very secure in the hands of those who were unable to exercise decent self-control.

These impressions were confirmed when efforts were made to translate the so-called "peace offensive" of the Soviet Union into action. Concrete proposals were put forward for the international control of atomic weapons. It was proposed to take a census of national armaments, so as to get a base on which proportionate reduction of armament might proceed. It was then the Soviet Union that blocked progress. It absolutely rejected any international verification or effective control.

It soon became apparent that the Soviet delegates' publicly exhibited zeal for peace lacked substance. The processes of the United Nations revealed to all the world a dangerous hypocrisy which needed to be exposed.

EDUCATION ADVANCED

Through its debates and informal discussions, the United Nations serves greatly to educate its delegates as to the point of view of others. Often the United Nations is referred to contemptuously as a mere debating society. I reject the word "mere." A thorough exchange of views about points of difference is precisely what is needed at the present stage of international development.

The great difficulty in the way of developing world order is that there are many different views as to what is right and what is wrong. Few controversies can be settled by action which reflects a common judgment of right and wrong. Often international proposals involve the attempt by a majority to impose upon a large minority results which the minority feels to be unjust. Under such circumstances, international processes must be used cautiously, lest they provoke violent resistance which might precipitate general war.

The most urgent task today of any world organization is education to bring about a better understanding and a reconciliation of different viewpoints, to find common moral and intellectual denominators. Often—indeed, usually—a frank and full discussion discloses merit in the other person's viewpoint that has not been appreciated.

The debates which take place within the United Nations— and I refer not merely to the formal recorded debates but to the private arguments that take place—almost always lead to changes of position. The United States Delegation has brought to the United Nations many proposals that it had drafted in advance with a genuine desire to meet the point of view of others. Usually, however, we have found that we had overlooked factors of genuine merit. To the best of my recollection, every proposition ever put forward by the United States Delegation has been altered as a result of the debates. That alteration generally has represented not a "deal" to get votes by compromise, but the recognition of overlooked merit in the point of view of others.

In order to get positive results in the United Nations Assembly, it is necessary to frame proposals in a way that will attract support from many different nations all over the world. This fact draws nations closer and closer together. It is a unifying process. It reflects the great merit of representative government.

Whenever elections are held in a free country, the political leaders of rival parties try to put their case in a way that will command the support of a majority. This usually draws the opposing parties closer together; and often great differences of principle shrink, and the leaders of opposing parties find it more and more difficult to state their positions in sharp contrast.

That is precisely the kind of unifying force that we need in world affairs, and it is provided by the United Nations.

"Things that are equal to the same thing are equal to each other." The "same thing" in the United Nations is the majority viewpoint that is represented perhaps most of all by the "small" states. At San Francisco, the reporters used to talk about the "Big Five" and the "Little Forty-five." It is the "Little Forty-five," now grown to a "Little Fifty-four," that represent the ability to get resolutions adopted.

The smaller nations put a high value on peace, justice, and liberty. They rely more on moral than on material force, perhaps because they have less of the latter. But the great powers cannot get anywhere in the United Nations Assembly except through proposals that appeal to the basic instinct of those who make up the numerical majority. As nations of different viewpoints each appealed to that instinct, they themselves come nearer together. In such a way the United Nations Assembly further serves its task of being a "center for harmonizing."

ENDING "NEUTRALITY"

At the beginning of the postwar controversy between "East" and "West," there was a Communist-promoted "whispering campaign" to spread the view that the differences between the Soviet Union and the United States were merely episodes in a typical "great power" struggle. The United States was supposedly trying to dominate the world and was threatening the world with disaster because it looked upon the Soviet Union as a possible rival.

Under such circumstances, it would be both natural and appropriate for the nations not directly involved to stay aloof and not to identify themselves with either of the two great contestants.

That was part of the Soviet technique designed to keep the non-Communist nations divided, so that they might be overcome one by one.

At the first meetings of the United Nations Assembly, the point of view was quite generally accepted that the struggle was indeed merely a struggle between two great powers such as had been typical over the past, when Rome and Carthage, England and Spain, and France and Germany, for example, were rivals. Even Mr. Bevin for a time said that the role of Britain was to be a "bridge" between the Soviet Union and the United States.

If that point of view had prevailed, it would have been difficult to forge the solidarity that helped countries such as Greece, Turkey, Iran, and Korea to withstand Communist tactics of infiltration and incitement to civil war.

At the first Assemblies of the United Nations some of the small powers felt considerable embarrassment in voting with the United States, particularly when the result was an overwhelming vote against the Soviet Union. They agreed with us, but felt that it would have been better if more nations had voted with the Soviet Union, merely to give an appearance of greater "neutrality." Likewise, at the first meetings of the Council of Foreign Ministers it was not supposed to be "cricket" for the United States' representatives to talk, in advance and privately, with the representatives of China, France, or England. There was supposed to be "neutrality."

However, the proceedings in the United Nations Assembly led to a rapid evaporation of this groping for "neutrality." By actual conduct, demeanor, and action, the United States completely contradicted the Soviet insinuation that the struggle going on in the world was precipitated by the ambition of the United States to gain dominance in the world. The struggle came to be seen, most of all, as involving the small countries that wanted to stay free. "Neutrality" in spirit and in voting came to an end. There developed a spiritual solidarity among most of the non-Communist nations which was open, and of which none was ashamed. The common tie is not a desire to serve the "power lust" of the United States, but a desire to preserve freedom and liberty and equal rights for all independent nations.

As against this background, it is interesting to refer again to the March 10, 1939, speech of Stalin from which I have already quoted. In it he stated that it was "neutrality" that had enabled Hitler, Mussolini, and the Japanese war lords to redivide the world in their favor and to extend their power at the expense of England, France, and the United States, which he then described as being the "non-aggressive states." It was "neutrality," he said, that made inevitable a second world war. As Stalin pointed out, the League of Nations in that 1938-1939 period was impotent to do away with the spirit of neutrality which left each country alone to "defend itself from the aggressors."

The United Nations may do better in that respect. It has provided intimacy of association and insight into national purposes. Out of that has come quickly a solidarity in spirit such as the world has never before known.

Whether or not that solidarity will persist remains to be seen. Governments act not merely in terms of what they want, but in terms of what they dare. There is a manifest preference for solidarity as against neutrality. But that assumes that solidarity can increase security.

If there is doubt about it, then fear may break the ranks of those who, in their hearts, reject neutrality and prefer to stand together against aggression, direct or indirect.

The United Nations cannot, alone and of itself, assure the solidarity needed to assure security. That depends also upon the member nations themselves and upon what they do, within the framework of the Charter, in the exercise of "the inherent right of individual or collective self-defense." But the United Nations has already shown the capacity to provide the moral foundation, the spiritual solidarity, which is indispensable for collective security.

CHAPTER SEVEN

COLONIAL EVOLUTION VS. VIOLENT REVOLUTION

The colonial areas have been the theater of dramatic political action.

At the time of the San Francisco Conference, we calculated that more than 700,000,000 people—about a third of the world's population—lived in a state of political dependency upon the "West." That resulted from the fact that for several centuries the nations of the West had been materially, intellectually, and spiritually dynamic. Through developments like the Industrial Revolution the Western powers, with England in the front rank, had invented tools that multiplied human energy many times and made it possible to produce what others wanted but could not get. Goods were produced which venturesome traders carried to the four corners of the earth.

Because most of these peoples could not pay English pounds sterling on the barrelhead, credits were extended and large investments were made in the undeveloped countries in the form of railroads, ports, irrigation projects, and the like. In order, however, for this process to work, there had to be a good measure of political security and monetary exchangeability. So the Western powers went on to provide government for peoples of the world who had not yet developed the political stability needed for trade and investment.

This extension of Western dominance never resulted primarily from mere force. There was, to be sure, some fighting by Western armies in Asia and Africa. But those wars were minor. The great wars of modern times have been the wars among the

Western powers themselves, not wars of the West against peoples of other civilizations. The political ascendancy of the West came about primarily because the West had something to offer which others wanted. Western ascendancy was not so much the work of generals as it was of diplomats, merchants, and missionaries.

Often the Christian missionary was the first to enter other lands. He was inspired by a concept of the nature of man that was fresh, although it had had its beginning in Judea, where East and West met. All men, he believed, were the creation and concern of a universal God Who had endowed every person with the right to develop in accordance with the dictates of his individual reason and conscience.

Merchants and engineers went, too, from the West to all the world. They gave distribution to the products of Western inventiveness and developed forgotten and hidden natural resources.

I do not suggest that all Westerners were consciously seeking a great universal goal of human betterment. The Western societies accepted the elemental fact that self-interest, be it individual, family or group, is the dominating human motive power, and if that is repressed very little happens. But Christian belief so conditioned material self-interest that, for the most part, individuals could not get self-satisfaction for themselves without at the same time promoting the general good.

There were some Westerners who became arrogant in terms of race, and wanted to perpetuate a condition that could make little men seem big if only their color were white. Some amassed wealth from an unfair exploitation of subject peoples. The dependent peoples had many legitimate causes of grievance, and ample occasion to assert themselves. But the religion and the economic and social philosophy of the West made Western colonialism something different from the colonialisms that had preceded it. There was a self-liquidating feature.

The colonial position of the West has always been considered by Soviet leaders to be its Achilles' heel—the point through which a mortal blow could be struck. They saw that the nations of

Western Europe needed the raw material resources that could be drawn out of the colonial areas: oil, rubber, tin, and the like. They saw that some Western countries needed colonial markets for goods such as textiles. Also, they realized that there was a rising tide of nationalism and an increasing desire on the part of peoples to assume control of their own destinies. The Soviet leaders thought this could be developed by propaganda and infiltration into a violent revolution which would serve two purposes: it would engage the Western powers in an exhausting military effort to put down civil insurrection; and it would in the end detach the colonies, under conditions of such bitterness that they would naturally come into the orbit of Soviet Communism, which could claim moral solidarity with the revolutionists.

Stalin said in 1924, "The road to victory of the revolution in the West lies through the revolutionary alliance with the liberation movement of the colonies and dependent countries." That policy directive laid down twenty-five years ago appears on page 52 of his *Problems of Leninism,* to which we have so often referred. It has been intensively followed. Upon it Soviet Communism has made a vast expenditure in terms of money and of top political thinking. When Mr. Molotov retired as Minister of Foreign Affairs on March 4, 1949, he apparently did so because the Politburo felt that he should devote his entire time to working out the Soviet Communist program for revolution in Asia—a task so important that it deserved the concentrated attention of the best international brains that the Soviet government could command. Therefore he was freed from participation in time-consuming and often unproductive meetings of the Council of Foreign Ministers and of the United Nations.

When the fighting in World War II drew to a close, the greatest single political issue was the colonial issue. If the West had attempted to perpetuate the *status quo* of colonialism, it would have made violent revolution inevitable and defeat inevitable. The only policy that might succeed was that of bringing independence peacefully to the more advanced of the 700,000,000 dependent persons.

This postwar issue first came to a head in the spring of 1945.

The Dumbarton Oaks Proposals had not contained any provisions for dealing with the situation. That was one of the significant gaps. It had, however, been contemplated that, shortly before the San Francisco Conference, the representatives of the Dumbarton Oaks powers would meet at Washington to draw up a program for trusteeship to replace the mandate system of the League of Nations, which had been devised for colonial areas detached from Germany and Turkey after World War I.

However, sharp differences of opinion arose within the United States government as to whether there should be trusteeship of the mandated Japanese islands in the Pacific and, if so, on what terms. The government was unable at that time to present a United States proposal or a United States position to other governments. The situation was the more difficult because of President Roosevelt's death and the sudden transfer of responsibility to President Truman. The result was that prior to San Francisco there was no international agreement of any kind with reference to the handling of the colonial problem.

The San Francisco Conference thus took up the problem without the benefit of any preparatory understandings. It wrote three important chapters of the Charter dealing with the colonial situation generally and with trusteeship in particular: Chapters XI, XII, and XIII. For this, much credit goes to Commander Stassen, who had this field as his particular responsibility at San Francisco. It was a difficult task, for the colonial powers and the Soviet Union differed sharply in opinion. Between these two forces, Commander Stassen was an able negotiator.

Negotiating skill, however great, could not have brought about a positive result except for the fact that the entire colonial development by the West had in it what I have called a "self-liquidating" element, because Christianity had largely influenced the colonial attitudes of the West. The result, at San Francisco, was that it was not necessary to put great pressures upon the colonial powers to accept the idea of ultimate self-government or independence. That was an idea to which they were receptive. Indeed, largely on British initiative the provisions of the United

Nations Charter were made far more comprehensive than the comparable provisions of the League of Nations.

The original idea had been to provide merely for an international trusteeship system which might take over the few non-self-governing areas which had been under League of Nations mandate and certain additional territories which might be detached from Italy or Japan under the peace treaties. Actually, this concept was broadened in the Charter of the United Nations to deal with all non-self-governing peoples.

Chapter XI lays down the basic and all-inclusive principle:

Members of the United Nations which have or assume responsibilities for the administration of territories whose peoples have not yet attained a full measure of self-government recognize the principle that the interests of the inhabitants of these territories are paramount, and accept as a sacred trust the obligation to promote to the utmost, within the system of international peace and security established by the present Charter, the well-being of the inhabitants of these territories . . .

The Charter goes on to spell out the obligation of colonial powers, among other things,

(b) to develop self-government, to take due account of the political aspirations of the peoples, and to assist them in the progressive development of their free political institutions, according to the particular circumstances of each territory and its peoples and their varying stages of advancement.

The acceptance of these principles by all the colonial powers was a great act of enlightened statesmanship. It pointed the way, and the only way, to frustration of the Soviet Communist program of violent revolution.

In addition to the general declaration of Chapter XI of the Charter on all non-self-governing territories, provisions were made by Chapters XII and XIII for an international trusteeship system. The provisions are complicated and represent compromises that were arrived at with difficulty. There was to be a Trusteeship Council divided evenly in membership between nations administering trust territories ("colonial" powers) and nations not administering trust territories ("non-colonial" powers). Then there were provisions for "strategic" trusteeships under the primary authority of the Security Council and "non-strategic" trusteeships which were to be primarily under the responsibility of the General Assembly.

"Strategic" trusteeship was devised in an effort to meet the views of the United States regarding the Japanese mandated islands. Our government did not want to annex these islands outright. It did want to be in a position to assure that these islands, which had been taken from Japan at the cost of so much American blood, could not again be used as steppingstones for an attack upon the United States. So, "strategic" trusteeship under the Security Council was invented. The United States had veto power there, and could block any Security Council action which it felt might impinge on United States security.

At San Francisco, this trusteeship matter was closely followed by the representatives of our Joint Chiefs of Staff. Also, the subject gave concern to the members of Congress who were on the Delegation. In Congress there was then a vocal demand that the United States annex the Japanese mandated islands. This whole matter was charged with political dynamite, and it might even have prevented a ratification of the treaty by the United States Senate. For that reason, the United States Delegation insisted that the Charter should carry no binding commitment to put the Japanese mandated islands even under "strategic" trusteeship.

The United States delegates at San Francisco could not, each of them, follow in detail all aspects of the deliberation. Each had particular tasks in particular committees, and no one could report in detail to the Delegation as a whole. But in relation to trusteeship there was one ritual. It had been early agreed that trusteeship would not apply automatically to any territory, but that "it will be a matter for subsequent agreement as to which territories in the foregoing categories will be brought under the trusteeship system and upon what terms."

At the daily meetings of the United States Delegation, Senator Connally and Senator Vandenberg would always put to Commander Stassen this question: "Are you sticking to the 'subsequent agreement' provision?" Commander Stassen would regularly reply in the affirmative. Then the meeting would go on.

When the Charter had been signed and came to the Senate for ratification, the political wisdom of the Senators was proved. This Charter clause, providing for no commitment with reference to the Japanese mandated islands or other territory, eliminated what otherwise might have been a serious obstacle to ratification.

Another compromise clause to reassure worried nations was the provision that any trusteeship agreement must be acceptable to any state "directly concerned, including the mandatory power."

These two clauses, while they helped get the Charter agreed to and ratified, did, as we shall see, create great difficulties in the way of establishing the trusteeship system.

The United Nations met for organization in London in January and February, 1946. At that time, all the principal organs of the United Nations were established except the Trusteeship Council. It was not possible then to set up the Trusteeship Council, because half of the membership had to be Member nations that were administering trust territories and there were no "trust territories" and could not be until there had been trusteeship agreements.

There was no obligation on any nation to put territory into the trusteeship system, because, as we have seen, this was "a matter for subsequent agreement." Also, there could not be any trusteeship agreements unless the agreements were approved not only by the General Assembly of the United Nations—or the Security Council in the case of "strategic" trusteeship—but also by "the states directly concerned." So at London on February 9, 1946, the General Assembly adopted a resolution inviting the nations holding mandates to submit trusteeship agreements not later than the Second Part of the First Session, which was to be held in New York in the fall.

When the Assembly reconvened in New York on October 23, 1946, an immense effort was made to bring about the establishment of the Trusteeship Council.

That required that a number of nations which held mandated

territories should be willing to put the territories into the trustee-ship system; that there should be negotiated and concluded agreements, of the nature of treaties, between these nations and the United Nations Assembly; and that a way should be found to limit the Charter concept of "states directly concerned" so as not to give the Soviet Union, in effect, a veto power over all the agreements.

The United States could have taken the lead in establishing the trusteeship system by quickly proposing for trusteeship the Japanese mandated Pacific islands. However, continuing dis-agreement between the different departments of our government delayed action. All the other countries holding territory covered by League mandates, except the Union of South Africa, indicated willingness to negotiate agreements converting the mandates into United Nations trusteeships that they would administer. These nations were the United Kingdom, France, Belgium, Australia, and New Zealand. They submitted proposed trusteeship agree-ments covering eight areas in Africa and the Pacific. New Zealand took the lead in this matter, and allowed itself to become the "guinea pig." Its action is a tribute to the broad international viewpoint of Peter Fraser, the Prime Minister, and Sir Carl A. Berendsen, the principal New Zealand delegate to that Session of the United Nations.

The willingness of these colonial powers to make trusteeship agreements was a great step forward. But it still left much to be accomplished. Each of them had a veto power on the terms of its own trusteeship agreement, because, as has been noted, the Char-ter provided expressly that the trusteeship terms must be agreed to by the mandatory power.

It soon developed that the terms upon which the mandatory powers were willing to turn mandates into trusteeships were ob-jectionable to many of the Delegations, probably to a majority of them. The greatest controversy revolved around whether the administering authority should have the right to establish military bases in the trust territory. The colonial powers insisted on that right.

Further complications arose from the fact that the Soviet

Union insisted that, as a great power with world-wide interests, it was automatically "directly concerned" in all the trusteeship agreements, and that there could not be a trusteeship agreement unless it approved the terms. It further indicated that it would never agree that the administering nations had the right to establish military bases in the trust territories.

Other nations would have liked to be considered as "directly concerned," and thus to have a veto power. The Arab states, looking forward to the time when the Palestine mandate might be dealt with, were particularly anxious for precedents that might give them a veto over the future disposition of Palestine.

The United States Delegation took an active part in trying to get the Trusteeship Council established. It seemed to us that it was urgent to arrive at this result. The Trusteeship Council could be a very important agency in helping to bring about the peaceful evolution of dependent peoples to independence. We knew that the Soviet Union did not want to see this happen. It wanted violent revolution in the colonies, and it was seeking to block the establishment of the Trusteeship Council for the very reason that, if there were no Trusteeship Council, the non-self-governing peoples would feel that they had been abandoned by the United Nations, and that the only way to realize their aspirations was to take matters into their own hands and use violence under the leadership offered by the Soviet Union.

It seemed for many weeks that no positive result was possible. At one stage, the committee working on the matter asked Mr. Novikov, the Soviet Ambassador to Washington, who was acting for the Soviet Union, to negotiate privately with me. The regular proceedings were suspended to permit this. He and I did confer, together and with Mr. Gromyko, and he and Mr. Gromyko in turn conferred with Mr. Molotov.

In the course of these talks it was intimated that the Soviet Union would agree to any disposition of the Japanese mandated Pacific islands that the United States wanted, and would, in general, go along with setting up the Trusteeship Council if the United States would support the Soviet Union in its desire to get a colonial base on the Mediterranean. Also, it was intimated that the Soviet Union might wish to be treated as a "state directly concerned" in a future trusteeship of Okinawa, or any other Japanese territory that could be used as an air base against Vladivostok.

I reported this to Secretary Byrnes and, with his immediate concurrence, promptly rejected the idea of any such deal.

This episode interestingly revealed the suspicion that arises as soon as the Soviet Union gets the "two power" talks with the United States which it always seeks. The British delegate called to see me and asked for a written pledge that the United States would not give the Soviet Delegation any private commitments or assurances to support their claim to be a "state directly concerned" in relation to former Italian colonies. I gave him that assurance.

My private talks with Ambassador Novikov came to no good end, and the situation reached a point where it seemed necessary to attempt to get the votes to override Soviet objections so that there might be enough trusteeship agreements to set up the Trusteeship Council. We of the United States Delegation then worked out a formula whereby the members of the General Assembly would, in effect, record their view that approval by any nation of the trusteeship agreements then before the Assembly would not involve a waiver of its right to be considered as a "state directly concerned" in relation to any future trusteeship agreement or any alteration of the present trusteeship agreements.

This formula, on being approved by the Assembly committee, made it possible to get the eight trusteeship agreements approved by the Assembly by a vote of 41 to 6 with 5 abstentions. Only the Soviet bloc voted against approval.

The vote in committee had been very close on questions of military bases (18 to 14 with 6 abstentions). Undoubtedly a majority of the delegates would not have accepted these provisions for bases except that rejection would have meant no Trusteeship Council at all.

The Soviet Communist bloc fought the trusteeship agreements to the bitter end, and announced that their nations would boycott the Trusteeship Council because, they asserted, the trusteeship agreements were illegal and unconstitutional, particularly in that they provided for military bases in violation of the United Nations Charter.

During the initial period of the negotiations described above, the position of the United States Delegation had been awkward because the United States, itself in possession of mandated territory, could not make up its mind to put this territory under United Nations trusteeship. We seemed thus to be in a position of urging others to do what we were not willing to do.

Toward the beginning of the Session, I had discussed the situation with President Truman, with the State Department, and with Secretary Forrestal. President Truman was responsive to my presentation of the case, and pushed the matter vigorously in Washington. A decision was announced by him on November 6, 1946. The decision was that the United States would "place under trusteeship with the United States as the administering authority, the Japanese Mandated Islands and any Japanese Islands for which it assumes responsibilities as a result of the second World War." It proposed for the Japanese *mandated* islands a strategic trusteeship to be approved by the Security Council.

The statement of this position greatly improved the moral authority of the United States Delegation in dealing with the question, and it was perhaps indispensable to a successful conclusion.

On February 27, 1947, after the adjournment of the Assembly, the United States submitted to the Security Council its proposed trusteeship agreement for the Japanese mandated islands, which was approved on April 2nd. Somewhat to our surprise, the Soviet Union did not exercise its veto power to block the agreement. It presumably realized that if this trusteeship agreement were blocked by Soviet veto, the result would be outright annexation of the islands by the United States. Also, the Soviet Union had never shown a great interest in the Japanese mandated islands except as a basis for bargaining. It had much more concern with North African trusteeships, and with a possible trusteeship of Okinawa in the event that the United States should "assume responsibility" for it, as was, perhaps, indicated by the President's statement of November 6, 1946.

The establishment of the Trusteeship Council was a notable step in implementing the policy of peaceful evolution of colonial peoples to self-government. The actual territories that the Council administers do not themselves contain a large percentage of the non-self-governing peoples. However, all the areas that were mandated under the League of Nations have become independent or been transformed into United Nations Trusteeships, except Southwest Africa. The Trusteeship Council, by its supervision and by its visits to trust territories, exerts a powerful influence for high standards of colonial administration, and this, in turn, has an influence in all the colonial areas.

The most spectacular strides forward have been made, not through the trusteeship system itself, but through voluntary action under Chapter XI of the Charter, which deals generally with "Non-Self-Governing Territories" and binds all member nations administering any such territories to develop "self-government" and to assist the peoples in "the progressive development of their free political institutions."

Since the signature of the United Nations Charter on June 26, 1945, political independence has been given to nearly 600,000,000 non-self-governing people. These include the peoples of India, Pakistan, Burma, Ceylon, the Philippines, Indonesia, Jordan, Israel, and French Indo-China. Of the present members of the United Nations, no fewer than seven are nations whose peoples were under alien control when the Charter was signed. Within about five years, nearly four-fifths of the 700,000,000 people who in 1945 were dependent on the West have won political independence and many more have been placed under United Nations Trusteeship. All this has occurred peacefully, except for sporadic fighting in Indonesia, Palestine, and French Indo-China.

The situation in French Indo-China is the least satisfactory at the moment of writing. It illustrates what Soviet Communists hoped would happen on a great scale throughout the entire colonial area. In Viet Nam there is a Communist-led revolution. The French are attempting to put it down by force.

While this situation represents only a small fraction of the total "colonial" problem, it already assumes great importance. It is a serious drain on French economy and on France's ability to become again a military power in Europe. About 150,000 French troops have been fighting in French Indo-China. They represent the best trained and most reliable troops that France has. The money cost is estimated to be the equivalent of about $500,-000,000 a year. This is a sizable sum when French needs for reconstruction at home are so great.

The French government is, belatedly, trying to work out of the situation by granting a large measure of independence to the Viet Nam government of Bao Dai. Agreements to this end were approved by the French Chamber of Deputies on January 28, 1950. But the French may have acted too late. The Communist leader, Ho Chi Minh, has been recognized by the Soviet government, the Yugoslav government, the Communist government of China, and others. His regime may be able to carry on a long and costly struggle, with the outcome in doubt.

The present effort is to multiply instances like Viet Nam. The Chinese Communists, following the return of President Mao Tse-tung from Moscow, began (February 21, 1950) broadcasting to the peoples of southwest Asia calling upon them to rise up against their present political leaders who were termed "colonial puppets" and "lackeys" of the "imperialists." The broadcast said "the people cannot attain liberation without armed struggle." Where the present government controls strong armed forces "the liberation movement should take the form of legal and illegal mass struggles, which must, however, be coordinated with armed struggles proceeding in other more favorable environments." These struggles, it was said, must be carried out in cooperation with the Soviet Union. "Only by leaning to one side—the side of the world democracies and peace-loving forces headed by the Soviet Union—can any country either achieve or maintain genuine independence." This, incidentally, does not sound like "Titoism."

These occurrences reveal the magnitude of the menace.

We can be grateful for the wise statesmanship that, on the whole, has guided the postwar policies of the Western colonial powers. We can be thankful for the moderation that, on the whole, has been shown by the leaders of the liberated peoples. We also should not forget those spiritual leaders who in the past implanted in Western colonial policies the basic concept of human liberty so that, from the beginning, Western colonialism had a liberating quality. The religion of the West and the economic and social philosophies of the West combined to promote a peaceful withering away of political rule by the West and its replacement by self-government. The great happenings of the last five years were a fulfillment, not an improvised reversal, of what went before.

The pagan empires of the past had a rule that was not illumined by ideals of liberty and freedom. Those conquerors had no belief in a universal God Who was as much concerned with the ruled as with the rulers. They did not believe that each person, whatever his race, color or present condition of servitude, had a God-given right to develop freely in accordance with the dictates of his individual reason and conscience.

It was the religion of the West that made the colonial system of the West profoundly different from the empires of the past. Those empires were wholly based on a material concept. When the rulers weakened, the ruled fought themselves free. They turned on their masters and destroyed them. That is the way in which civilizations of the past have gone down in ruins. Western civilization may perhaps escape that fate.

CHAPTER EIGHT

REGIONAL ASSOCIATIONS

The United Nations was designed to be a "world," a "universal," organization. It had a responsibility to seek to maintain international peace *everywhere*. It could, therefore, admit of no rival.

But did that require that the United Nations should be an *exclusive* agency, the only agency, for maintaining international peace? Could there, perhaps, also be *regional* associations for peace?

There were already nations and federations of states that maintained domestic and interstate order. Also, many nations had historically drawn close together. There were, for example, the Pan American Union and the British Commonwealth. Was it not possible that within such groupings peace could be organized with more authority and more dependability than on a universal basis?

This question was important because the United Nations Security Council was hobbled by the veto. Some veto was inevitable in a universal organization, given the present state of the world. It did not, as we have seen, doom the United Nations to futility. But the veto did reflect difficulties in the way of action by a *world* organization which would not necessarily be found in the way of action by a *regional* organization.

President Wilson had faced this same problem when he founded the League of Nations. He did not solve it to the satisfaction of the Senate and, in consequence, the Monroe Doctrine was one of the rocks on which the League of Nations was shipwrecked.

The United Nations narrowly escaped being wrecked on this same Monroe Doctrine rock.

When we met at San Francisco we were confronted by two conflicting and irreconcilable acts which had recently been taken by our government. One was the Yalta decision of February 11, 1945, which spelled out the veto rights of the five big powers. This decision, when read in conjunction with the Dumbarton Oaks Proposals, meant that no peace enforcement action could be taken under regional arrangements without a vote of the Security Council in which all five of the Permanent Members concurred. Let me illustrate what that would mean.

If the Communist Party should win control of the government of a single South American country, then that government, with Soviet Communist connivance and support, could wage a war of aggression against its neighbors, and the United States or any other signer of an American pact could not take forcible action for peace unless the Soviet Union concurred.

That was, in essence, what had been agreed to at Dumbarton Oaks and Yalta.

But meanwhile, in February–March, 1945, an Inter-American Conference on Problems of War and Peace in Mexico City had adopted the "Act of Chapultepec," under which a regional agency within the Americas was to be established with responsibility for the maintenance of peace in that area. The Act laid down the principle that an attack on any one of the American States should be regarded as an act of aggression against the others, and it recommended the conclusion of an inter-American treaty establishing procedures whereby any acts of aggression within the Americas should be met by collective sanctions, including force.

The conflict between the Dumbarton Oaks–Yalta formula and the formula of Chapultepec was not fully seen until after the San Francisco Conference was under way. It was pointed out by Nelson Rockefeller, who had principal responsibility for liaison with the Latin-American delegates. He knew that a revolt was brewing among them because they believed that the hopes and promises of Chapultepec would be nullified by subjecting

American regional action to possible Russian veto. On the evening of May 5, 1945, he discussed the matter with Senator Vandenberg. The Senator that very night dictated a letter to Secretary Stettinius, urging most strongly that a way be found to permit an American regional association to act free of Russian veto.

The problem was not easy to solve. The Dumbarton Oaks Proposals, plus Yalta, suited Mr. Molotov very well. It gave the Soviet Union an effective veto over any regional action in the Americas or elsewhere. The United States government felt that it could not alter what had already been agreed to, unless released from the agreement by the Soviet Union. Mr. Molotov was planning to return to Moscow in a few days. Obviously it would be difficult to get any concessions after he had gone.

Mr. Molotov had acted in this matter with great shrewdness. In the very first days of the conference he had obtained the agreement of the United States to a provision (Article 53) the effect of which was that, irrespective of Security Council approval, the Soviet Union could act under the network of "non-aggression pacts" that the Soviet Union was negotiating with other European nations—Poland, Yugoslavia, etc. That network now includes China. The United States accordingly would not have any veto power over Soviet action in what might be a zone of special Soviet concern. But we had not been alert enough to ask then for a corresponding exemption in favor of an American regional collective security system. So, our negotiating position was weak.

However, we set to work. For some days this topic became the first and, indeed, the exclusive order of business. It was serious, because the Latin-American countries were threatening to walk out on the San Francisco Conference unless we could salvage the possibility of having a self-operating Inter-American regional system. That we could not get without Molotov's approval; and we had little to trade for it.

A further complication was the fact that some members of the United States Delegation felt that the United States ought not to carve out any further exceptions to the rule of the Security Council. They felt that if the Dumbarton Oaks and Yalta Proposals were further opened up to permit independent, regional enforcement action, then world organization would never come into effective being; the world would be divided into spheres of influence of large states surrounded by groups of smaller states; these regional groups would take on the character of armed camps, and the possibilities of a universal order would vanish.

The differences within the United States Delegation were such that the matter had to be referred to President Truman and a memorandum was sent to him, listing the pros and cons. His response instructed the Delegation to try to work out a formula which would permit of an Inter-American system that could act for peace free of Security Council veto.

Then we faced the task of finding an appropriate formula and getting the Soviet government and the Latin-Americans to accept it. There were many suggestions. The formula finally agreed upon is that which now appears as Article 51 of the Charter and which provides for a "collective" right of self-defense. The first sentence of this article reads:

"Nothing in the present Charter shall impair the inherent right of individual or collective self-defense if an armed attack occurs against a Member of the United Nations, until the Security Council has taken the measures necessary to maintain international peace and security."

In order to get Soviet approval, it proved necessary to proceed rather drastically and to depart from what might be called the best diplomatic manners. Mr. Molotov had gone back to Moscow, May 9, 1945, without having agreed. We could not get the agreement of the remaining chief delegate, Mr. Gromyko. Finally, Secretary Stettinius and I drafted a press statement which he issued (May 15, 1945) publicly committing the United States to the equivalent of the present Article 51. We felt that only in this way could the Soviet hand be forced.

The tactic succeeded. The Soviet delegates at first refused to accept the text we had publicly sponsored. Eventually they gave in.

The Latin-American delegates were not wholly satisfied with our proposed language. It was hard for them to believe that two words, "collective self-defense," could solve so big a problem. They would have preferred an explicit reference in the Charter to the Act of Chapultepec and its proposals specifically excepting them from the veto-bound rule of the Security Council. They acceded, however, to our formula after a dramatic meeting in the penthouse at the Hotel Fairmont. There Senators Connally and Vandenberg used all their powers of persuasion, and they were great. They pledged the honor of the United States to the early consummation of the Inter-American agreement that had been contemplated by the Act of Chapultepec. One of my vivid memories is of that penthouse meeting, with Senator Connally standing half crouched, with arms outstretched, and shouting to a circle of Latin-American diplomats: "You must trust the United States!"

Secretary Stettinius, with the approval of the President, formally and publicly pledged, "After the conclusion of the Conference at San Francisco, it is the intention of the United States Government to invite the other American republics to undertake in the near future the negotiation of a Treaty," as provided for in the Act of Chapultepec.

The Article 51 formula was formally accepted by the San Francisco Conference, and thus was born the possibility of "collective self-defense"—a possibility of incalculable value.

Without this provision the Soviet Union would have had an unlimited right to prevent organization of effective defense agreements against its own possible aggression; and then the United Nations Charter might have proved a positive menace, rather than a blessing, for mankind. It could have been an instrument usable by an aggressor in aid of aggression.

Quite apart from the Soviet aspect of the question, a basic principle was involved. It is illustrated by the creation of the United States itself.

The United States is a union of sovereign States which came about when our thirteen States sought collective security. This creation of our Union and its subsequent development has served peace better than preservation of the separate status of the States. But our regional Union might not have been possible under conditions such as those laid down at Dumbarton Oaks and at Yalta; the Great Powers of that day, Russia, England, France, and Spain, would each have had a right of veto over any enforcement action by our States for collective defense.

It is, of course, important to have a world organization that is universal in its scope and in its interests. It should never be pushed into the background by regional concerns. But it is at the universal level that cohesion is most slowly achieved. It would be folly to say that that slow pace must govern even regional action.

THE RIO PACT OF 1947

The Conference of the Americas, which on May 15, 1945, had been promised "in the near future," did not take place so promptly.

The reason was the increasing confusion in relations between the United States and the Perón regime in Argentina and disagreement within our government as to how that situation should be dealt with.

On October 3, 1945, the State Department announced that, in view of recent developments in Argentina, the United States favored the postponement of the Inter-American Conference which had been scheduled to meet in Rio on October 20th.

On January 11, 1947, Senator Vandenberg spoke of the necessity of "refreshing" inter-American solidarity. He felt the Rio Conference should be held promptly. He feared a Communistic upsurge in the Americas if the American nations continued to drift apart.

On June 3, 1947, President Truman stated that the United States was prepared to consult with all American republics on the subject of a mutual defense pact, and on July 1st Brazil, as host, set August 15th as the date for the conference. That was more than two years after the San Francisco events which we have recorded.

Both Senator Vandenberg and Senator Connally were members of the United States Delegation, which was headed by Secretary of State Marshall. Former Senator Austin, who had become United States Representative to the United Nations, also was a member of the Delegation. He had represented the United States with distinction at the Mexico Conference which had drawn up the Act of Chapultepec.

At Rio there was signed on September 2, 1947, the Inter-American Treaty of Reciprocal Assistance. It embodied the Chapultepec pledge of "one for all—all for one." It bound the parties to participate in an "Organ of Consultation" which, in the event of aggression either from within or from without the Americas, could by a two-thirds vote require action, including economic sanctions, by the member nations. However, "No State shall be required to use armed force without its consent."

The area of the Americas was charted. It included Canada and Greenland, although neither the Dominion of Canada nor Denmark, the sovereign of Greenland, was a party to the pact.

The Rio Pact was a significant development in American foreign policy.

Originally the Monroe Doctrine had been merely a statement by the United States as to what *it* would do if any nation outside the Americas should attempt either annexation in the Americas or extension there of its political system. It was originally looked upon by the United States as a program of self-defense, and was in part directed against Russian expansion along the northwest coast of the North American continent. It also tended to put the United States in the position of a protector, in its own interest, of the countries to the south of us. They had nothing to say about it.

As these countries had grown in power and influence, they had come increasingly to resent the inferior status in which the Monroe Doctrine seemed to place them. They felt it was more dignified and more consistent with their own self-respect to be equal partners in an integrated system of regional security. The Rio Pact involved acceptance of that point of view by the United States. It was a wise and forward-looking step. It put our relations with our southern neighbors on a basis of mutual aid, and both we and they can be the gainers from this new relationship.

The Rio Pact was also significant because it actually put to work Article 51 of the United Nations Charter.

Before that Charter came into force, there had been a number of regional associations of a somewhat loose character. There was the British Commonwealth of Nations; there was the Arab League which had been formed by the Arab States in March, 1945, just before the San Francisco Conference was convened; there was the network of "non-aggression" pacts between the Soviet Union and other "friendly" countries. There was, however, nothing comparable to the security system established by the Rio Pact of the Americas. Its carefully drawn provisions established with precision the nature and scope of the understandings, and set up machinery to implement them.

The Rio Pact set a precedent from which the United States went on to develop the even more significant North Atlantic Pact.

NORTH ATLANTIC PACT

During the winter of 1947–1948 there was fear in Western Europe. That was the period when the Communist parties in France and Italy were openly violent. They organized political strikes and committed many acts of sabotage. They boasted openly, "The Red armies will soon be here." They sought, and won, adherents to their Party by promising that members would be safe from punitive action when the Soviet Union did take over. Premier Queuille of France told me that he estimated that two out of five members of the French Communist Party were members through fear. Many had plans for flight to other parts. Spain was looked on as a possible haven, on the theory that the Pyrenees might be the limit of the first wave of Soviet assault. Those who could were trying to secrete money abroad so that, if they had to flee, they would have funds on which to live.

All of this interfered greatly with economic recovery. It seemed that only a decisive pronouncement by the United States would check the fear that was inspired by Moscow.

In April, 1948, I was taking an early spring vacation on an island in Lake Ontario when I received, through a Canadian lighthouse, a radio message that I was wanted for a conference at Washington. I arrived at Blair House on April 27th, and met Secretary Marshall, Under Secretary Lovett, and Senator Vandenberg.

The four of us discussed the situation. We all agreed that some United States action was called for to allay the rising tide of fear in Europe. What form should it take?

Mr. Lovett suggested that the best solution would be a pact modeled after that of the Americas, which would formalize the community of interest within the West that had been demonstrated during two world wars.

I was at first doubtful about so formal a treatment of the situation. I knew that it would be difficult to draw the line for inclusion within, and exclusion from, the pact and thought at first that it might be better to start our European commitment by a Presidential Declaration like that of President Monroe. It could perhaps be formalized later.

After a full exchange of views, Secretary Marshall and Under Secretary Lovett decided to proceed along the lines of a North Atlantic regional pact. Senator Vandenberg indicated that he felt that the Senate liked the idea of regional associations and would be disposed to approve in principle a further developing of such associations for collective defense.

This estimate was verified on June 11, 1948, when the Senate adopted by the overwhelming vote of 64 to 4 the "Vandenberg Resolution," which stated it was the sense of the Senate that the United States should pursue among other objectives:

(2) progressive development of regional and other collective arrangements for individual and collective self-defense in accordance with the purposes, principles and provisions of the Charter;

(3) association of the United States, by Constitutional process, with such regional and other collective arrangements as are based on continuous and effective self-help and mutual aid, and as affect its national security.

The State Department then undertook initial discussions with Canada, the United Kingdom, France, and the Benelux countries—Belgium, the Netherlands, and Luxembourg. The negotiations were primarily conducted by Under Secretary Lovett at Washington. Secretary Marshall and I were in Paris at the United Nations Assembly during the fall of 1948, and I did not follow the matter closely. I did, however, suggest to Secretary Marshall that nothing definitive should be done until after the Presidential elections. It seemed undesirable that a firm commitment should be made as to the details of this matter until it was clear which of the major parties would have the primary responsibility of carrying the project to conclusion. Secretary Marshall said that no definitive commitments would be made until after November 2, 1948.

Following the November election, the matter was pushed. The seven original sponsoring nations decided to consider enlarging the scope of the pact to include the Scandinavian countries— Iceland, Norway, Denmark, and Sweden; also Italy and Portugal. Sweden decided not to join, considering a Scandinavian Pact preferable. The others accepted.

This expansion of the original group involved many close questions and difficult decisions. The inclusion of Norway seemed to some unnecessarily provocative of the Soviet Union, as Norway has a common frontier with the Soviet Union and the Soviet Union would have strongly, and understandably, resented the establishment along that common border of air bases that were open to use by the United States. The Soviet government did, indeed, make a strong protest to Norway, and on February 1, 1949, the Norwegian government gave assurance that it would not enter into any agreement with any other countries obligating Norway to grant bases on Norwegian territory unless Norway was attacked or threatened with attack.

Norway has always had close ties with England, and has considered itself a distinctively "North Atlantic" country. It wanted to join the pact, and its joining would make more likely the joining also of Iceland and Denmark. Iceland had proved to be a useful point from which to patrol the North Atlantic during the Second World War. Also, the inclusion of Denmark would bring in Greenland, already included in the American area defined by the Rio Pact. Denmark, with Norway, might take effective action in the event of war to block the exit of Russian submarines through the Skagerrak.

The inclusion of Portugal brought in the Azores, which had proved valuable as a base during the Second World War.

Italy also was included, although not a North Atlantic nation. France attached importance to the possibility of a common defense with Italy of the passes through the Alps. Also, the inclusion of Italy involved a desirable recognition of Italy's reformation from Fascism into one of the free countries of the West. This recognition was timely because the Italian government was facing serious Communist opposition and had to face up to the probable liquidation of Italian colonial aspirations in North Africa.

Whether or not all of these decisions were wise, only time will tell. Certainly there were some good reasons for them. They resulted in a North Atlantic Treaty which, on April 4, 1949, was signed by the United States, Canada, and the ten Western European countries.

The heart of the treaty is Article 5, which provides that "the Parties agree that an armed attack against one or more of them in Europe or North America shall be considered an attack against them all," and that in that event each of the parties will take forthwith "such action as it deems necessary, including the use of armed force, to restore and maintain the security of the North Atlantic area."

The North Atlantic area, for the purposes of the treaty, includes the territory of any of the parties in Europe or North America, the Algerian Departments of France, the occupation zones of any party in Europe (for example, in Germany), any islands of any party in the North Atlantic, and "the vessels or aircraft in this area of any of the Parties." The treaty provided for a Council and committees, including a Defense Committee which would recommend the measures to implement the treaty.

The treaty met with considerable opposition in the Senate. But after prolonged hearings and debate, and after proposed amendments had been beaten down, ratification was finally voted on July 21, 1949, by the very substantial majority of 82 to 13.

The North Atlantic Treaty is a major development in the organization of peace. It makes clear that hereafter an invasion of Western Europe from Russia or Germany will be treated as an act of war upon the United States. It is the theory and hope of the proponents of the treaty that by thus making clear in advance what we will do in the event of an attack on Western Europe, that attack will not, in fact, occur.

Many believe that if the Kaiser had known in advance that his attack on France by way of Belgium would have brought England, and then the United States, into the fray he would never have made that attack. Because he did not know this with certainty, he took a chance. He lost, and it was not his loss alone, but the loss of all of us.

Many also believe that if Hitler had known that his war would involve the United States he would not have started it. Not knowing, he took a chance. He lost, and again so did we all.

The North Atlantic Pact, plus the Pact of the Americas, removes any uncertainty as to the concern of the United States with the regions that are defined. There is no longer any excuse for miscalculation or for the taking of chances.

The treaties are not all gain, for by increasing certainty in some areas they increase uncertainty in other areas. We shall consider some of these angles later. But the two pacts do provide the parties with valuable insurance against piecemeal aggression. The United States is committed to no more than what almost certainly it would do if, for example, the Soviet Union were to launch an armed attack against either Western Europe or the Americas. Also, it is not just a one-sided arrangement. The United States might be attacked first, and we should then desperately need the help of allies and the bases they could make available.

We can fairly judge that the Rio and North Atlantic pacts are steps along a path that leads in the direction of peace.

CHAPTER NINE

FILLING IN THE ECONOMIC VACUUM

When Europe was liberated in 1945, it was feeble and reeling. It could not stand without support.

It had taken three grievous blows in quick succession. There was World War I. That had greatly depleted the man power and financial strength of France and England.

Then there came the world-wide economic depression that began in 1929 and lasted for several years. This had dislocated production and distribution, had caused widespread unemployment, and had shaken the peoples' confidence in the economic practices of the West.

Then came the third blow, World War II. France was conquered, her currency debauched, and French spirit seemed momentarily broken except as General de Gaulle, Jean Monnet, and a few others in exile kept alive the idea of "Free France." England underwent a terrible ordeal which drained the vitality of the people and almost completed the exhaustion of her foreign investments. England, France, and Holland faced the loss of colonial areas which had long been a source of economic strength. When victory came, the Soviet Union put its Iron Curtain through the middle of Europe and cut off normal access to the food and raw materials of Eastern Europe. Throughout the Continent, mental and moral doubts turned into deep despair.

Except as strength came from outside, Europe was largely a vacuum—a military vacuum, an economic vacuum, and a moral vacuum.

At first there was only one dynamic source from which to fill that vacuum. That was Soviet Communism.

From the Communist standpoint, the situation in Central and Western Europe was ideal. It was a moment such as Stalin had looked forward to when, in discussing "strategy and tactics," he called for "the selection of the moment for the decisive blow, of the moment for starting the insurrection so timed as to coincide with the moment when the crisis has reached its climax . . . and maximum consternation reigns in the ranks of the enemy" (p. 64).

The 1946-1947 period seemed to meet the specifications. That was apparently the judgment of the Politburo.

Russia itself had, of course, suffered greatly from the war. But that great heartland was still pulsing with energy that could be mobilized and directed by the Communist leaders.

From Finland to Albania and from the Ukraine to the Elbe, where Russian armies were, or threatened, the Communists were potent. It seemed that there was a good chance of extending Communist dominance to all of the Continent. Their plans had been made long in advance, and the moment for action had come.

The only other source of dynamic power was the United States. But victory had left us momentarily uninterested.

Americans have come to look upon war as a kind of gigantic prize fight. The objective is to knock out your opponent. If you do knock him out, the job is done. Then it is in order to go home, break training, and enjoy yourself until you may have to go into training for a return bout.

When victory came in World War I and World War II, it found the United States without any political objectives to be implemented by victory. The program was to get home, to demobilize and try to make up for the good times that had been lost because of the necessities of war.

Fortunately, after World War II we did not remain long in that mood. Soviet tactics were so flagrantly threatening that they involved an overreaching. They slapped our faces until we waked up from our postwar daze. Awakening was, however, a gradual process, and it took the Moscow meeting of the Council of Foreign Ministers (March–April, 1947) and its attendant circumstances to arouse the leaders and the people to the fact that the peril was great and called for positive policies of large scope.

The French situation at the time was parlous. The 1945-1946 elections had given the Communists about 30 per cent of the votes and about one-third of the deputies. They were the largest single political group. Communists were strongly represented in the government and headed important ministries, including in 1947 the Ministry of Defense. The Communist Party had won control of the central labor union, the C.G.T., and through it could strangle French production by calling strikes of the workers in the French industries, the coal mines, and the government itself. French fear of Germany was exploited by the Communists, who asserted that the United States would seek to rebuild and rearm Germany at the expense of France.

The United States Delegation, on its way to Moscow, stopped for two days in Berlin. We then had the welcome opportunity of conferring with General Clay and his associates, who had been doing preparatory work from the standpoint of our military government in Germany. On March 7, 1947, Secretary Marshall held at Berlin a policy conference attended by General Clay, Ambassador Murphy, State Department Counselor Benjamin Cohen, and myself. We discussed a memorandum I had prepared, analyzing the European situation. It emphasized the danger from either a Germany subject to "political penetration" by the Soviet Union or a Germany "independent of both East and West" which would have "an enormous bargaining power." My memorandum concluded that "the European settlement should seek primarily to solidify and strengthen Western Europe."

There was general acceptance of the view that Germany should not be dealt with as an isolated problem. Secretary of State Marshall, although he had held that office only a few weeks, had an immediate grasp of the total strategy involved. He frequently remarked that "localitis" was one of the most difficult problems with which he had had to deal in planning a military campaign, and that he hoped to avoid that when he was planning peace.

When we arrived at Moscow we began the discussion of a peace treaty for Austria and the establishment of a German government, with which peace might be made. Some progress was made on an Austrian treaty. There was, however, total disagreement regarding Germany. Mr. Molotov insisted upon the establishment of an all-powerful central government at Berlin. The Soviet leaders felt confident that if all political power were centered in one place, preferably Berlin in the Soviet Zone, they could get control of Germany by getting control of that central power.

The United States Delegation felt the danger of centralized power. We called for a federal system in which the German states would have much of the power. We insisted on sticking to the directive of the Potsdam Declaration signed August 1, 1945, by Truman, Stalin, and Attlee to the effect that there should be a "decentralization of the political structure and the development of local responsibility."

From the standpoint of agreement on Germany, the Moscow Conference was wholly negative in its results. The conference did, however, have important by-products.

It aroused the United States to the scope of Soviet ambitions on the Continent of Europe. We saw at first hand the determination of Soviet leaders to dominate both Germany and France. We saw that France was the key to thwarting that, not only because geographically it lay between Germany and the Atlantic, but also because only with French good will could there be developed an integrated West into which Germany could be drawn.

The French Delegation had come to Moscow with little hope of fruitful cooperation with the United States and England, and feeling that they would have to seek help from the Soviet Union. To change that mood was a primary purpose of the United States Delegation at the Moscow Conference. We tried to dispel the notion that the United States was committed to a program of building up a strong Germany at the expense of French recovery. We found many ways to do that.

The United States and the United Kingdom agreed at Moscow to support provisions in the German peace treaty that would make the Saar into an autonomous area having economic and financial ties with France.

The United States agreed at Moscow that more Ruhr coal

should go to the reconstruction of France, as a need having priority over the reconstruction of Germany.

The United States agreed on a control of the Ruhr industrial basin which would provide "a European solution in a Europe which includes Germany."

In general, we tried to support France's proposals on Germany wherever they seemed to have merit, and many of them did seem to have much merit.

In contrast, the Soviet delegates indicated that they put their primary reliance upon winning control of Germany, figuring that France was already riddled by Communism and that if they could get Germany all Europe would be "in the bag."

By the end of the Moscow Conference, there was a marked change in the relations between the French and the Soviet Delegations. Perhaps that change can be best illustrated by the story of two dinners.

At the opening of the conference, Mr. Molotov gave a welcoming dinner in honor of the other delegates. He sat at the middle of a narrow table. At his right sat Mr. Bevin, and at his left, Secretary Marshall. Immediately opposite him sat Mr. Bidault. The attitude of Mr. Molotov toward Mr. Bevin and Secretary Marshall was formally correct. Toward Mr. Bidault, he was effusive. Mr. Bidault responded in kind. They repeatedly toasted each other. They leaned nearer and nearer, until it almost seemed that they would fall into each other's arms.

That typified French-Soviet relations as the conference began.

At the close of the conference there was another dinner, a farewell dinner given by Marshal Stalin at the Kremlin for the three visiting foreign ministers and their top advisers. It was an impressive occasion. With two exceptions, all the members of the Politburo were in attendance. Mr. Molotov, at Marshal Stalin's request, acted as toastmaster. He toasted Mr. Bevin and General Marshall and various other persons. Finally he made a belated toast to Mr. Bidault, couched in language that seemed to all of us to be a deliberate insult.

That typified French-Soviet relations as the conference ended.

In the radio report which I made on my return from Moscow,

I said, "We did not come home empty-handed." I spoke of "the establishment of closer relations with France," and continued: "As we studied the problem of Germany in its European setting, we became more and more convinced that there is no economic solution along purely national lines. Increased economic unity is absolutely essential to the well-being of Europe."

Secretary Marshall has intimated that it was on the plane flying home from Moscow that he began to form in his mind the idea of what is now known the world over as the "Marshall Plan." No doubt others had similar ideas at much the same time. Events were compelling us to think in that direction. But the Moscow Conference was, to those who were there, like a streak of lightning that suddenly illumined a dark and stormy scene. We saw as never before the magnitude of the task of saving Europe for Western civilization. We saw the need of economic and moral support and the need of a program that would be both comprehensive and creative.

Moscow was the logical prelude to the idea that Secretary Marshall gave the world shortly after his return. Also, it educated Mr. Bevin and Mr. Bidault to the importance of quickly grasping hold of the Marshall "idea" and seeking, from their side, to convert it into a Marshall Plan.

The essence of the Marshall idea on June 5, 1947, was that the United States would consider a long-range program for filling in the economic vacuum in Europe. But the European countries which would receive our aid must themselves cooperate so that there could be a common program. The United States did not want to be in the position of building up one country at the expense of another, or of emphasizing political and economic divisions and rivalries which ought to be done away with if there was to be general economic welfare.

The Marshall proposal was open to all Europe, including the Soviet Union. Czechoslovakia and Poland were eager to share the benefits of the program. But the Soviet Union refused to participate and vetoed participation by any Communist-controlled country. Mr. Molotov pretended that the plan was a sinister plot of the United States imperialists. More likely, he did not want the satellite peoples to learn at first hand of the marvel of American productivity, or to sense the American spirit of generosity. The Soviet Union dared not allow a lifting of the Iron Curtain. In consequence, only the countries of Western Europe came together to qualify as recipients of Marshall Plan aid.

It was no easy task to translate the Marshall "idea" into a concrete European Recovery Program which might run for five years and involve the United States' giving away as much as $20,000,000,000 in goods. Also, it would take time for our people to learn the need of making such an effort, wholly without parallel in time of peace.

But circumstances were making an insistent call—so much so that, on November 10, 1947, a plan of "interim aid" to France, Italy, and Austria was put before Congress. It was not possible to wait until the five-year program had been fully developed.

The Interim Aid program was pending in Congress when the Council of Foreign Ministers next met in London in November–December, 1947. The French internal situation was then in an upheaval that was approaching a climax. The "middle" parties seemed to be losing control of the situation. It seemed probable— many thought it certain—that General de Gaulle would come to power, and that the Communists would oppose him with arms, thus touching off a full-scale civil war in France.

With Secretary Marshall's approval, I left the London Council meeting on December 4, 1947, and went to France for a personal check of the situation. It seemed to me—and to him—that that was more important than hearing Mr. Molotov repeat what he had said at Moscow six months before.

In Paris, I conferred with President Auriol, Prime Minister Schuman, Minister of Interior Moch, and such leading political figures as Léon Blum and Léon Jouhaux, who inclined to the "left," and General de Gaulle, who inclined to the "right." Also, our Ambassador, Jefferson Caffery, gave me much valuable information.

The situation was indeed desperate. Rail transportation was disrupted. Indeed, the train on which my wife and I traveled had had to be rerouted because the tracks ahead had been blown up. In Paris, there was no electric light, power, or running water, except intermittently. Industry was at a standstill, and essential utilities, if they operated at all, did so by the help of the French Army and Marines, who also patrolled the railroad tracks. The government was handling the situation courageously, but its members eagerly welcomed any sign of moral support from the United States. Also, they needed assurance of economic support in the form of coal, and assurance of future aid which would permit them to promise reconstruction despite the ravages of Communist sabotage.

Interim Aid legislation was then nearing passage, and Congress was thinking of attaching some conditions that worried the French government, because the conditions could be misconstrued to give plausibility to the Communist propaganda that the United States was trying to turn France into an American colony.

I got a telephone connection to my brother, Allen, in the United States, and through him conveyed to Senator Vandenberg and to Representative Herter an idea of the critical nature of the situation. The result of their efforts was that the Interim Aid program was assured without conditions which would have played into the hands of the French Communist Party.

President Auriol and Prime Minister Schuman regarded my trip to Paris, made with Secretary Marshall's approval, as a symbol of United States concern in the maintenance in France of a non-Communist government. It seemed that, in time of need, the United States had sought to show publicly its sympathy. This thought was widely conveyed by the non-Communist press and moving pictures. Crowds followed me everywhere.

The French Communists attacked me viciously. The large Communist Parliamentary group met on December 6, 1947, and adopted a resolution condemning my trip as "odious" United States interference with the political independence of France.

By early December, the fury of the Communist effort had begun to wane. The French people had come to realize that they were being victimized by a political movement which had been launched from Moscow by Thorez, the head of the French Communist Party. They were encouraged by the assured economic support of the United States, visibly evidenced by the arrival of shiploads of coal.

Thus France passed through its most severe crisis since the liberation. A major Communist bolt had been shot and had not proved fatal.

When I later testified before the Senate Foreign Relations Committee in connection with the European Recovery Program, I was able to say that the timely grant of Interim Aid to France had been a decisive element in helping the French nation to preserve its free institutions.

By the beginning of 1948, the preliminary work on the Marshall Plan had been done and the matter was taken to Congress. The original Administration project had not been well conceived. To Senator Vandenberg, then Chairman of the Foreign Relations Committee, fell the heavy burden of rewriting the legislation in a form that would make it workable and acceptable to the Congress and to the country. This he did in a way that entitled him to share with Secretary Marshall the credit for the ultimate result.

One thing that Congress did was to make explicit the *policy* behind the legislation and the ultimate result sought.

The task, as I saw it and as I testified before the Senate Foreign Relations Committee, was to bring about increased economic unity in Europe. It did not seem that the non-Communist parts of Europe, deprived of colonies and cut off from normal access to the resources of Eastern Europe, could survive as a series of sixteen separate economic compartments with an average population of about 13,000,000 per country. These nations were, at the time, separated not only by tariff and quota barriers, but by separate currencies which were overvalued and could not be freely exchanged.

Prolonged American generosity might suffice to keep the peoples of Western Europe alive. But it could not give them self-respect or the possibility of developing the economic strength needed for their own independent survival. That could happen only if there were increased economic unity between the upwards of 200,000,000 industrious people participating in the European

Recovery Program who possessed, as among themselves in Europe or in Africa, immense natural resources.

So the policy statement of the Act, as rewritten by Congress, emphasized the importance of developing a large single market such as we have in the United States; and it incorporated language which I suggested to the effect that the "continuity of assistance provided by the United States should, at all times, be dependent upon continuity of cooperation among countries participating in the program."

The European Recovery Act was voted by Congress in March and approved by the President on April 3, 1948. Interim Aid was already flowing, so that there have now been over two years of the European Recovery Program. Under it, within these two years, over $10,000,000,000 in money and goods has been made available by the United States to Western Europe, including Greece, Turkey, and Western Germany. This is in addition to normal trade, the proceeds of the British loan of 1946, War Department aid to our Zone in Germany, and gifts, totaling hundreds of millions, from religious groups, charitable organizations, and individuals.

The European Recovery Program has not accomplished all that was hoped, or even all that might reasonably have been expected. But it has poured goods into Europe at such a rate that the economic vacuum has, to a large extent, been filled. Productivity in the participating countries has, broadly speaking, recovered so that it equals or surpasses prewar production. Instead of a famine of coal and steel, there is a growing surplus. Hope has been reborn, and there no longer exist the vast areas of human desolation which seemed to offer Soviet Communism the chance to strike a "decisive blow."

It has been a costly operation, and it is not yet finished. But the results justify the cost. The Soviet Communist program of indirect aggression against Western Europe has, for the time being, been thwarted.

CHAPTER TEN

FILLING IN THE MILITARY VACUUM

Do the Soviet leaders plan to use their army for conquest? That is *the* question of questions. Perhaps no one knows the answer. If anyone does, it is the world's best guarded secret, locked in the innermost recesses of the Kremlin.

Nevertheless, the rest of the world must make some assumptions. We need a working hypothesis, for we ourselves have to make plans. If it is assumed that the Soviet Union plans an early invasion of Western Europe, it would be folly to ship arms to Europe to fall into Russian hands. If it is assumed that the Soviet Union is determined *not* to make an armed attack, then perhaps we can let up on our own military expenditure. If the answer is "Maybe, but not now," still another course may be indicated. We have to make certain assumptions because we ourselves have to act in some way.

Fortunately, our assumptions need not be pure guesswork. A number of relevant facts are known.

First of all, we know that Soviet leaders attach the utmost importance to a strong military establishment—and they have it.

The first post-war Five Year Economic Plan was essentially one for the development of heavy industry suitable for war purposes. That was despite the fact that the people were pathetically in need of household goods.

In Russia in the spring of 1947 I was struck by the shortage of household goods in the shops of Moscow. The shop windows were mostly filled with papier-mâché dummies. What was on the shelves was mostly loot from Germany. The Soviet Zone of Eastern Germany had apparently been stripped bare of china, glassware, silver, furniture, etc., and that "war booty" could be bought in Russia. But there was little else of such consumers' goods.

Each of our parlor suites at the Hotel Moskva boasted a piano. But all these pianos were German pianos. In the bathrooms, with washbowl and tub, there was only one metal stopper. At first I thought this was an oversight, and I tried to get a second. But I found that there were not enough stoppers to allow one each for the washbasin and the bathtub even in the best hotel in Moscow, a hotel which had just been renovated for the reception of the Foreign Ministers' Council, and where, I might add, the service was efficient and courteous.

Despite such a scarcity in household goods, the first post-war economic effort was, as I say, not one for the fabrication of peace goods, but of the heavy goods needed for war.

We now know that the Russian scientists and industrialists, with the help of scientists brought from Germany and the help of spies, have developed atomic weapons and done so with surprising rapidity. I was in a position to know, in the spring of 1949, that our top official experts were then convinced that it would probably be five years or more before the Russians would be able to make atomic bombs.

Richard L. Davies, a Philadelphia industrialist, believed that the Russians would have atomic bombs by 1949, and I was sufficiently impressed by his reasoning to give sponsorship to that forecast. In an address made in Toronto on March 8, 1948, I said, "Competent authorities now say that this year—1948—may be the last during which any single country will have any effective monopoly of the knowledge of how to use atomic energy." However, Mr. Davies was not able to get official attention or credence. There seemed in official quarters to be a "superiority" complex and a feeling that, because it had taken us many years of stupendous effort to make the first atomic bomb, the Russians, even with German help, would not for a very long time be able to match us.

The outcome shows that there has been a dangerous tendency to underestimate the scientific knowledge, the industrial "know-how," and the willingness to sacrifice that make up the Soviet military effort.

We know that the Soviet high command is developing a navy. It seems to be concentrating on submarines of the new German seagoing *Schnörkel* type. It claimed in 1949 to have 250 operational submarines. Also, it is building some cruisers. It has a major air force. It should be assumed that the Soviet government has gone into the possibilities of hydrogen bombs and of bacteriological warfare. It continues to maintain a large standing army.

So, fact number one is that the Soviet leaders have a powerful modern military establishment.

A second fact is that Communist doctrine does not give primary emphasis to conquest by direct military aggression. In that respect Communism differs sharply from the Nazism of Hitler and the Fascism of Mussolini. They relied primarily on military action.

Stalin talks about the Soviet military establishment as being designed to defend the Soviet Union rather than to aid the worldwide offensive of the Soviet Communist Party. That, of course, is no guarantee that the Red Army and Air Force will not launch an attack. Communist doctrine teaches that any end is justified if it helps Communism reach its goal of world mastery. Violence, at least civil violence, is accepted as a proper, and indeed necessary, means to that end. Soviet Communists certainly have no *moral* inhibitions against using an army to advance their purposes, and some of their authoritative writings suggest that, in the end, this may be necessary. But Soviet Communist doctrine does not emphasize conquest by military invasion. This perhaps is because of—

Fact number three: the fact that the Soviet Communists have effective means of conquest other than through direct military aggression. Soviet military power is used by Communists to frighten non-Communists. But Communists are not dependent, like Hitler, upon an actual use of military power. The Nazi doctrine was based largely upon race supremacy. It was designed to make the Germans masters of the world. Obviously that was not a doctrine which readily gained voluntary acceptance abroad. It was a doctrine which could be spread only by military conquest.

Soviet Communism is a doctrine which, theoretically, could gain world-wide acceptance without military conquest. It has in it elements of universality, because it pretends to seek the welfare of the "masses." The "masses" are any majority who think they would be better off if they could despoil any minority. These are to be found everywhere. So Communism promotes *class war* —civil war—more than national war. Indeed, it tries to avoid stirring up nationalism, except in the colonial areas where "Independence" is a slogan for stirring up revolution against the colonial powers.

One of Soviet Communism's great blunders was its stirring up of nationalism in Yugoslavia. Generally it avoids anything that suggests a war of nation against nation, because it may arouse national loyalties which are stronger than class loyalties. War between nations and war between classes are two different kinds of war that do not go readily hand in hand. Communism is committed primarily to class war.

To promote class wars, Soviet Communism has developed over the years a world-wide organization thoroughly trained in the arts of propaganda, penetration, espionage, sabotage, and subversive warfare. The organization, while headed up in Moscow, is international. In every country of the world this organization operates, and everywhere its secret agents get into positions of great influence in what Soviet Communists call "mass organizations," such as labor unions, and also in parliaments and governments.

The effectiveness of these methods is shown by the fact that Communism, through governments, political parties, and labor unions, now has dominant influence over about one-third of the entire human race.

With two exceptions, the expansion of Soviet Communist power has been accomplished without any direct use of the Russian army.

One exception is the dismemberment of Poland in September,

1939, when, to use Molotov's words, "it needed only one swift blow to Poland, first by the German army and then by the Red Army, and nothing remained of this ugly offspring of the Versailles Treaty." [1]

The other exception is the Soviet war against Finland of 1939–1940.

These two instances show that when Soviet leaders think it expedient, they will use the Red Army for aggression. But in both these cases they were in competition with Hitler.

Even though the Red Army has not often been used for open aggression, the Soviet Communists have made great propaganda use of that possibility in aid of their "indirect" aggression. It helped the Communists in Czechoslovakia to take over complete power in 1948. It has greatly aided the French Communist Party to build up its strength. But that is talk which—during the last five years, at least—has not been turned into reality.

A fourth fact is that the Soviet Communist Party has fanatical designs for world conquest; and the Party is quite a different thing from the Soviet State, the Red Army, or the Russian people.

The distinction is not always easy to follow, because Party leaders are usually also State leaders, and vice versa. But the distinction has reality. Stalin is very emphatic about it. He says that "not a single important political or organizational question is decided by our Soviet [the State] . . . without guiding directions from the Party" (p. 135). But "this does not mean that the Party can be identified with the Soviets, with the state power. The Party is the core of this power, but it is not and cannot be identified with the state power" (p. 138).

The significance of the distinction becomes clearer when we realize that the Communist Party of the Soviet Union has a membership of about 6,000,000. That is about 3 per cent of the total population and perhaps 5 per cent of the adult population. More than 90 per cent of the Russian people are not "Communists,"

---

[1] Quoted from Molotov's Report to the Extraordinary Fifth Session of the Supreme Court of the U.S.S.R., Oct. 31, 1939 (English translation as published at Moscow).

and the Russian army is not a "Communist" organization. Indeed, the Communist Party felt during World War II, and feels at the present time, compelled to keep a close watch on the Red Army and its generals by means of its own political commissars.

In total war, the Communist Party would have to depend upon an army and upon people who are themselves only to a small extent Communist, and who do not at all share the fanatical beliefs and global ambitions of the members of the Communist Party. Russian troops prefer to stay at home.

Some of the highest and most competent authorities in Europe have recently told me that they do not believe that the Communist Party would dare to order the Russian armies to march into Western Europe as an invading force unless Russia had first been attacked, so that it was clear to the Russian people that the operation was necessary for self-defense.

Because of the four facts I have mentioned, most well qualified persons are inclined to feel that there is no imminent danger of the Red Army's being marched out of Russia against Western Europe or Asia in a war of aggression. The position of Yugoslavia is somewhat different, because it involves defection within what Soviet leaders consider their political orbit.

It would indeed seem foolish for the Soviet leaders deliberately to precipitate a fighting war with the militarily powerful United States, when Soviet Communism is still making vast gains in a "cold" war where their techniques are as superior to ours as guns are to bows and arrows. Also, they are making gains as rapidly as they can digest them.

Nevertheless, it would be folly to risk the safety of our nation and our civilization upon the accuracy of what, at best, are educated guesses.

It is never safe to assume that our type of reasoning will guide the future action of those who have unlimited ambitions affected by personal rivalries, who have despotic power, who control a vast army and air force, who have no moral scruples, and who, because they operate a police state, can act with much less prolonged preparation of public opinion than is required in a free society.

The United States, since it woke up to the hostile nature of Soviet Communism, has wisely assumed that it is not safe to gamble everything on the chance that the Soviet will not attack. We have for several years been spending over $10,000,000,000 a year on our military establishment. Several hundred million dollars a year go into atomic development and the effort to create a substantial stockpile of atomic bombs. This lethal item is budgeted, somewhat ironically, as for "National Resources, not primarily agricultural."

Many have believed that the supremacy of the United States in atomic weapons was a main defense of Western Europe. Churchill, in this country on March 13, 1949, said:

"It is certain that Europe would have been Communized like Czechoslovakia and London under bombardment some time ago but for the deterrent of the atomic bomb in the hands of the United States."

Up to 1949 this was the accepted strategic concept for Western Europe. It was not thought that it would be worth while to attempt to fill in the military vacuum which had existed in Western Europe ever since the Germans disarmed the French and the Allies disarmed the Germans.

The North Atlantic Treaty was originally designed to implement that strategic concept. It was felt that the Red Army would not march into Western Europe if it were made clear in advance that the United States would immediately counterattack with its air power and atomic bombs.

However, the governments of Western Europe did not feel happy to be completely exposed to an attack against which the only defense was the dropping of bombs on Russia by air from the United States. As Foreign Minister Schuman put it to me in the winter of 1948–1949:

"It is not good enough for us to know that if we are invaded the United States will go to war and win the war. If we are invaded again—and this time by the Russians—that will be the end of Western civilization so far as we are concerned. A United States victory will, for us, be meaningless."

Furthermore, as economic recovery progressed under the European Recovery Plan, it seemed that Western Europe could afford to develop some military power of its own.

During 1948 the military leaders of the different Western countries began to explore that possibility.

The nucleus of this exploration was the five-power Brussels Pact of March 17, 1948, between the United Kingdom, France, Belgium, the Netherlands, and Luxembourg. Under the pact a Joint Staff Headquarters was set up at Fontainebleau; and in December, 1948, United States officers were assigned to work with it.

Out of this came the Military Assistance Program. The plan was, in essence, that the United States should assist the European signers of the North Atlantic Treaty with certain types of modern equipment so that they might develop a coordinated system of defense of their own homelands.

The fact that this program was in the making in the spring and summer of 1949 was the principal reason why there were difficulties in securing the ratification of the North Atlantic Treaty.

Only a few Senators would have objected to a commitment by the United States to go to war in the event of a Soviet invasion of Western Europe. There was objection to the new strategic concept which involved our helping to fill in the military vacuum in Western Europe. Many felt that this would be excessively expensive to the United States, and that in no event would it be possible to develop in Western Europe a force that would be significant in relation to the force that the Soviet Union could bring to bear.

Actually, of course, there was nothing in the North Atlantic Treaty that committed the United States to any particular strategic concept. I was in the Senate at the time, and argued there in the debate that the two issues were quite distinct; that after the North Atlantic Treaty came into force a specific military assistance program would be brought to the Congress, and then it could decide whether or not the United States should help to develop a military force in Western Europe.

There was nothing novel in the idea of giving arms to European countries threatened by attack from Communist countries. Under the Truman Doctrine of 1947, Congress had already authorized the United States to supply arms to Greece and Turkey. However, the extension of such aid to Western Europe was more costly and the reasons for it more debatable.

The Administration's original Military Assistance bill sought a grant of power virtually without limit as to amount and scope. It covered the whole world. It was so sweeping that it aroused widespread objection in both Houses of Congress and in both parties. After an exchange of views in which I participated with Senator Connally and Senator Vandenberg, the original bill was withdrawn and a totally new bill was proposed, along lines I suggested to the State Department. Even in the second bill, however, it seemed that the powers and the sums requested were excessive.

Senator Vandenberg and I introduced amendments to meet these objections. Also, we proposed to tie the Military Assistance Program closely into the North Atlantic Treaty and the recommendations of its Council and Defense Committee. Merely to rebuild small, unbalanced national military establishments in each of the countries would be a waste of money and effort. The only chance of getting worth-while results out of the limited resources available was to have a coordinated program under which each participant would carry the particular responsibility allotted it under a common defense program.

The amendments we proposed were accepted by the Administration, and with these amendments the bill was adopted by a substantial majority in both Houses of Congress. Under the bill, $500,000,000 was made available for expenditure in the fiscal year ending June 30, 1950. Contracts during that period for a like amount were authorized, so that the work could be gotten under way in respect to future deliveries. Also, substantial deliveries of United States surplus military equipment were authorized.

Thus the United States adopted the policy of gradually filling in the military vacuum which World War II had created in Western Europe.

That is sound policy in a world where, unfortunately, arma-

ments are not yet internationally controlled. It is inherently a
defensive policy, for it would not be possible in any predictable
time to build up in Western Europe a military establishment
which would have any *offensive* significance. Indeed, it cannot
quickly have much *defensive* significance, except against indirect,
internal aggression. But the fact that the peoples of Western
Europe are not left wholly naked from the standpoint of their
own defense should be a stabilizing influence. It is a step toward
regaining normality; it decreases the risk of panic, and in that
respect decreases the risk of war.

CHAPTER ELEVEN

BIPARTISANSHIP IN FOREIGN POLICY

We have, up to this point, discussed a number of postwar policies. All these policies have made a contribution to peace, and their good possibilities are not yet spent.

But no policy can promote peace unless it actually becomes a dependable reality.

Some of the policies we have discussed found expression in treaties. That was true of the United Nations Charter, the Rio Pact, and the North Atlantic Pact. Treaties, however, only become operative if they are ratified by the United States Senate. That takes a two-thirds vote.

Some of the policies we have discussed require the United States to appropriate large sums of money. In order for the United Nations to be a going concern, the United States has been putting up about 40 per cent of the United Nations' regular budget. Military and economic aid to Greece, military aid to Turkey, the European Recovery Plan, and the Military Assistance Program, together, cost around $6,000,000,000 a year. The money only became available when Congress appropriated it.

Most of the policies we have discussed are not just United States policies, that we could carry out alone. Their success depends upon the governments of foreign countries cooperating with us. That involves them in great risks. To decide to cooperate with the United States is no easy decision for those who live in exposed areas such as Norway, Denmark, Iran, Turkey, Greece, and South Korea. Indeed, all the European members of the North Atlantic Pact are taking serious risks. The governments of the nations in Asia that have newly won independence all face the menace of Communist penetration and civil war. The personally "safe" thing for the leaders of such countries might be to turn to Communism or try to be "neutral," or perhaps retire into exile.

Everyone in an exposed area who makes common cause with others to resist Soviet Communist aggression and to preserve free institutions risks not merely his office, but his life. Such persons take these risks primarily because of their beliefs. But the risks are reckless and hardly worth taking unless United States leadership and support can be depended upon. The entire postwar program which we have been reviewing would collapse like a house of cards if the governments of the still free peoples felt that there was such division within the United States that the policies we have discussed did not have assured continuity, at least in their broad outline.

The ratification of treaties, the appropriation of money, the assurance of continuity all require bipartisan cooperation.

At no time during the five years since fighting stopped could a treaty have been ratified without the support of Republicans.

At no time during these five years could the necessary appropriations have been voted without a large measure of bipartisan support, because even when the Democrats or the Republicans had a paper majority, internal party divisions prevented its being, of itself, a working majority. During two of the five years in question, the Republicans have had a majority in both Houses of Congress. For a considerable period prior to November 2, 1948, it was generally assumed by foreign governments that a Republican would be elected President and that the Republican Party would control not merely the Congress, which it then already controlled, but the executive administration of foreign affairs.

The election of November, 1948, did not come out as most foreign governments had anticipated. But it was close enough to leave foreign governments feeling that they would not want to risk much in reliance on United States policies unless these

policies had substantial support by both parties in the country
and in Congress.

The United States cannot successfully bring about a coalition
for peace unless the two major political parties cooperate on
major policies.

Because that fact has been realized by leaders in both parties,
there has been developed since the war a policy known as "bipartisanship."

Bipartisanship is not easy to define, nor is it easy to produce.
It requires the President to bring responsible members of the
opposition party into the making of his foreign policies; and it
requires these members of the opposition party to cooperate
loyally to get support in the Congress and in the country for the
policies that have been worked out together.

That procedure seems to cut across two fundamental American principles. One is that the President, and the President
alone, has the responsibility for the current conduct of foreign
affairs. The other is that, under a two-party system, it is the duty
of the opposition party to be a watchdog rather than a teammate.

Because bipartisanship in foreign policy thus cuts across our
basic constitutional and traditional political views, it ought to be
used only sparingly and when the needs and perils are so great
that exceptional measures are demanded.

In time of war we practice a large amount of bipartisanship.
Victory is so desperate a need that the Administration in power
usually seeks help from qualified persons without regard to their
political party, and members of the opposition party gladly respond. Congress votes almost as a matter of course for what a
war Administration says is necessary. Everyone concedes that
there must be a large measure of national unity to meet grave
national peril from without.

Winning a war is important. But winning peace is equally
important. Also, the winning of a "cold" war is as important as
the winning of a "hot" war. In each case our liberty, our free
institutions, are at stake. There has been ample justification for
the bipartisanship which has in fact been practiced during postwar years with respect to parts of our foreign policy. Indeed,

there are other parts, such as Far Eastern policy, where bipartisanship might usefully have been practiced.

Postwar bipartisanship had what might be called its "birth" in August, 1944. Then Governor Dewey, as Republican candidate for President, asked me to go to Washington on his behalf to confer with Secretary Hull, acting on behalf of President Roosevelt, on the then projected United Nations Organization.

The prelude to that request was Governor Dewey's publicly expressed anxiety lest the Big Three at Dumbarton Oaks think of peace as a continuing military alliance of a few big powers. He urged that more recognition be given to the smaller powers and more attention be paid to the moral qualities they could contribute.

Secretary Hull replied that Governor Dewey misconstrued what was planned at Dumbarton Oaks. Further, in the course of a press conference, he remarked that he would be glad to tell Governor Dewey about the actual plan.

Governor Dewey accepted that idea and asked me to confer with Secretary Hull in this matter. The governor was greatly concerned lest the United Nations incur the fate of the League of Nations and be lost in partisan controversy within the United States. The danger was the greater because the issue of world organization was now being precipitated in the middle of a bitterly fought Presidential campaign.

Secretary Hull agreed to meet me, after first clearing the matter with President Roosevelt. The President, he records, was, however, "skeptical" of whether it would be possible to arrive at any agreement with the Republicans.

Secretary Hull in his memoirs says:

"I have seldom worked harder on any project than on the preparation for and conduct of the conversations with John Foster Dulles."

I, too, worked hard, for I, too, felt that much depended upon the success or failure of our endeavor.

I conferred at Albany with Governor Dewey. On my return to New York Mr. Willkie spent an afternoon at my home. Our talk was somewhat strained, for Mr. Willkie had not yet decided

to support the Republican ticket. But he did respond to Governor
Dewey's and my invitation to talk over the future of world organization, in which he was deeply interested. I went on to
Washington, and conferred first with the Republican members
of the Foreign Relations Committee—Senator Vandenberg, Senator Austin, and others. Then, on August 23, 1944, I met with
Secretary Hull.

I had hoped that we would agree within a few hours. Actually,
we had three days of almost continuous conference. The Secretary seemed to me very stubborn. Perhaps I seemed that way to
him.

We had no disagreement on the basic proposition that it was
so important to create world organization that the effort ought
to have the support of all Americans, without regard to party.
We both saw that the effort would surely fail if it had a partisan
Democrat label that subjected it to Republican attack. That
would prevent the two-thirds Senate vote required for ratification.

However, Secretary Hull and I found it difficult to put down
on paper any agreement. He wanted an agreement broad enough
to cover not only the creation of world organization but *all* subjects relating to the future peace, including, for example, the
arrangements that might be made with Russia for the future of
Poland, a topic then much discussed.

Governor Dewey was adamant against that, insisting on the
right to debate generally all aspects of foreign policy. I agreed
with him emphatically.

Secretary Hull also objected to any reference to "bipartisan"
agreements, preferring the word "nonpartisan." He feared, or
at least Mr. Roosevelt's political advisers feared, that the word
"bipartisan" might concede the Republicans an equal status in
a project that was now presumed to be politically profitable.

There was also the question of the extent to which Governor
Dewey and I should be kept informed as to what was going on
at Dumbarton Oaks. Much as we sympathized with the idea of
creating a world organization, we also realized that, unless it was
the right kind of world organization, it could do more harm than
good. We were unwilling to give a blank-check endorsement.

To meet the third point, Secretary Hull gave me the confidential texts that were being worked upon so that I could at least know what the situation was to date.

Secretary Hull and I never came to a complete agreement. We did agree that I, on behalf of Governor Dewey, should be kept currently informed of developments, and that the Governor's and my views with reference to the nature of the proposed Charter should be taken into account.

I agreed that in our press communiqué we would use the word "nonpartisan" rather than "bipartisan."

With respect to the scope of the agreement, Secretary Hull held to the position that the whole matter of future peace was a " 'nonpartisan' subject which must be kept entirely out of politics." I insisted that there must be "full public 'nonpartisan' discussion of the means of attaining a lasting peace."

Our final joint communiqué of August 25th, after expressing our respective views, concluded with this paragraph:

The question of whether there will be complete agreement on these two respective views and their carrying out will depend on future developments.

Future developments were satisfactory. Both Presidential candidates supported the program for creating the United Nations, and the only controversy to which our accord of August, 1944, has given rise is over which party deserves the higher credit for this first great step in what, with all respect to Mr. Hull, I continue to call "bipartisanship." The controversy revived again in the course of the 1948 political campaign.

There is enough credit for all. Both Republican and Democrat leadership took a course which put the welfare of the nation and the world above what each, at the time, thought was partisan advantage.

After my August, 1944, understanding with Secretary Hull, he continued to keep in touch with a bipartisan Congressional group, and I followed the major developments at Dumbarton Oaks. From time to time I made certain suggestions, some of which were adopted. I was not, however, satisfied with the way that part of the understanding worked. Secretary Hull cooperated in good faith. But it was not possible, without actual participation in the Dumbarton Oaks discussions, to exert any effective influence on what was done.

This experience made it clear to me that any bipartisan effort ought to give the opposition party member an opportunity to share in the formulation and development of policy.

My understanding with Secretary Hull and its successful operation, coupled with the active cooperation of Senator Vandenberg in the Senate and Representative Eaton in the House, made it logical that the United States Delegation to the San Francisco Conference should be bipartisan in character. This occurred when President Roosevelt appointed to the Delegation Senator Connally and Senator Vandenberg of the Foreign Relations Committee, Congressman Bloom and Congressman Eaton of the Foreign Affairs Committee, and Mr. Stassen, then serving as Commander in the United States Navy. This was a sharp contrast to the Delegation that President Wilson appointed to the Paris Peace Conference of 1919, where only the very tenuous Republicanism of Henry White was present.

At first I was not asked to serve with the Delegation. It seemed that President Roosevelt then held a certain rancor against Republicans who had been actively identified with the Dewey Presidential campaign. However, Secretary Stettinius, Senator Vandenberg, and others thought that my presence would be desirable, and President Roosevelt came to see it the same way. Thus, with the President's approval, Secretary Stettinius named me as a senior adviser to the Delegation.

While at San Francisco I worked in particular intimacy with Senator Vandenberg. We came to be looked upon as a "team." Already, of course, I had had close relations with Governor Dewey, so that now the three of us were drawn together in a way that gave the Republican Party a powerful and coordinated leadership in relation to foreign affairs.

The United Nations Charter was submitted to the Senate on July 2, 1945, and it was agreed to on July 28th by the overwhelming vote of 89 to 2.

This contrasts strikingly with the fate of the League of Nations in the Senate. The outcome was generally considered as a triumph for the bipartisan approach which had been followed for the preceding twelve months.

The fact that leading members of the Republican Party had helped to make the United Nations Charter had not led to secrecy or cut off public enlightenment, as some had feared. On the contrary, there was widespread discussion and public understanding. The public approval was greater than with respect to any major foreign policy since the pronouncement of the Monroe Doctrine.

The success of bipartisanship in creating the United Nations led to efforts to continue that policy with respect to the operation of the United Nations and the negotiation of European peace terms.

When the first meeting of the Council of Foreign Ministers was held in early September, 1945, Secretary Byrnes asked me to accompany him as a Republican adviser. I accepted, after conferring with Senator Vandenberg and Governor Dewey.

The fact that I was at London with Secretary Byrnes as a Republican and with powerful Republican backing enabled me to play an important part in the momentous decision to end the policy of seeking to get agreement with the Russians by "appeasing" their aggressive ambitions.

Since then the policy of "appeasement" has become generally unpopular. But that particular mood had not clearly developed by September, 1945. Without my presence, Secretary Byrnes could not have known that he could come home with what, superficially, was a total failure without being subjected to criticism by the opposition. Because I was there, he knew that to make concessions would involve Republican attack, while not to make them would encourage Republican support. I made it clear that that was my own view, and that I believed it would also be the view of Dewey, Vandenburg, and other Republicans when I reported the circumstances to them.

Thus the Secretary of State was able to make a momentous

and clear-cut decision with confidence that it would have bi-partisan backing.

When the United Nations Assembly first met, the United States Delegation was bipartisan; and that quality has been preserved up to now. The Delegation of ten, including alternates, to the First Part of the First Session, included four Republicans —Senator Vandenberg, Representative Eaton, former Senator John G. Townsend, Jr., and myself.

Senator Vandenberg, Representative Eaton, and I were re-appointed to serve at the Second Part of the First Session, which was held in New York in the fall of 1946. This, however, was the last time that Senators or Representatives served on the Delegation. It was difficult for members of Congress to find the time to serve also as members of the United Nations Assembly. Furthermore, Senator Vandenberg, after he became chairman of the Foreign Relations Committee following the Congressional elections of 1946, felt that it would be embarrassing for him to serve as a delegate because the United Nations Participation Act of 1945 requires delegates to act and vote under "instructions" from the President. That legal process of "instructing" delegates by Presidential order has rarely been used in practice, and delegates have much opportunity to use their own independent judgment in arriving at policies. But Senator Vandenberg felt that, as the foreign affairs leader of a coordinate branch of the government, he ought not to put himself in a position to be required by law to follow the President's judgment rather than his own.

The delegates to the United Nations Assembly have, however, continued to include Republicans. I was a delegate at all of the regular sessions up to that which opened in September, 1949, when I myself was serving in the United States Senate. I was replaced in that Delegation by John S. Cooper, a former Republican United States Senator from Kentucky.

Thus, as regards the United Nations Assembly, the tradition of bipartisanship, as begun in August, 1944, has been consistently preserved.

It should also be noted that the permanent American representative to the United Nations, since the resignation of Mr. Stettinius in 1946, has been Warren R. Austin, formerly Republican Senator from Vermont. This is perhaps not an example of "bipartisanship" because Mr. Austin is serving on a full-time basis as a Presidential Ambassador, and does not in any way speak for, or represent, or commit, the Republican Party. The fact that a distinguished Republican was so appointed is, however, an illustration of nonpartisanship in foreign policy.

Bipartisanship has also continued with respect to the meetings of the Council of Foreign Ministers and some special conferences. As has been noted, Senator Vandenberg and former Senator Austin were delegates to the Rio Conference which negotiated the Pan-American Regional Pact. Senator Vandenberg attended the Paris Peace Conference in the summer of 1946 and took some part in the Council of Foreign Ministers' meeting in New York in the fall of 1946. I also took some part in that meeting; but I was principally engaged at that time in the United Nations Assembly that was held concurrently. I attended with Secretary Marshall the Moscow session of the Council of Foreign Ministers in March–April, 1947, and the London session of that Council in November–December, 1947. I attended with Secretary Acheson the next meeting of the Council of Foreign Ministers at Paris in May–June, 1949.

There have been sharp differences of opinion as to the wisdom of this practice of bipartisanship which has grown up during the five years since August, 1944.

There is a question as to its wisdom from the standpoint of the nation, and also from the standpoint of the Republican Party.

As to its wisdom from the standpoint of the country, I have no doubts. It has, in my opinion, made an indispensable contribution at a critical period. In the area where there has been this kind of bipartisanship, the Administration has been able to proceed with confidence, knowing that policies which were threshed out with responsible Republican participation would be accepted by the Congress and by the nation. In that way we have avoided the spectacle of a nation sharply divided at a time when our own peace and safety and the safety of friendly peoples were dependent upon presenting a united and resolute front to potential enemies.

Just as the Presidential election period of 1944 showed, dramatically, that bipartisanship was necessary to create world organization, so the election period of 1948 showed dramatically that bipartisanship was needed to prevent a major defeat in the "cold" war that Soviet Communism was waging.

Perhaps because 1948 was a Presidential election year, when internal division and consequent paralysis could be expected, the Soviet Union stepped up its pressures in Europe. In March, 1948, General Clay advised the Chief of Staff that he had given up his position that war was impossible, and felt that we could no longer preclude its possibility. Shortly thereafter the Soviet forces in Eastern Germany began gradually to cut the Western access to Berlin by railroad, canal, and road. Thereby, as we have seen, the Soviet leaders attempted to compel the Western Allies to retreat from that advanced base.

The blockade got into full operation about the time that the Presidential campaign was getting under way. It was countered by the airlift. But the airlift was vulnerable to Soviet interference. The big question in the minds of friendly governments and peoples in Europe—and no doubt also in the minds of the Russians, although they were less communicative—was whether the uncertainties and division of a Presidential election would prevent our nation from acting strongly abroad.

I was at that time (July, 1948) called into confidential conferences with the State Department on measures that might be taken to counter the blockade. Thus informed of the facts, including the military estimate of the situation, I was in a position to advise Governor Dewey, the Republican candidate. Also, Senator Vandenberg, in Michigan, was kept informed by telephone.

One of the first acts of Governor Dewey after his nomination was to ask Senator Vandenberg and me to discuss the Berlin situation with him. The three of us met at the Governor's farm at Pawling, New York, on July 24th. After our talk he issued a statement reading:

The present duty of Americans is not to be divided by past lapses, but to unite to surmount present dangers. We shall not allow domestic partisan irritations to divert us from this indispensable unity ... In Berlin we must not surrender our rights under duress.

Again, on September 10, 1948, we conferred in New York. Senator Vandenberg reported our meeting to the press and said that Governor Dewey, if elected, would carry on the United States policy in Berlin.

If at that time the Republican leadership had given the slightest sign of weakening, the result might have been disastrous. But there was no such weakening.

Republicans were privately critical because, at the time of the German surrender, and in days when there was no Republican participation, the Administration had neglected even to ask for a clearly defined Western corridor of access to and egress from Berlin. If bipartisanship had not subsequently developed, the Republican Party would probably have capitalized on this grave negligence of a Democrat Adminstration. But the active practice of bipartisanship in these European matters through a period of four years had created a sense of fellowship and solidarity, and an understanding of the national peril. So, when this critical moment came, the two major parties were united, the nation was united, and the calculations of our enemies were confounded.

I went to Paris with Secretary Marshall to attend the fall Assembly of the United Nations, which opened September 21st. We found there the Foreign Ministers of most of the nations of the world, and they were gravely concerned lest the ability of the United States to act should be paralyzed during the rest of the election period and the ensuing transition period which would follow the anticipated Republican victory.

The circumstances of that occasion impressed on me, vividly and indelibly, the immense responsibility for leadership that devolves upon the United States. If at any moment our leadership seems to falter, panic spreads among all the free nations. At Paris, many began by doubting that the United States would have continuity of policy or the capacity to act strongly. Members of friendly governments felt that not only their personal safety, but the very existence of their countries as free nations, depended upon a continuity of American policy and a continuity of vigorous action; but they felt that that continuity could not be relied on, and many were uncertain as to what future United States policies might be if, for example, there were a Republican victory. Would that mean a return to "isolationism"? If so, they felt they would be engulfed by the Communist wave almost at once. Some, indeed, were considering whether they ought not, in advance of the election, to get on a more friendly basis with the leaders of Soviet Russia.

Secretary Marshall and I cooperated closely to dispel the rising tide of doubt and fear.

I was in regular contact with Governor Dewey. On October 3rd I flew back to New York for a long day's conference with him, and when I was in Paris we had almost daily exchanges through a private "telecon" arrangement which the State Department had set up for that purpose.

As illustrative of the almost daily communication between Governor Dewey and myself, I give below the texts of two private messages I sent to him on October 13th and of his reply on October 15th:

For Dewey:

Hoffman yesterday asked my views regarding German plant removals for reparation purposes. This is actively in dispute with British who are pushing dismantling and removal. Hoffman is discussing with Bevin in London today and the issue can have serious repercussions in Congress unless satisfactorily resolved. I said that in view of ERP it seemed to me that reparation claims and national ambitions should be subordinated to creation in Western Europe of maximum economic productivity and that that should be the test of whether plants should stay as is or be shifted.   Dulles

For Dewey:

Turkish Minister of Foreign Affairs today called to get reassurance regarding your attitude. I referred to your earlier support of aid program which last July you authorized me to recall to Turkish Ambassador when he saw me in New York. I added that I felt the American people regarded highly as a precious thing in the world the

apparent resolution of Turkish people to stand up and fight, if necessary, to preserve their independence.   DULLES

FOR DULLES FROM DEWEY:

Governor agrees your position regarding dismantling contained in
your message Number 19. Governor also agrees your position taken
with Turkish Minister Foreign Affairs and the statement you made to
him as in your message 20.

In the light of the explicit concurrence of Governor Dewey
in my statement to the Turkish Minister of Foreign Affairs, I
saw the Minister again; and the total result was that his initial
doubts were turned into renewed courage and hope.

Through conversations of this kind with the representatives
of the more exposed countries, I helped them to realize that
Governor Dewey's election would not mean a reversal of the
policy of extending them moral support and material aid.

On week ends, I traveled to Vienna, Berlin, Copenhagen, and
Stockholm. I sought to reaffirm at those exposed points my confidence in a continuity of the strong European policy that had
developed under bipartisan auspices of the past, and to reassure
those who might be wavering.

I attached particular importance to my trip to Germany. The
Berlin blockade was at a critical point. Winter was setting in.
The days were short, and the nights were long and dark and
cold. There was virtually no coal for heat and no light for
reading. There was large-scale unemployment, because there were
no materials with which to work. The big question was: Would
Western Berlin morale hold out? The Germans in Western
Berlin seemed loyal, although they felt that, if the airlift failed
and the blockade succeeded, their lives—certainly their freedom
—would be the price of that loyalty.

General Clay was, in the eyes of the German people, the
symbol of the determination of the United States to stand fast.
But there was widespread gossip that he and I were unfriendly.
There were rumors, which found their way into the press, that if
Governor Dewey should be elected General Clay would go.

These rumors were, of course, totally without foundation.
Their origin was, no doubt, the fact that General Clay and I

had had some differences of opinion as to the respective roles of France and Germany in the program for European reconstruction. The differences, however, were only such differences as are normal between persons who approach a difficult problem from varying backgrounds. Our personal relations were of the best, and I had the highest respect for his character and intelligence. I spoke frankly to him of the rumors about our relations and remarked on one occasion that, from my standpoint, the only trouble was that he was too strong and able a person to be in charge of a limited theater like Germany; his great abilities would inevitably lead to the overemphasis of any area for which he was primarily responsible. What was needed, I said, was a larger, not a lesser, theater for his responsibility.

The gossip about the relations between General Clay and myself could have hurt the situation in Western Berlin. It needed to be put to rest. So, with General Marshall's approval, I took a Saturday and Sunday to go to Germany. I first met with General Clay and Ambassador Murphy at Frankfurt on October 15th, and sat beside the General at the meeting he and the British commander, General Robertson, had with the German leaders of the two zones—"Bizonia." The next day, I rode the airlift to Berlin and spent Sunday with him there. We were seen together, photographed together, and had a press conference together. It was made perfectly plain to the people of Western Berlin, and indeed of all of Germany and to the Soviet leaders, that a Republican electoral victory would not involve any repudiation of General Clay or of the policy to hold fast in Berlin.

As November, 1948, approached, Secretary Marshall and I had a number of talks in Paris about the situation that would develop if the American people voted a change of Administration. We felt that it would be dangerous not to make plans for this contingency. Otherwise, there could be a period of indecision and impotence on the part of the United States which Soviet leaders might use to win new victories by indirect, and perhaps even direct, aggression.

On such matters, I was also in close touch, by the telecon, with Governor Dewey through my brother Allen, who was with him on his campaign train. The result was that Governor Dewey was in a position such that, if elected, he could have helped to assure a transition from Democratic to Republican Administration without damage to our international position or collapse of the cooperation of free nations under United States leadership. The contingency we prepared for did not happen. But in view of the then estimate of probabilities it would have been almost criminal not to have had plans to meet that eventuality.

The only disturbing incident during these days was the report that came to us in October that President Truman might send Chief Justice Vinson on a special mission to Moscow. This took those in Paris by surprise, and, perhaps because the President's intentions were not fully understood, many foreign Delegations were disturbed, particularly the British and French.

We had been working together intimately with the British and French governments so as to present a united front to the danger that flowed from the Soviet blockade of Berlin. The United States was taking the strongest line. The French and, to a lesser extent, the British had been reluctant to break off the August discussions at Moscow regarding Berlin, which at one time had seemed to produce an agreement with Stalin. The French were on the same continent with the Russians; they were themselves virtually unarmed, and only a few miles away was a powerful Red Army in Germany. They naturally felt anxious. The terminating of the three-power Moscow talks had come about largely because of the strong conviction of the representatives of the United States that there was no sincerity of purpose on the Soviet side, and on that account it would be dangerous weakness to continue direct talks. Also, the United States was taking the strongest line against "appeasement" attitudes in the United Nations Security Council. Various compromises were considered by the Security Council neutrals. These might have led to a lifting of the blockade, but, in our opinion, only at the expense of giving the Soviet Union such an economic strangle-hold over Western Berlin that, in fact, the population would become subservient to Soviet influence and the Western allies driven out.

The British and French, sometimes against their better judgment, cooperated loyally to maintain a solid three-power front. Therefore, it surprised them to learn that our government might undertake single-handedly to resume talks at Moscow. This in itself would have been a Soviet victory, for Soviet diplomacy constantly seeks to bring about two-power talks that will drive a wedge between the British, French, and ourselves.

Secretary Marshall flew back to the United States and discussed the situation fully with the President; and, as a result, the idea of a Vinson mission to Moscow was dropped and three-power confidence reestablished.

The incident illustrates that when a Presidential campaign occurs during a period of great international tension, it is important to preserve the reality of bipartisan cooperation. If, at a time of national peril, two Presidential candidates should compete in making novel and unseasoned proposals, designed primarily to win votes, the end of that campaign would leave our foreign relations in a shambles.

The fact was that from the standpoint of foreign policy, subject to the minor exception noted—which was quickly corrected—the campaign of 1948 was conducted on a high level by both sides. No damage was done. On the contrary, the net result was that by Election Day the foreign delegates, both those that were friendly and those that were unfriendly, were more than ever convinced that the American nation was solidly united on the main lines of its foreign policy.

That impression was confirmed by an incident that occurred shortly after the election. Up to November 2nd many foreign delegates had expected that I would be increasingly responsible after that date for United States foreign policy under the direction of a Republican President-elect. As it was, November 3, 1948, found me merely a member of a party that had been defeated at the polls and would have no chance to reverse that verdict for four years. Both Mr. Vishinsky, the head of the Soviet Delegation, and Mr. Katz-Suchy, head of the Polish Delegation, gloated at meetings of the United Nations Assembly. They suggested that, instead of being Secretary of State, I should now be going back to the private practice of law, for which, they suggested, I was much better qualified. My influence and prestige, which had been high, had sunk to a low point. I had, indeed, serious doubt as to whether I could usefully continue to carry responsibility in the United Nations for the very heavy tasks which had been assigned to me up to that time. I so indicated to Secretary Marshall.

Secretary Marshall was then himself about to return to the United States. He had been unwell, and there was pressing need for him to have a major operation. After the election he felt it necessary to return for his operation. That would leave the Delegation without a chairman.

Then, on November 18, President Truman designated me to be Acting Chairman of the United States Delegation.

That was a fine and generous gesture, made at the moment of victory toward one of the defeated opposition. I was, and always shall be, grateful for this action. It immediately restored my waning prestige, and enabled me to carry to a successful conclusion the various matters that I was already charged with, and to assume others in the absence of Secretary Marshall and Ambassador Austin, who, on account of illness, had also returned to the United States.

The President's act had far more than merely personal consequences. It was a demonstration, under circumstances that made it dramatic, of the reality of national unity in the field of foreign relations.

The defense of free institutions did not falter during that critical winter of 1948-1949. We, and others, stood firm. That was possible because, as regards the United Nations and European policies, there had been solid cooperation during four years between Truman, Byrnes, and Marshall on the one side, and Dewey, Vandenberg, and myself on the other side. The cooperation had borne good results that stood our nation in good stead at a time when otherwise there might have been disaster.

Bipartisanship in foreign policy has limitations and drawbacks. It is difficult to operate. But during the period from August, 1944, through 1949 it operated to promote the security and peace of the United States and of the world.

PART III

THE MEASURE OF OUR FOREIGN POLICIES

CHAPTER TWELVE

THE FIVE-YEAR SCORE

We have reviewed the principal postwar foreign policies of the United States—policies devised under the pressure of events to counter the Soviet Communist program of world conquest by fraud, terrorism, and violence.

Are these policies adequate? Can we depend on them to frustrate evil methods so that these methods will be abandoned as inexpedient and the possibility of lasting peace emerge? These are the questions we shall try now to answer.

After nearly five years of "cold" war, if we make up the score, we find successes and failures.

Let us consider first our minus score—the successes that Soviet Communism has gained by its methods.

CENTRAL EUROPE

Soviet Communism, in the five postwar years, has consolidated its position in large areas of Central Europe, notably Poland, East Germany, Czechoslovakia, Hungary, Rumania, Bulgaria, and Albania.

From a military standpoint, these areas have become more closely integrated in the orbit of the Soviet Union.

From an economic standpoint, their connections with the West have been almost completely broken, and their trade is almost exclusively within the area of Soviet dominance.

From a national, cultural, and spiritual standpoint, the old loyalties have been weakened through purges and terrorism. To accomplish this the Soviet Union has often had to install persons of Russian nationality in positions of importance within these states, particularly to direct the operation of the secret police. The processes of terrorism have caused fear and discontent; but on the whole they have worked. The Communist police have found new ways to make political prisoners numb and pliant confessors to what they have not done. Similarly, on a vast scale, they have found ways to terrorize their subjects into a like numbness.

In spots there is brooding resentment which marks potential danger to Soviet Communism; but, on balance, its hold on these areas has been strengthened during the last three or four years. To think otherwise would be wishful thinking.

Hungary

The most spectacular accomplishments have been the Communist seizures of complete power in Hungary and in Czechoslovakia. In Hungary the election of November 4, 1945, showed the Communists to be a small minority. The "small landowners" won a large majority in the Parliament. But the Communist minority, by tactics which startlingly illustrate the Communist methods, won control. They infiltrated into the police and "justice" departments, and from there tried and condemned non-Communist leaders. They terrorized Prime Minister Nagy into resignation and exile as the only way to assure the safety of his four-year-old son, who was then brought from Hungary to Switzerland to join him. Then they took over. President Tildy, who had held on, finally resigned in July, 1948, when his son-in-law was threatened with prosecution as a "spy."

Czechoslovakia

The Communists carried on a comparable operation in Czechoslovakia in February, 1948. Its success was more surprising, because Czechoslovakia had closer ties with the West than any other Central European nation.

Czechoslovakia had been born in the West by action of France, England, and the United States during World War I. The group led by Thomas Masaryk was recognized by President Wilson on September 2, 1918, as a *"de facto* belligerent government."

My close personal relations with the Czech leaders date from that year, when the United States Treasury agreed to make an advance to the *de facto* government to enable it to function, and I went to the Treasury Department with Mr. Masaryk to identify him as he received the first check to the order of the Czechoslovak government.

At the Paris Peace Conference of 1919, where the United States took a leading part in establishing the new state, I worked intimately with Mr. Beneš, the Minister of Foreign Affairs. He, representing a group of new states which had formed part of the Austro-Hungarian monarchy, and I, representing France, England, and the other creditor nations, worked out together the program of contribution by the "succession states" to the cost of their liberation.

Immediately after the conclusion of the Versailles Peace Treaty, I went to Czechoslovakia and negotiated a cotton credit on behalf of the Federal Reserve Bank which enabled the spinning industry of Czechoslovakia to get quickly into operation.

The intimacy of relations between the Czechoslovak government and the West continued until the Munich deal with Hitler. At that time Mr. Beneš had succeeded Mr. Masaryk as President, and the governments of England and France, with the acquiescence of the United States, put strong pressure upon his government to cede important parts of Czechoslovakia to Germany. He gave in, against his better judgment.

When this sacrifice failed to stop the Second World War, and Czechoslovakia was completely taken over, Mr. Beneš went into exile. I talked with him in London in 1942, during the war. He was an embittered man, reflecting the spirit of an embittered people.

Mr. Beneš had placed great hope in the League of Nations. The failure of the League, and the power politics played at Munich, had made him feel that no small country should ever thereafter put hope in "collective security." Events proved, he felt, that small nations could survive only by becoming satellites of great powers which would protect them.

From then on, the Czechoslovak foreign policy was to align the country politically with the Soviet Union. On December 12, 1943, the Czechoslovak government-in-exile, acting through Z. Fierlinger, its Ambassador in Moscow, made a treaty of "Friendship, Mutual Assistance, and Postwar Cooperation" with the Soviet Union. Subsequently, when the defeat of Germany was imminent, President Beneš went to Moscow to plan there, with Czechoslovak delegates, the reorganization of the Czechoslovak government. Upon leaving, on April 1, 1945, he thanked the Russians for their promised help and said, "In the future we shall go together with you, our brothers." An American diplomat in Prague told me that President Beneš had said that experience forced him to believe that, in an emergency, the Western powers would always sacrifice Czechoslovakia to save their own skins.

It was, however, the belief of Mr. Beneš and at least the hope of Jan Masaryk, the first President's son, who became Minister of Foreign Affairs, that the Soviet Union would be satisfied if Czechoslovakia became *politically* allied with it and maintained solidarity with it in *international* affairs. They thought that Soviet Communism would keep its hands off their internal affairs. So Jan Masaryk, as the principal delegate of Czechoslovakia to the United Nations, consistently voted as desired by the government of the Soviet Union. As he once remarked to me, Soviet proposals often smelled so bad that he had to hold his nose with one hand while he raised the other hand to vote for them. But he did it.

It soon developed that Soviet leadership does not understand the idea of partnership. There must be subjection. Czechoslovakia became more and more subjected to the local Communist Party. In February, 1948, the Communist Party in Czechoslovakia seized complete power in a bloodless revolution. President Beneš died of a broken heart, and Foreign Minister Masaryk of murder or suicide.

That was a great and frightening victory for the ruthless methods of Soviet Communism.

Germany

Soviet Communism has also strengthened its hold upon the Soviet Zone of Eastern Germany. This area is of the utmost importance tactically and strategically. It offers an opportunity to gain control of all Germany, and with that control to achieve easy domination of the entire Continent. The Communist stranglehold on Eastern Germany has not been gained by love, but only by fear and ruthless use of power.

Through holding an important part of Germany and having there a puppet "all-German" government, the Soviet leaders are in a position to extend their influence throughout Germany. They can be emotionally eloquent about German unity, and they promise that unity provided the Western Germans get rid of the occupying forces of England, France, and the United States.

The Soviet Union is in a position to propose an ending of military occupation. It dares do that because it has created an armed and disciplined Communist group in East Germany which it believes will be loyal to it and do its will.

It is in a position, when it finds it expedient, to offer to restore to Germany the important agricultural and industrial areas, including Upper Silesia, which, for the time being at least, it has given to Poland in compensation for the Soviet annexation of Eastern Poland.

The Captive Churches

Throughout Soviet-dominated Central Europe, some progress has been made in weakening the anti-Communist religious influence. Communist leaders have recognized that the church leaders were the greatest obstacle and their greatest source of danger. They have tried in Central Europe to deal with that as they dealt with religion in Russia following the 1917 Revolution. The trial and conviction of Archbishop Stepinac in Yugoslavia (October, 1946) and of Cardinal Mindszenty in Hungary (July, 1949) are symbolic of terroristic methods. The policy has not been to wipe out all religion, but to make it innocuous from the standpoint of Communist programs and policies.

The Constitution of the Soviet Union provides for "freedom of antireligious propaganda" and "freedom of religious worship." The intent is to confine religion to acts of worship, primarily ritualistic, and to exclude any teaching or preaching that might influence the political and social life of the community. There may be personal "faith," but it cannot permissibly be translated into "works" that Soviet Communism does not like.

In Russia the Communist leaders have imposed a working arrangement of this kind on the Orthodox Church. In return for teaching people to reverence Stalin as their leader on earth, the priests are allowed to conduct services of worship of God in heaven.

I attended an Easter service in one of the few remaining churches in Moscow. The church and the streets around were packed with an estimated crowd of twenty thousand people. They stood from ten o'clock at night until after three o'clock in the morning. From time to time priests would appear on the church balcony and bless the people. It was an impressive demonstration of the surviving thirst of the people for spiritual sustenance. But also, it demonstrated the confidence of Communist leaders that the Church was no longer an obstacle to the realization of their unmoral program based on an atheistic view of the nature of man.

ASIA

On the Continent of Asia, Soviet Communism has made its greatest gains. These are indeed spectacular.

Through the Yalta Agreement of February 11, 1945, Stalin won the support of Roosevelt and Churchill for the preservation of the *status quo* of Outer Mongolia under its Communist government, and its *de facto* detachment from China; the "safeguarding" of "the preeminent interests of the Soviet Union" in the Chinese Eastern Railroad and South Manchurian Railroad and in the port of Dairen; and the restoration of the lease of Port Arthur as a Russian naval base. At the time, this arrangement was kept secret from China.

At the San Francisco Conference in the following May, T. V. Soong, the Chinese Premier, asked me whether any of the secret

agreements reached at Yalta related to China. I reported our talk
to Mr. Stettinius, who as Secretary of State had been at Yalta
with President Roosevelt. He told me that he did not know of
any such agreements and that I might so advise Mr. Soong. I
did so.

Mr. Soong shortly afterward went to Moscow and concluded,
August 14, 1945, a treaty with the Soviet Union which, in sub-
stance, confirmed the sacrifice of Chinese interests agreed upon at
Yalta.

That episode influenced the attitude of the National Government of Generalissimo Chiang Kai-shek and Premier Soong much
as the events of 1938 had influenced the Czechoslovak Government of President Beneš. It shook the historic belief of the
Chinese that they could count upon the loyal friendship of the
United States. It made immensely difficult the task of General
Marshall, late in 1945, when he went to China as Special Representative of President Truman.

When Japan surrendered, the surrender terms authorized the
Soviet armies to accept the surrender of the Japanese in Manchuria and in North Korea. That put the Soviet troops into occupation of Manchuria and North Korea, and it gave them control
of great amounts of war material which had been accumulated
in Manchuria by the Japanese when they thought that they might
carry on a war on the mainland even after their islands had been
lost. These supplies of arms and ammunition were turned over
by the Soviet Union to the Chinese Communist Army, and greatly
increased its strength.

Then the Generalissimo, distrusting the military advice of
General Marshall, attempted to liberate Manchuria and to defeat
the Communist troops that were there. The Nationalists could not
use Port Arthur and Dairen because these ports were now in
Soviet hands. They tried to fly their troops to Manchuria. In the
process, the military strength of the Chinese Nationalist Army
was dissipated, its personnel and equipment were largely lost, and
its prestige greatly damaged.

The United States then judged the cause of the Nationalist
government to be lost, partly because of its loss of military

power, and partly because it had lost the confidence of the people. Its armies had been undisciplined and the government had not been able to prevent a vast currency inflation. United States military, economic, and moral support was largely withdrawn, and the Red armies of China soon overcame all organized opposition on the Chinese mainland.

Thus the 450,000,000 people in China have fallen under leadership that is violently anti-American, and that takes its inspiration and guidance from Moscow. The Soviet Union has effective political control in the northern areas of Manchuria, Mongolia, and Sinkiang, which contain vast natural resources. If these areas can be exploited by Chinese man power, it will greatly improve the economic position and the industrial power of the Soviet Union.

Soviet Communist leadership has won a victory in China which surpassed what Japan was seeking and we risked war to avert.

Whether the fruits of the victory will prove illusive remains to be seen. But Soviet Communism has now the chance to consolidate a vast contiguous area extending from the river Elbe in Germany to the China Sea, with more than 700,000,000 persons and immeasurable natural resources.

THE COLONIAL WORLD

The Western colonial powers did, on the whole, parry the first thrust of Soviet Communism by quickly granting independence to many colonial peoples who otherwise would have fought for it in alliance with Soviet Communism.

It would, however, be premature to judge that this peaceful evolution marks a permanent setback for Soviet Communism. It cannot now quickly snatch another great victory, like that won in China; but it is still in a strong position from which to make further major gains.

The governments that have been established in new nations such as India, Pakistan, Burma, Ceylon, the Philippines, the United States of Indonesia, and Indo-China are vulnerable to indirect aggression by Soviet Communism.

We have seen how minority Communist parties have succeeded

in taking over governmental power in countries such as Hungary and Czechoslovakia, where free political institutions had seemed securely established. We know how difficult it is, even in the United States, to check Communist penetration. Can the governments in the new nations withstand the pressures to which they surely will be subjected?

The peoples are inexperienced in operating free political institutions. Most of them face a condition of starvation—a condition that will grow worse if Soviet Communists get to control or disrupt the economy of the "rice bowl" area of Burma and French Indo-China. There is widespread misery which affords Soviet propaganda great opportunities.

We must furthermore take into account that in all these countries the Chinese have historically exerted a great influence. China in the East stands for an honored tradition. It has deeply influenced the culture and thinking of the entire area. The fact that a Chinese government is now Communist and that Chinese embassies, legations and consular offices in many countries will be manned by Chinese Communists, will give the Communists in this area added prestige in their effort to extend Communist sway in the new freed lands of Asia.

To sum up, China with its population of about 450,000,000 has already come almost wholly under a rule which takes its guidance from Moscow. In Asia and the Pacific there are about 600,000,000 more people whom Soviet Communism does not yet dominate, but whom it has a good chance of dominating.

If it should win this further area, or any substantial part of it, then Soviet Communism would control considerably more than half of the total population of the world.

AFRICA

In the Continent of Africa the influence of Soviet Communism has grown over the past five years.

The greatest present opportunity is probably in the Union of South Africa. There, a minority of whites is surrounded by a sea of colored people. The whites believe that they can survive only by holding the natives down with a rule of iron. In addition to the natives there is a large Indian population; and the Indians, like the natives, are discriminated against by the ruling class.

This situation has been annually agitated in the United Nations Assembly. India has taken the lead in attempting to secure recognition in the Union of South Africa of the "human rights and fundamental freedoms for all without distinction as to race, sex, language, or religion" which are to be observed, according to Article 55 (c) of the United Nations Charter.

Adjoining the Union of South Africa is Southwest Africa, a former German colony which had been detached from Germany under the Treaty of Versailles and given, under League mandate, to the Union of South Africa. It has now been incorporated *de facto* within the Union and it is the only mandated territory which has not either been given independence or been placed under United Nations trusteeship. The Union of South Africa has objected to the United Nations considering either the problem of its Indian population or the problem of Southwest Africa.

There is danger in the Union of South Africa that its policy may touch off an explosion that will spread the fire of revolution throughout Africa and shake the colonial rule of England, France, and Belgium. (Incidentally, the Belgian Congo is our principal source of uranium for atomic bombs.) However, the South African government has been adamant in its policy of "white supremacy" and has not been receptive to advice. This was true even when Field Marshal Smuts was its head.

It must be admitted that the whole population of South Africa is in a difficult position. It feels deeply that it stands for a Christian civilization that affords the "native" and Indian populations much better living conditions than they could otherwise get, and that if it were voluntarily to accept submergence it would inaugurate a new era of darkness for an awakening Continent.

One cannot talk with South African whites, as I have talked with Field Marshal Smuts and other personally fine members of the government, and fail to be impressed with the deep sincerity of their views. But also one is impressed with the fact that those views are both wrong and obsolete in the world today. The policy of the Union of South Africa is, in fact, giving Communism the opportunity to precipitate a bloody struggle.

This opportunity is not limited to South Africa. In French North Africa also there are repressive political conditions that Soviet Communism is vigorously and hopefully exploiting.

LATIN AMERICA

In the countries of Central and South America the Communist parties have steadily increased their strength. The growth has been favored by the economic dislocations that followed World War II. During that war the United States was paying high prices for mineral and agricultural products from Latin America. The result was an inflation and an unhealthy prosperity. Then the abnormal war purchases ceased, leaving the governments with the difficult task of readjustment to a peacetime economy.

Soviet Communism has not, however, made any major effort in Latin America, except in the normal way of spreading propaganda and helping to invigorate the local Communist parties. The Communists are particularly influential in Guatemala; and Communists may have precipitated the violent rioting that nearly wrecked the Bogotá Conference of 1948.

But Soviet Communism does not attempt to do everything everywhere at the same time. The task of the Party, as Stalin has laid it down, is:

To locate at any given moment that particular link in the chain of processes which, if grasped, will enable us to hold the whole chain and to prepare the conditions for achieving strategic success.

The point here is to single out from all the problems confronting the Party that particular immediate problem, the answer to which constitutes the central point, and the solution of which will ensure the successful solution of the other immediate problems. (P. 68.)

Mr. Vishinsky repeated this guiding principle on December 19, 1949, when he emphasized that action should be pointed toward the principal strategic objectives, not toward a "secondary" one.

South America has, for the time being, been treated as a secondary theater.

However, the over-all trend in Latin America has created a

situation out of which Soviet Communism can manufacture distinctive successes if and when the Party judges that the effort is worth while.

In some Latin-American countries there has been a trend toward fascism. Argentina is a notable example. Also, in many Latin-American countries political control is more than ever in the hands of military groups. These groups have more power than ever because our Defense Department has built up military strength in some of the countries on the theory that the Americas should be treated as military allies under the Act of Chapultepec and its successor, the Rio Pact. These trends away from representative government increase the opportunities of Communism.

ATOMIC WEAPONS

The development of atomic weapons by the Soviet Union must go down in the ledger as a great success.

The Soviet Union, by quickly bringing our monopoly to an end, radically altered the strategic situation to its own advantage. United States ability to deliver bombs in Russia is now largely neutralized by the ability of the Soviet to deliver atomic bombs in the United States and Western Europe. Perhaps the position is more than neutralized, for our economy may be more vulnerable than that of the Soviet Union to atomic attack.

The gain to the Soviet Union is not merely in the fact that it now has atomic weapons. It has increased greatly in prestige because it has treated its accomplishment as perfectly natural and normal. It has allowed the fact of its possession of the bomb to leak out through foreign sources. The American people first learned of it in a statement by President Truman on September 23, 1949.

The Soviet attitude was one of surprise that anyone was surprised that Russia had atomic weapons. Of course it would have them. Why not? The Soviet leaders' calm assumption of Soviet scientific and industrial superiority impressed peoples throughout the world more than any heralding of the development by blaring trumpets.

Mr. Vishinsky discussed this matter on December 19, 1949, at

the celebration of Prime Minister Stalin's seventieth birthday.
He treated the Soviet "mastery of the secret of atomic energy"
as primarily a peacetime economic development, of which the
atomic bomb was a minor by-product. He referred to this as a
"gigantic success for the Soviet state" because, "in a period of
all kinds of devaluations, the Soviet Union has accomplished the
most important devaluation—devaluation of the atomic bomb."

It is significant that the speech was released only in February,
1950—after President Truman's announced decision that the
United States would seek to develop hydrogen bombs—giving the
implication that if the United States insisted on an armament
race the Soviet Union could and would match us, although it preferred to concentrate on economic development. This was effective propaganda.

Mr. Vishinsky makes extravagant statements when he speaks
for foreign consumption. However, the statement quoted was not
originally intended for foreign consumption and is close to being
sober truth. The rapid Soviet development of the atomic bomb
is indeed "a gigantic success for the Soviet state"; and the ending
of the United States monopoly in this field will have widespread
repercussions which cannot yet be fully foreseen.

One possibility that we can and must foresee is that the possession of atomic weapons greatly increases the area within which
the Soviet Communist leaders and the leaders of local Communist parties can exert terroristic threats.

We have seen that talk about the Red Army has strengthened
Communist influence and Communist parties in France, Italy,
and in other countries which are geographically subject to Red
Army invasion. Now there is far more scope for the use of such
terroristic methods, and increased likelihood of winning over the
governments and peoples of countries which are highly vulnerable to atomic attack by Soviet Russia.

THE MINUS SCORE FOR COMMUNISM

Soviet Communism does not win victories everywhere, all the
time. It has suffered some checks and reverses, partly through
its own inherent defects and partly because constructive policies

and tactics at times have frustrated its evil methods of aggression.

We turn now to the Communist *minus* score.

Yugoslavia

The greatest failure of Soviet Communism has been in Yugoslavia, itself a Communist-dominated country. Non-Communists have had little or nothing to do with this. It resulted from a defect that is inherent in the present Stalin brand of Communism.

Marshal Tito is a Communist. But his Communism differs from Stalin's. It is a brand that Stalin and the leaders of the Soviet Communist Party consider to be rank heresy.

The heresy is supposedly akin to that of Bukharin, the Soviet Communist leader who was executed in 1938. He had been a defendant in the trials in which Mr. Vishinsky won world-wide fame as prosecutor and producer of "confessions."

In March, 1948, vituperative exchanges began between the Cominform and Tito. He was accused of adopting the "heresy" of Bukharin that it is possible for Communism to have "peaceful growth" in relation to Capitalism. Tito, in reply, denounced Soviet Communism for its "foul methods" and asserted that he was holding to the true faith. They continued to argue violently about what was the "true" creed and what was "heresy." The Communists take these things very seriously.

The dispute is not merely vocal. The Cominform, under the leadership of the Soviet Communist Party, has been seeking a "purge" of Tito; and there have been attempts to stir up violence in Yugoslavia similar to the attempts previously made by Yugoslavia to stir up guerrilla war in Greece. There have even been hints that there might be full-scale international war and the use of the Red Army.

In a totalitarian society, where there are no free elections, the only method of resolving political rivalries is violence. So every three or four years, more or less corresponding to our presidential election periods, there is a test by purge within the Communist leadership. For example, Trotsky and Stalin became rivals, and

Trotsky was driven into exile and eventually assassinated in Mexico in August, 1940.

In a sense, the feud between Tito and Stalin was a thing to be expected; but it had a deeper cause.

The Soviet Communist Party had demanded that the Yugoslav Communist Party should apply rigidly the precise pattern of life that was designed by the Soviet Communist Party in Moscow. Moscow called for a solution of the farm problem in Yugoslavia along the lines that had been adopted in Russia, eliminating the independent farmers. It demanded that the Government of Yugoslavia should treat the Western "imperialist" nations as "enemies" with whom there could be no tolerant intercourse. By thus imposing a distinctively Russian pattern on Yugoslavia, the Soviet Communist Party tried to force a square peg into a round hole. It did not fit; and by trying forcibly to make it fit the Soviet Communists did violence to the patriotic sentiment of the people and to their traditional way of life.

The Soviet Communist program for dealing with farmers caused deep resentment in Yugoslavia. Also, the country badly needed industrial and mining equipment which it could not get from Russia but could get from the West. Therefore, Tito, himself a ruthless dictator, felt that he could raise the flag of revolt and have the backing of the Communist Party and the people of Yugoslavia.

The result has been a great breach within the ranks of the Communist countries and a check to the success of Soviet Communistic methods, in which it has exposed a basic weakness.

The Soviet Communist program is too rigid to be readily exportable. Conformity is demanded to an absurd degree. There must be conformity not only in basic creed but in all sorts of practices; not only in economic and social fields, but even in the realm of art, science, and literature. Such compulsory conformity is bound to lead to widespread unrest, discontent, and even revolt in peoples with distinctive loyalties to church and state and their own traditions, whose social and economic problems cannot be solved by applying without deviation the particular solution that has been framed in Moscow.

It is unlikely that we have seen the end of the Stalin-Tito feud. Under Communist practice, the end comes only when one or the other is liquidated. Until that happens, there is an open wound in the side of the Communist bloc.

Communist leaders must now divert to an internal problem the top planning and large effort which would otherwise be devoted to expanding the frontiers of Communism.

Western Europe

The onward rush of Soviet Communism in Western Europe has been checked, and the situation stabilized for the time being.

Soviet Communism made three major thrusts in Western Europe:

One was made in France during November and December of 1947 by means of political strikes and sabotage. Another was the effort to win the Italian elections of April, 1948. The third was the blockade of Berlin, begun in 1948.

The French and Italian thrusts were primarily "probing" operations. The blockade of Berlin was probably expected to succeed. All three failed, primarily because those who were directly threatened wanted a society of personal liberty, and because other free peoples showed a spirit of solidarity with them. That is a big "plus" for the way of peace, and a big "minus" for the way of Soviet Communism. However, Soviet Communism does not accept the first result as final. It bides its time and with good reason, for Western Europe is still plagued by grave problems that have not been resolved. The position is greatly improved over that in 1947 and 1948, but there still remain reasons for anxiety.

The West still has no recognized corridor of access to Western Berlin; and, even if it had one, blockade or interference with transit by railroad, road, and canal could recur at any time.

At the Paris meeting of the Council of Foreign Ministers in May–June, 1949, we asked the Soviet Union to agree to a definite corridor of access, the Helmsted Autobahn. The request was rejected contemptuously by Mr. Vishinsky. He laughed in our faces when he first heard it.

The economic life of Berlin is stagnating. There is large unemployment, and the morale has gone down from what it was during the exciting days of the airlift.

Germany as a whole presents problems which, if not so immediately acute as Berlin, are even more fundamental.

The Germans concededly are the heart of the problem of Europe. They are regaining strength, despite all obstacles. What will they do with that strength? Will they use it to end the artificial division of Germany by the Iron Curtain? If so, will the Iron Curtain be pushed back to Poland or moved forward to France? Will the Germans start to bargain between East and West? That is a possibility that is bound to attract the many Germans who still feel that the future of Germany is to be found in nationalism and who want to see their nation restored to greatness.

Never before has a people so numerous (between sixty-five and seventy million) and so potentially powerful had so unique an opportunity to bargain between two opposing groups. If the Germans would combine again with Soviet Communism as they did in the fall of 1939, that combination could sweep Europe. The victory of a Soviet-German alliance would be so certain that it is doubtful indeed whether there would be any organized resistance. That is a prize that a revived, nationalistic Germany can offer Soviet Russia—at a price.

A revived Germany can also be a great asset to the West. By attracting Eastern Germany into its orbit the West can gain an advanced strategic position in Central Europe which will undermine the Soviet Communist military and political positions in Poland, Czechoslovakia, Hungary, and other neighboring countries. So a revived nationalistic Germany has much to offer the West—at a price.

If Germany revives with nationalistic impulses, it is unrealistic to imagine that the Germans will not use their unique position for bargaining to improve their lot.

When we consider the organization of a military defense of the West, the problem of Germany again emerges. What will be the defense line? Will it be the Rhine?

If our defense line is the Rhine, nearly sixty million Germans to the east of it will have to be abandoned. If the West abandons them, will they not make the best terms they can with the Soviet Union?

If we plan to hold a line of defense along the Elbe, what can we hold it with? Can Germany be held against the Soviet Union, except perhaps by German troops? Does that mean the rearmament of Germany? Will France consent, and what dependence can be placed on rearmed Germans? Can we be sure that they will shoot in what we think is the right direction?

There are as yet no agreed answers to these questions posed by Germany.

When we turn to Europe west of Germany, we find more problems that await solution.

In France and Italy there are still powerful Communist parties, representing about a quarter of the total electorate and with corresponding representation in the parliaments.

This is not as bad as it sounds. The Communist parties in France and Italy are not like the Communist Party in the Soviet Union, which is a small, highly trained, iron-disciplined, fanatical group.

In France and Italy the Communists have attempted to organize a popular front party. Many of the members are not orthodox, and vote as members of the Communist Party in protest against the other parties or to show that they want what the Communist Party promises.

Behind these large voting blocs in France and Italy there is a small, hard core of orthodox Communists who have penetrated deeply into the national life. They can exert a strong influence, politically and through labor unions, and they can steal military secrets. They can give Soviet Communism much help if and when another thrust is decided upon.

There has been an amazing economic recovery in the countries of Western Europe, so that their productivity is, generally speaking, equal to or above the prewar level. That is a tribute to the possibilities of a free society. But it is not enough—not nearly enough.

Western Europe (together with Greece and Turkey) is subdivided by the national policies, practices, and currencies of the eighteen different nations not behind the Iron Curtain. Each nation has developed an economic isolationism that far exceeds any that it has practiced in modern times.

All but a few have national currencies which are artificially valued and are practically non-exchangeable with any other currency.

Each country imposes not merely tariff restrictions but quotas on what may be brought in from abroad.

Many of the countries have gone in for a form of socialism or near-socialism that requires insulation from other countries. An economy that is mostly "planned" cannot admit of forces that the planners do not control. Therefore, high walls must be built, with only a few doors which can be closely patrolled by the government to make sure that the economy is immune from any natural forces.

Let us look at England.

The United Kingdom developed a population of about fifty million on an island which has few natural resources except coal and fish from the sea.

As one Englishman put it to me: England is a lump of coal in a bowl of fish. Nevertheless, England became great; and, for a century and more, it dominated the world.

That was because of the inventiveness, the resourcefulness, and the venturesomeness of her people.

It was in England that the Industrial Revolution began. The English found out how to put their one natural asset—coal—to work to run machinery which could multiply many times the productivity of human effort.

They manufactured goods on a great scale. They built ships to carry these goods through the seven seas of the world. They developed trading companies to distribute their goods. The Bank of England made its money—the pound sterling—into a world money, backed by gold. It was acceptable and exchangeable everywhere, so as to make possible an exchange of goods throughout the world. The English risked their profits by investing them in railroads, ports, irrigation projects, roads, and waterways in many lands. With a great navy they policed the trade of the world and helped maintain political order where their investments lay.

Never has the world made material, social, and indeed moral progress equal to that during the century of British dominance between the Napoleonic Wars and the First World War.

Through that dominance, England thrived. The greatest wealth of modern times was accumulated in England, and from all over the world there flowed to it the finest of everything: tea from the East, cigars from Havana, wines from France, porcelain from China, rugs from Persia. Its population grew by leaps and bounds. This ship of state called "England" was manned by officers and crew who were hard-working, courageous, resourceful, inventive, and venturesome. They had set full sail in a turbulent sea.

Now, however, all is changed. The captain and crew often act as though they were in charge of a derelict drifting to no discernible haven, with no dependable means of propulsion and only limited supplies of food and water.

Under such circumstances "socialism" is natural. When men, women, and children are adrift they usually divide the food and water on an equal basis.

That is what is happening in England. The discipline and stoicism are admirable; the leadership is capable and high-minded. But there is discouragement of the inventive and venturesome qualities which made England great and prosperous in the nineteenth century, and alone enabled it to support its population.

Necessity, it is said, is the mother of invention. Chance of gain also stimulates invention and venture. But will inventions and venture come adequately from a society where there is no hard necessity because everyone is provided for on a survival basis, and where steeply graduated taxes make it impossible for anyone to gain appreciably more than the means for bare survival?

There may be an affirmative answer. I hope there is. Perhaps it is to be found in a development of the vast resources of Africa. Certainly we are entitled to hope that a people who in the past have shown such great qualities will find a way of escape from the dangers that press on it. It would, however, be folly to believe that what has so far been done in the way of "European recovery" is a permanent solution to the economic problems of England.

Virtually no progress has been made in achieving in Europe the single market and the economic cooperation which were envisioned by the European Recovery Act. The result is that, in spite of a successful relief operation which has gained time and has prevented immediate catastrophe, there is no long-range solution. Under present conditions economic illness is bound to be recurrent, giving Soviet Communism new opportunities.

In the problem of military defense, while progress has been made, it is not along lines which hold any assurance of success.

No one of the countries of Western Europe is able to develop a military establishment which would be formidable on its own account. Under the North Atlantic Treaty they are supposed to operate under some plan for coordinated defense with other Western countries. But this arrangement does not eliminate unreliability. A national force which operates under political command can be surrendered at the decision of the political government. That happened in France in June, 1940, despite the Anglo-French alliance. Since this is so, no one country wants to have its own defense dependent upon some other military force under a foreign political command which may or may not be dependable in time of stress. So the English want a defense of their own, the French want a defense of their own, Benelux wants a defense of its own, and so forth.

It is not possible, with the resources available, to build a formidable and effective defense out of a series of politically distinct military establishments.

The European Recovery Plan, the North Atlantic Treaty, and the Military Assistance Program have not created in Western Europe a solid and dependable defense against the indirect aggression of Soviet Communism or against a possible armed attack by the Soviet Union. But these measures have at least provided a serious obstacle to the realization in Western Europe of the ambitions of Soviet Communism.

Greece

In Greece the check to Soviet Communism has undoubtedly been a serious and unexpected blow to the hopes of Soviet Communism. It seemed reasonable that the Greek government could not support indefinitely the tremendous expenditure of man power and economic resources involved in putting down a guerrilla war that was constantly fed from the great Communist hinterland north of the Greek border.

If Greece had fallen, much would have fallen with it. Control of Greece and of the Greek islands would have carried a dominance in the eastern Mediterranean even greater than Molotov sought when he asked for Tripolitania. Turkey would have been virtually surrounded and cut off from the West, and made an easy prey.

In Greece, Communist ambitions have suffered a serious, though perhaps not permanent, frustration.

The United Nations

In the United Nations, the Soviet Union has suffered a series of defeats. It has been isolated, and seldom finds outside support for the positions that it advocates. It has become normal in the General Assembly for the Soviet Union to get 6 votes, with from 40 or 50 against, and a few abstentions. The 6 are formed by the vote of the Soviet Union itself, of its two states the Ukraine and Byelorussia, and Czechoslovakia, Poland, and Yugoslavia. Now even Yugoslavia cannot be relied upon, so that sometimes the vote on the Soviet side is only 5.

It would be a mistake, however, to treat these lopsided votes as necessarily an accurate measure of the position of the Soviet Union in the United Nations. The Soviet Union often seems to wish and seek the voting results which we mention.

Time after time, those of us who have worked in the United Nations have been amazed at the way in which the Soviet Delegation has deliberately alienated votes. By even the slightest concessions, it could often have got many votes. Certainly the members of the Soviet Delegation are smart enough to know that.

The explanation seems to be that Soviet leaders, for purposes of their own, wish to present the picture of a Communist world encircled by hostile elements. When the Soviet Delegation introduces a resolution to condemn warmongers, or a resolution calling for disarmament, and that resolution is voted down by a vote of 45 or 50 to 6, Communist propaganda uses the fact to show the "masses" that the Communist nations are the only really peace-loving nations, and that they are surrounded by war-loving capitalists. The very fact that Communism stands alone is made into an asset. We can fairly conclude that the methods of Soviet Communism have failed in the United Nations; but we cannot rate the failure as very great because, in a sense, it is invited by the Soviet Union for its own purposes.

Also, it is a failure that could readily be retrieved if that should become Soviet policy. It would be particularly easy with Communist China in the United Nations. There are several other member states from Asia which might vote with China when they would not vote with the Soviet Union. Also, by a slight change of tactics, it could pick up a good many votes from other areas and become a very substantial minority within the Assembly.

The fact is that votes of 5 or 6 to 45 or 50 do not by any means measure the real influence of Soviet Communism in the world. A ratio of 1 to 13 would more accurately measure the balance that the Soviet Union could probably achieve, with Communist China in the United Nations, if it really tried to roll up a maximum vote.

We can take solid satisfaction from the results so far achieved in the United Nations. But it is wise to avoid any great elation over the overwhelming votes that have been recorded against proposals heretofore put forward by the Soviet Union.

THE NET SCORE

As we thus go over the world scene and score the pluses and minuses for the methods of Soviet Communism, we find that the pluses greatly outbalance the minuses. Soviet Communism has suffered one serious setback in Yugoslavia. It has been held back in Western Europe by a great exertion and expenditure on our part which, nevertheless, still leaves the situation precarious. In the rest of the world Soviet Communism has had success wherever it has exerted itself strongly; and it has had great success in China.

There has been a very definite shift in the balance of power in the world, and that shift has been in favor of Soviet Communism.

The area covered by the North Atlantic Pact and by the Truman Doctrine for Greece and Turkey has a total population, including the United States, of more than 350,000,000. This area includes the traditional hard core of Western civilization, and within it we have made the maximum expenditure of money and effort.

The population of the further area in the Americas covered by the Rio Pact aggregates about 100,000,000. This area is not so strongly held.

The areas not covered by the North Atlantic Pact, the Truman Doctrine for Greece and Turkey, or the Rio Pact have a total population of about 1,700,000,000. Of these, already more than 700,000,000 have been brought under the control of the Communist government of the Soviet Union and affiliated Communist governments. They have good chances of success in much of the remaining area whenever they may be disposed to move strongly.

Population figures are not in themselves conclusive as to power. Population together with natural resources makes potential power; but developed power may still be a long way off. From the standpoint of actual economic productivity, the balance is still in favor of the non-Communist world. However, the success of Soviet methods is to be measured in terms of their ability to advance their own program. That program has been from the beginning one of encirclement which would leave to the last the overthrow of the hard core of Western civilization, first by encirclement and then by weakening.

The program of encirclement has made great strides, and it is apparent that the policies so far devised do not frustrate gains by Soviet Communism through its combination of fraudulent propaganda, terrorism, class war and civil war, and finally a cutting off of the people from contact with outside sources that might give them spiritual encouragement and hope for ultimate freedom from despotism.

If any one of us were sitting in the Kremlin as a member of the Politburo checking over the score of the last five years he would conclude that these methods worked very well indeed, and he would see no reason to abandon or to alter them materially.

That, no doubt, is the view of the Politburo. It was expressed in an editorial by the official paper *Izvestia* on January 1, 1950, concluding:

The New Year has come to us as a welcome and dear guest. We have celebrated it with the joyous feeling of creators and builders. . . . With faith and hope the downtrodden people are looking to the great Soviet Union—mighty and spiritually close to the working people of all lands. Around the U.S.S.R. the camp of the fighters for peace, democracy, and socialism is growing and becoming stronger.

The forces of this camp are multiplying day by day. The camp of democracy and socialism today includes the Great Soviet Union, democratic Poland, Czechoslovakia, Bulgaria, Rumania, Hungary, Albania, Northern Korea, the Mongol People's Republic, where the workers are building socialism and have achieved hitherto unheard-of successes in improving the economy, culture, and science, the Chinese People's Republic, created by a great people which has cast off the burden of the imperialist and feudal yoke, and the German Democratic Republic, the formation of which marks a turning point in the history of Europe. . . .

The sun of freedom and Communism shines brightly for the world today. Communism is conquering, Communism will triumph!

A Happy New Year, comrades, a very Happy New Year!

CHAPTER THIRTEEN

WHY SOVIET COMMUNISM WINS

There are basic reasons why Soviet Communism is scoring great gains:

One is that Soviet Communism saturates the world with propaganda that has universal appeal.

A second reason is that the Soviet Communist Party has perfected a superb organization to conduct indirect aggression throughout the world.

A third reason is that Soviet Communism has the advantage of the offensive. It has no counteroffensive to fear, either in propaganda or in "cold war." It can push its redivision of the world, picking the time and place for its offensive and knowing that it can consolidate its gains at leisure.

Marxism is materialistic and atheistic. But the Communist Party sees clearly the power of ideas, and the leaders attach great importance to slogans that appeal to men everywhere, particularly to the so-called "masses" whose power Soviet leaders hope to harness.

The party of the proletariat must rely upon . . . such a social idea as . . . is capable of setting into motion broad masses of the people. (P. 603.)

So Soviet Communists have devised a program that has a tremendous appeal to all men everywhere who feel oppressed or cheated by the existing order and also to some of the idealists who want a better world.

The Constitution of the Soviet Union well illustrates the Party propaganda line. Here are a few excerpts:

Article 118 provides: "The right to work is ensured by the socialist organization of the national economy, the steady growth of the productive forces of Soviet society, the elimination of the possibility of economic crises, and the abolition of unemployment."

Article 119 provides: "Citizens of the U.S.S.R. have the right to rest and leisure."

Article 120 provides: "Citizens of the U.S.S.R. have the right to maintenance in old age and also in case of sickness or loss of capacity to work."

Article 121 provides: "Citizens of the U.S.S.R. have the right to education."

Article 122 provides: "Women in the U.S.S.R. are accorded equal rights with men in all spheres of economic, state, cultural, social and political life. The possibility of exercising these rights is ensured to women by . . . prematernity and maternity leave with full pay, and the provision of a wide network of maternity homes, nurseries, and kindergartens."

Article 123 provides that "any advocacy of racial or national exclusiveness or hatred and contempt, is punishable by law."

Article 125 provides for "(a) freedom of speech; (b) freedom of the press; (c) freedom of assembly."

Article 127 provides: "Citizens of the U.S.S.R. are guaranteed inviolability of the person."

Article 128 provides: "The inviolability of the homes of citizens and privacy of correspondence are protected by law."

The Soviet Communist world program tempts men everywhere with these social promises as set out in the Constitution of the Soviet Union.

Internationally, the Soviet Communists promise peace as against the program of war which is attributed to the "capitalist," the "bourgeois," the "imperialist" states, which are ruled by "warmongers."

The following quotation from an editorial in *Pravda* on December 21, 1949, written in connection with Stalin's seventieth birthday, illustrates the typical Communist "peace propaganda" line:

Our leader and teacher Comrade Stalin has sounded a great appeal for peace among peoples. This appeal sinks ever deeper into the hearts of the people. No gangster of the pen from the camp of the warmongers will succeed in disparaging the Stalin policy of friendship among peoples; he will not succeed in obliterating the sacred word of peace inscribed upon the banners of the freedom-loving peoples.

The mighty movement for peace and against the instigators of a new war is developing ever greater breadth and strength. The peoples of all countries regard Comrade Stalin as the great defender of peace.

Most readers of this book will know that social conditions within the Soviet Union do not in fact correspond with the word picture given by the Soviet Constitution. Also they will know that, if Soviet leaders perhaps do not plan international war, that is true only to the extent that they believe they can get more advantage out of class war or civil war.

But most of those to whom Communist propaganda is directed do *not* know the real facts, and they are easily misled by the constant repetition of appealing word pictures by past masters in that art.

In Canada, England, and the United States there have been some exposures of spying activities on behalf of Soviet Communism. Those glimpses show that Soviet Communists have been able to get treasonable cooperation from highly educated persons who, by birth and environment, were thoroughly steeped in the traditions of our Western society. They did not get the cooperation by crude processes of bribery—any such approaches would have been indignantly rejected. They got it because the persons had come to accept Soviet propaganda so far as to believe that disloyalty to nation would serve the higher cause of human welfare.

If Soviet propaganda and techniques can persuade "educated" persons that Communism means peace and a better world, how much more persuasive must that propaganda be to those of the "mass organizations" for whom the propaganda is primarily devised.

Before going to Russia in 1947, I read a guidebook to the city of Moscow issued in that city ten years earlier by the Co-

operative Publishing Society of Foreign Workers in the U.S.S.R.
It tells of the new buildings and structures and of the new people
"who at one and the same time are their creators and proprie-
tors," and whose works "vividly reflect the consciousness of the
working people that they are building 'their own' subway, 'their
own' factories, 'their own' municipal buildings and apartment
houses and are not working for the benefit of a private owner.
... Moscow is the city of emancipated and joyous labour, where
everyone works, studies and is an active builder of a new life."

I made some allowances; for guidebooks usually exaggerate.
I had, however, not imagined anything so drab, unkempt and run-
down as the reality. The roofs were leaking, the windows were
dirty, the areaways were dumping places for refuse and garbage.

It was a case of "What is everybody's business, is nobody's
business." In Moscow the residents took little interest in the
cleanliness and decency of their surroundings, for no one knew
where he would be living the next year.

I concluded that the guidebook had been written to guide, or
misguide, those who would never go to Moscow.

That is characteristic of Communist propaganda. It is for those
who will never compare what they hear and read with the reality.

When our people were carrying on what became known the
world over as the "Great American Experiment" we subjected
that experiment to the test of critical observation. We welcomed
visitors and immigrants from all over the world. Others learned
of what we did, not through official propaganda by ourselves, but
through the first-hand reports that visitors took home and through
the letters that immigrants wrote back to their relatives and
friends in the "old" country. We had no desire fraudulently to
spread our ideas or win leadership.

It is otherwise with Soviet Communist leadership. Its propaganda is a method of warfare. Methods are judged by their success, not by any sense of honor or responsibility toward the
"enemy."

At one meeting with high Soviet officials which I attended,
there was some discussion of the repatriation of Japanese troops,
promised by the surrender terms. The Soviet representatives ex-

pressed great surprise that we should take seriously that promise to repatriate. They said they had assumed that that provision had been put into the surrender terms only in order to induce the Japanese to surrender; and, since they had surrendered, the clause had served its purpose.

That cynical attitude is reflected in every aspect of Soviet Communist conduct of the "cold war." Their propaganda is fraudulent because the truth would not serve their present need. The Iron Curtain is an essential technique, not merely to cut off the peoples behind it from contact with the outer world, but also to prevent those outside, who are slated to be fooled by Communist propaganda, from learning the truth.

The comparison between our conduct of the Great American Experiment and the conduct of Soviet Communism may be historically interesting and may serve to increase our self-esteem. But the comparison does not alter the fact that Soviet Communism is getting results everywhere by professing beliefs which have a universal appeal. They catch the imaginations of millions and millions of people—those who want a better world, those who feel hopeless or despairing, those who feel that their lot could be improved by a successful class war against those more fortunate than themselves.

Such propaganda is the initial softening-up process. The follow-up is conducted by coldly and efficiently organizing toughness and terrorism.

The Soviet Communist Party has built up a world-wide organization of fanatical believers in the Stalin creed, believers that the end justifies the means, who accept "iron discipline" and are thoroughly trained for the conduct of "cold" war and indirect aggression. For this training the Party maintains schools in Russia; and it draws to these schools men from all countries of the world who are destined to be the top advisers in the army which stands ready, throughout the world, to carry forward the Soviet Communist program of world domination. They penetrate, usually secretly, into the labor unions, into the press, radio, and other vehicles of public opinion, into political parties, and into governments themselves. Each has an allotted task for which he is trained, and which is coordinated with the tasks of others by the Soviet Communist Party, as the "general staff" in this world-wide offensive. Many of these persons, particularly those who penetrate into so-called "mass organizations," develop a following which has no knowledge of the tie-in with Soviet Communism.

When Communist activity becomes strong and open, as in China, Indo-China, Greece, Czechoslovakia, and Hungary, the leaders are found to include those who have had their period of intensive training in the schools maintained by the Soviet Communist Party.

On January 1, 1950, I was asked to name the ten persons who had had the most profound influence on developments during the first half of the century. I listed Mikhail Borodin as one of the ten. The reporter who questioned me had not heard the name, and no doubt it means nothing to many other Americans. But Borodin in 1923 went from Russia to China to undertake the task of winning China to Communism. He attained a position of influence with the Kuomintang as "political adviser," and went on from that to establish a Communist government in Hankow; and he took a leading part in organizing the militant Chinese Communist armies that have been waging civil war in China for more than twenty years and have now won there a great victory for Communism.

One of his associates in China, who had trained in Russia, was Ho Chi Minh, who now leads the civil war in Viet Nam that is bleeding France.

This "cold war" army of the Soviet Communist Party conducted the guerrilla war in Greece; led the strikes and sabotage that nearly wrecked France in the winter of 1947–1948. It spreads the terrorism that frightens people into the Communist Party, or frightens them from opposing it; and it mans the secret police and conducts the purges when Communism gets into control.

Neither the United States nor any other non-Communist nation has any organization for taking the initiative in this "cold war," or even an organization adequate to expose Communist elements within our midst. As a result, Soviet Communism has the immense advantage of being able always to take the offensive. It is able to carry out Stalin's advice in "the strategic utilization of the forces of the revolution," which involves "the concentration of the main forces of the revolution at the enemy's most vulnerable spot at the decisive moment" (p. 63).

Soviet Communism is free to concentrate upon the offensive and to pick the time and place for decisive action because it does not have to worry about any counteroffensives, even though, within the existing area of its control, there are weak spots. Those whom Soviet Communism is fighting are tied down to defensive action on battlegrounds selected by Soviet Communism.

Most of the non-Communist countries operate on the theory that they are either at peace or at war. The United States, for example, has governmental departments manned for peace. The State Department is one. It conducts peacetime relations with other nations which we recognize, and with which we deal on a presumably friendly basis.

When we go to war, diplomatic relations are broken, our ambassadors come home, and the primary responsibility then passes to the War, Navy, and Air Departments, now combined into the "Department of Defense." They then conduct a fighting war.

Soviet Communism has invented an intermediate stage, a twilight zone between war and peace. The descriptive phrase "not war, not peace" is said to have been first uttered by Trotsky in connection with the Treaty of Brest-Litovsk. That was the peace that was supposed to end the war in which Germany and Russia were then engaged. Trotsky is gone, but the policy which he launched remains. It not only remains, but has been implemented in ever mounting degrees.

On our side, our Constitution and legal system rigidly insist that we are either at war or at peace, so that we are almost impotent when it comes to dealing with the "not war, not peace" condition in which we find ourselves. We are devoting billions in money and our highest talent to preparation for a fighting war —a war that may never come. Meanwhile, we are being encircled and the strength of our society is being undermined by the "cold war" that is here, and which could finally defeat us.

We have now seen the basic reasons why Soviet Communism has won and is winning great successes throughout the world. The "Great Soviet Experiment" is the most advertised, the most ballyhooed scheme for softening up the opposition that the world has ever known. That softening-up organization is, in turn, backed up by the most ruthless, unscrupulous, highly trained, omnipresent, secret army that the world has ever known. Finally, neither the propaganda nor the secret army has any effective competition or opposition from without, so that Soviet Communism holds the advantage of the offensive.

PART IV

WHAT NEEDS TO BE DONE

CHAPTER FOURTEEN

A SUMMARY OF NEEDS

There is no reason why we should be content with the present situation. The foreign policies which we have reviewed are good so far as they go. But they do not go far enough. They leave the world field wide open to successes by methods of fraud, terrorism, and violence.

We could of course gamble that, if we rest on the defensive and organize an inner citadel of the West or of the Americas, everything will turn out all right because the task of encirclement is so vast and Soviet Communist plans so grandiose that they will, sooner or later, collapse, even though we have no policies to make them do so.

Certainly the unpredicted and the unpredictable play a great part in human affairs, and perhaps we would be favored by luck.

Usually the lucky breaks favor those who are alert and vigorous under the impulse of a dynamic faith. Luck rarely sustains those who rely on it exclusively.

If the American people adopt luck as a substitute for enlightened policies and programs of their own, they may for a time be lucky; but, even so, in the end they will surely lose.

To rely on luck is wrong because it involves unconcern for the welfare of humanity. It means that we are indifferent to the moral enormities which are the inevitable consequence of what is happening and is threatening in much of the world.

It is stupid to rely on luck to bring about that which we can bring about ourselves, if we will. We do not need to gamble with our future. What we have already done proves our capacity to do more. The Berlin airlift and the European Recovery Plan are two concrete examples of faith and works which can be drawn on more deeply to check the progressive strangulation of human liberty in the world.

It is time to think in terms of taking the offensive in the world struggle for freedom and of rolling back the engulfing tide of despotism. It is time to think less of fission bombs and more of establishing justice and ending terrorism in the world.

We should all feel relief if methods of mass destruction were abolished. But that would not mean "peace." It might mean that we should die a little later rather than a little sooner; it might mean that we should die slowly rather than quickly; but it would not have much bearing on whether or not our world was to be one where myriads of human beings were degraded to the status of broken-spirited pack animals.

The situation today is comparable to that of 1942, although in geographic terms it is not as bad. Then the despotic power of the Axis had overrun Europe to the Atlantic, had conquered Burma, Malaya, and the islands of the Pacific—Indonesia and the Philippines—and had control of a large part of China.

Today Soviet Communism is held at the river Elbe in Germany; and, while it has overrun China, it is not yet in open control of Burma, Malaya, or any of the islands of the Pacific.

In the dark days of 1942 we were not thinking about "peace" in terms of some settlement that might temporarily allow us to go on existing as an oasis in a totalitarian desert. We were not thinking about how to save our necks, but how to save freedom.

We need more of that spirit today. If we had it, there would be far more chance of getting real peace. Security is the by-product, not of fear, but of great endeavor and great faith.

If we do develop that spirit, it will lead us to strengthen and invigorate those of our present policies which are sound and to develop new policies and programs of even greater scope and imagination.

First of all, we need, here at home, to put bipartisanship in foreign policy on a solid basis. For five years bipartisanship has given strength and continuity to the foreign policies it served. It has made them vigorous and dependable so that we could provide

effective leadership. We shall need bipartisanship even more if
we are to develop broader and stronger policies. But today it has
gravely deteriorated, and there is risk that we shall become in-
ternally divided at a time when continuity, dependability, and
invigoration of foreign policy are more than ever vital.

The United Nations has contributed to the solution of international disputes. It has deterred aggression by exposing potential aggressors. But the United Nations has settled down to a
somewhat stodgy routine at a time when it needs to be the arena
where the great world struggle for peace and justice is drama-
tized in a way that grips the imagination and steels the resolve
of free men everywhere.

Within the area of our strategic military concern, notably the
"West," we have had some good policies. But the West still remains gravely divided within itself. Our policies have not yet
eradicated from the West the seeds of its own disintegration, and
we are pinned down there by tasks that should be completed
so that we can pay more attention to the East. Therefore, even
within the inner citadel of the West our policies need to be
strengthened.

In the vast areas of Asia and the Pacific we have no adequate
policy, largely because China, always until now our friendly
partner, has been taken over by the allies of Soviet Communism.
That calls for new thinking about our relations with the peoples
of Asia and the Pacific.

We have been concentrating almost exclusively on preparation
for a "hot" war which may never come. Top policy decisions
have been influenced too much by the military, whose duty it is
to think primarily in terms of a shooting war. Meanwhile, we
can lose the "cold" war. There is imperative need for an over-all
strategy that takes account of all the realities, the nonmilitary
as well as the military.

We need, ourselves, a capacity to wage "not war, not peace." If
we continue without adequate organization or techniques for conducting the "cold" war which Soviet Communism presses on us,
some may come to feel, in desperation, that time is working
against us, and that it is better to have a shooting war at which

we should doubtless be more competent, and where the odds would still be in our favor. But another world war, whatever the military outcome, would make it almost certain that totalitarianism of some kind would be the victor over any survivors.

At the moment, we have little in the way of influence to project into the vast fields which lie beyond the reach of our military or economic power. We are not generating the dynamic faith, the ideas, needed to touch the spirits and to arouse the hopes of the peoples of the world who are the prey of predatory Communism. If we would break the ever tightening noose, there is need for spiritual qualities which can give our influence greater scope.

We shall discuss each of these needs.

CHAPTER FIFTEEN

A FUTURE FOR BIPARTISANSHIP

Bipartisanship in foreign policy is difficult to practice. The present omens suggest that it is not going to be practiced.

The bipartisanship of the past five years has depended more on personalities than on principles. Now there is a trend back to the professional view that bipartisanship is bad politics.

In 1944 the professional politicians, both Republican and Democrat, did not want to have bipartisan cooperation in world organization. Many Democrats opposed it because they thought that the Democratic Party should try to capitalize on the popular desire for a world organization and make it appear that only the Democratic Party had the will or the competence to achieve that result.

Many Republicans were opposed to bipartisanship because they believed that there was no advantage for the Republican Party in seeming merely to endorse what President Roosevelt was doing. They felt that, if the leaders of the Republican Party could not do better than endorse the leader of their political opponents, the people would be apt to do the same. They recalled that the Republican Party had won the elections of 1920 in large part because of the revolt against Woodrow Wilson and his internationalist policies, notably his advocacy of the League of Nations.

Always, within the Republican Party, powerful elements believed that bipartisanship was wrong as a matter of principle; that the duty of the opposition party was to attack and to expose, and that, when it collaborated in making foreign policy, it became estopped from discharging its proper role.

They also believed that, as a matter of practical politics, the Republican Party could not win by tactics of cooperation. It might be the fact—indeed, it was more or less conceded—that on matters where we helped to hammer out foreign policy, Senator Vandenberg and I made contributions which matched those of our opposites in the Democratic Party. The results represented an honest and a loyal effort in a spirit of partnership, and in reality the result bore the trade-mark of us all. Nevertheless, when the policies finally emerged they naturally and properly emerged as the policies of the President and his Secretary of State. In consequence, the policies were identified in the public mind with Democrats.

The Republicans could not attempt publicly to claim credit which might be theirs for the making of the agreed policies, for bipartisanship would never survive if it were merely a prelude to open quarreling as to where lay the principal credit for origination.

Because bipartisan cooperation is not a very usable asset for the opposition party, many leading figures in the Republican Party believe that bipartisanship has been, and always will be, a political mistake. The latest exhibit to support their thesis is China. A great misfortune has befallen us there. Republicans can point to that misfortune as demonstrating Democratic incompetence, and they feel free to do so because there never has been bipartisan cooperation in this area.

From the Democratic side, the future of bipartisanship is equally problematic and beset with political difficulties. There is a reluctance to have bipartisan cooperation participated in by persons who might thereby gain stature and, from a domestic standpoint, become more formidable political opponents.

There cannot be genuine bipartisan cooperation except through individuals who are stalwart members of the two parties, and who have the opportunity and the capacity to help shape foreign policy. Republican senators and representatives, Republican governors, and Republican political leaders generally will not go along with a foreign policy as "bipartisan" merely because someone who is nominally and formally a Republican was a member of the international delegation that produced the policy.

President Wilson attempted a sham bipartisanship when he appointed Henry White to his peace delegation in 1918. Mr. White was not a stalwart Republican; he did not have the confidence of Republican leaders, and it seemed obvious that he would play no real part in the decisions at Paris. This assumption proved to be quite correct. Mr. White, as I can testify from personal observation, was not consulted about any major decision that was taken at the Paris Peace Conference of 1919. He was an honorable and distinguished person; but his appointment did not make the delegation bipartisan, and the attempt to make it appear so created political irritation at home.

At the time of the Dumbarton Oaks Conference, Henry Fletcher was made a member of the United States delegation. He had in the past been a vigorous and trusted member of the party; but he was not then in a position to bring Republican influence to bear effectively on what was done at Dumbarton Oaks. His participation was largely formal, and the delegation was not made bipartisan by his membership in it.

Because politicians on both sides view bipartisanship with alarm, bipartisanship in foreign policy has a precarious future.

This ought to be changed.

Of course, the normal role of the opposition party should be to oppose. But these are not normal times. The United States faces, and will continue to face for some years, the greatest danger that ever confronted it. Our nation is in a position where, if we calculate on the basis of cold reason, time may well be on the side of those hostile to us, with the balance of power shifting in their favor. We have faith and hope that this will not happen, but we dare not ignore the warning of reason.

If we are to do what reason tells us we should do to escape the peril, the first step must be to find a way of assuring unity on the main features of our foreign policy, so that there can be confidence that our policies will be sustained and continuous.

As never before in our national history, we carry the responsibility for leadership. Most of the non-Communist governments face the future with trepidation, knowing that they are lost if they stand alone. But they are unable to work effectively together except under such leadership as the United States can provide.

Foreign policy today is very different from what it has been heretofore in our national history. We have a totally new responsibility. It is a frightening responsibility because, if we do not discharge it adequately, the whole non-Communist world will crumble and we may crumble with it. In a very real sense, we do not today live for ourselves alone. Our foreign policy is not just a United States foreign policy; it becomes the foreign policy of many nations and many peoples. Therefore, we cannot play with it as with something that is just our own. It is impressed with a trust for the benefit of mankind. That requires that we make of it something that is dependable and something that is consistent, for the fortunes and the lives of many peoples are risked upon it.

Our national policies will not attract the confidence of those whom we need as friends and allies if they have no better support than a precarious partisan majority in Congress. On January 19, 1950, the House of Representatives, which is overwhelmingly Democratic, voted down the Administration request for funds for Korea. The appropriation, as a practical matter, required Republican help for its passage; and the Republicans had been kept so much in the dark regarding a Far Eastern policy that most of them were unprepared to go along with an Administration request. The fund was subsequently voted. However, the effect of the original vote had repercussions far beyond Korea.

In an earlier chapter I have told at some length of the situation that existed in Paris in the fall of 1948, and of the near-panic that gripped all the governments of friendly countries lest our foreign policies, into which they had geared their own, might suddenly be shifted. Because of the bipartisanship then being practiced by Governor Dewey and President Truman, it was possible to allay that panic and to restore confidence and resolution.

If conditions had been otherwise, if the Republican candidate for President had been a believer in "isolation," campaigning against the foreign policies of the Administration, then, in the summer and fall of 1948, even the inner citadel of the West might well have fallen apart. Iran, Turkey, and Greece would have altered their policy of strong resistance to the indirect aggression of Soviet Communism. The peoples of Western Berlin would have decided to make the best terms possible with the Soviet Communists. Berlin would have been lost. Then, probably, Western Germany would have been lost, and after that the rest of the Continent would almost surely have been lost.

Both the Democratic Party and the Republican Party have a duty to put behind them dubious political advantage that would risk creating a situation where disasters of that magnitude could, and almost certainly would, befall us.

How is this to be brought about?

It can be brought about only by public understanding of the importance of bipartisanship and of the nature of bipartisanship, and by popular insistence that both parties do the necessary to provide it.

There is, I think, general public approval of bipartisanship in foreign policy. That is indicated by the fact that, in the 1948 presidential campaign, each party claimed the credit for initiating the practice in 1944. But the public must also understand the real nature of bipartisanship, so that neither party can get away with a hoax.

Also, the people must make clear, even before an actual election, their determination to turn overwhelmingly against whichever party is chiefly responsible for subordinating the safety of the nation to partisan advantage.

These principles should be kept in mind:

(1) The primary responsibility for bipartisanship rests upon the Administration in power. Under the Constitution the President, and the President alone, decides on how to conduct foreign affairs. He can conduct them alone or with others, as he desires: the decision is his. Without his positive action there can be no bipartisanship. The opposition party has no right or possibility of intruding itself. Bipartisanship can come about only through presidential invitation.

(2) An invitation to members of the opposition to participate in making foreign policy bipartisan is meaningless and is a sham unless it is made to loyal members of their party, trusted by party leadership.

(3) The opposition members selected to participate in making foreign policy bipartisan should be qualified by training and experience to make a genuine contribution and to take an active and constructive part in the formulation of foreign policy. If the opposition party is to cooperate with the Administration on foreign policy, the participation must be meaningful. Nominal participation is not good enough.

(4) The opposition participants must have opportunity to get in at the early shaping of foreign policies and must not be left out until the end, when matters have gone so far that there is little opportunity to do other than acquiesce. As Governor Stassen remarked, "Republicans should be in at the take-off and not merely at the crash landing." Often in recent years Republicans have been faced with Administration decisions which seemed unwise; but repudiation had disadvantages even greater than going along with what they deemed unsound. That was true of the loan to England of $3,750,000,000 in 1946. The conditions attached to the loan as regards repayment, trade, and currency exchangeability are revealing of how, in those days, even the best informed members of the Administration saw only "through a glass, darkly."

But when the loan terms first came to Republican attention, our government was so far committed that repudiation would probably have been more costly than acquiescence.

By appeals to patriotism, an appearance of bipartisan cooperation may temporarily be forced. But in the long run, that merely builds up smoldering resentment which will some day break out.

(5) In these foregoing respects, the Administration has the responsibility. If, however, the four preceding conditions are met, then the opposition party has a duty also. Obviously, no party can be expected to give a blank check, and there is no party machinery for doing so. The opposition party in this country, unlike the British opposition, has no officially defined leadership. "Titu-

lar" leadership is not enough. But if opposition members of the character and competence we have indicated receive the kind of opportunity we have described to help make the foreign policy, then the opposition members of Congress should not seek to make political capital by attacking the results, but should support them through treaty ratifications and Congressional appropriations as far as their convictions permit.

If the leaders of the opposition party refuse at this critical time, as a matter of partisan advantage, to accept a *bona fide* offer to make foreign policies cooperatively, so that those policies can command unity at home and attract adherence abroad, then those who take that position ought to be repudiated at the polls. Refusal by the Administration to make such a *bona fide* offer ought to ensure a like fate.

We are dealing here with the safety of the American nation and of the liberties and freedoms that are our most precious heritage. That concerns, most of all, the people themselves. They should make their understanding manifest by a will which even the most politically minded will respect.

CHAPTER SIXTEEN

DEVELOPING WORLD ORGANIZATION

The United Nations, as it now is, has a field of usefulness which is large, but limited. It can do much, but there is much that it cannot now do. Here are some of the things it cannot do:

The United Nations cannot suppress or reconcile the difference between the materialistic and atheistic philosophy of the Communist Party and the spiritual faith that animates the leaders and peoples of the non-Communist states.

The United Nations cannot stop those who hold strong beliefs from feeling a sense of mission and seeking to spread their beliefs in the world. Both Christians and Marxists, for example, feel it their duty to carry their creed into all the world.

The United Nations cannot compel the Communists to give up their belief in class war; or their use of fraud, terrorism, and violence so long as it seems that these methods get results. The Communist Party feels that duty and advantage require it to spread its power by any method that will work.

The United Nations cannot alter the determination of the free peoples to fight and die rather than be terrorized into a surrender of their own beliefs and free institutions which reflect a spiritual view of the nature of man.

The United Nations cannot do these things as it now is or as it could be remade. It takes more than a vote to calm a world scene made turbulent by those who combine fanatical beliefs with tremendous power. Even a "police" force would not suffice. Nor could peace and order be assured if the United Nations were made into a mighty military instrument whereby a bare majority would attempt, in alliance, to impose their will upon a powerful minority.

Certainly, the American people would never accept the kind of peace that depended upon enforcement by a Communist-dominated world police state. Also we had better assume that the Communists would not accept a peace that depended on enforcement by a world police state which we dominated. They would hate and fight our kind of world organization just as much as we would hate and fight subjection to their will.

To say these things is not to be fatalistic or to assume that nothing can be done. In a world where "cold" war is exterminating human liberty and where "hot" war might be waged with atomic bombs and hydrogen bombs, fatalism or complacency would be criminal.

There is plenty to be done. But the basic divisions and distrusts in the world cannot be obliterated by fiat, or by doing away with the "veto," or by bringing into being toy contingents as a United Nations "police force," or by giving that organization the vast military power it would require if it were to be the instrument whereby one-half the world seeks to coerce the other half.

The "civilized" part of mankind is in a grave plight. But we shall gain nothing if, in panic, we lose contact with realities and assume that, because there is great *need* of a quick, easy, and sure way to avoid war, there must *be* such a way. Unfortunately, practical possibilities do not always keep pace with needs. Sometimes they lag behind. That is the case today. Natural science has outstripped moral and political science. That is too bad; but it is a fact, and the fact does not disappear because we close our eyes to it.

Let us remember those who, after the First World War, felt intensely that war must be abolished, as we feel today. Then high-minded people invented the slogan: "Outlaw war." Under that noble impulse the United States and France brought all the nations to agree that they would not go to war, but would settle all their disputes peacefully. That was the Kellogg-Briand Pact. When it was signed there was great jubilation, and church bells rang. Many felt that at last the curse of war had been forever abolished, and that we had moved into an era of permanent peace.

Unhappily, the Kellogg-Briand Pact did not stop World War II by a single day. Probably it made the war come sooner, because many innocent and trusting people put their faith in the pact and felt that armament was unnecessary. Thus they tempted the aggressions of Hitler, Mussolini, and the Japanese war lords.

We should learn from that experience that it is not possible to abolish war by slogans or strokes of a pen. Indeed, we should all be suspicious of any formulas that promise quick, easy, and sure results. There is a strong presumption against them.

Fundamentally, world peace depends upon world law, and world law depends upon a consensus of world opinion as to what is right and what is just. If there is wide disagreement about what is right and just, there will always be risk of war. Human nature is such that men always have believed—and I trust always will believe—as President Wilson put it in his war message to Congress, "The right is more precious than peace."

Experience in the United Nations shows that there is considerable agreement about what is right. That is particularly true between those who are influenced by one or another of the great religions. All the great religions reflect to some degree the moral or natural law, and that makes it possible to find many common denominators of right and wrong.

The great difficulty today is that the Communist rulers, who control so much of the world, are animated by an atheistic creed which denies the existence of a moral law or a natural law. To them, laws do not reflect justice, but are ways whereby those in power win their class war. For their beliefs and ours, it is impossible to find a common denominator. They do, however, pay attention to other people's sense of right and justice, because that affects what they will do and how they will act in any given situation. That is always of interest, even to despots.

We shall do well to think of the United Nations as a place where discussion leads nations and peoples to form judgments as to right and wrong, judgments which will influence their future conduct. Every government is interested in those judgments and takes them into account. Votes in the Assembly have practical significance if they measure underlying power in the world that is swayed by moral judgment.

In a society of free institutions there are public debates in the light of which the people vote. Those votes reflect their judgment on the merit of the propositions that have been debated. If a vote shows a clear balance in favor of a certain policy, the opponents reconcile themselves to that policy, provided it does not impair their fundamental rights, because they know that it would be futile to contest forcibly. Voting in this sense provides a moral substitute for war.

At the present stage of world development we should try to evolve a world organization that will form moral judgments and reflect as adequately as possible the quantity, quality, and intensity of power which will back these judgments.

Some changes sought for the United Nations go in the wrong direction. They represent devices by which some nations hope to get results that they could not possibly get in any other way. Some persons would like to throw out Soviet Russia because we disagree with their representatives and they with us. A world organization without Soviet Communists would be a much more pleasant organization. But they have power in the world, and if the United Nations gets away from that reality it becomes artificial and exerts less influence. The United Nations should mirror more accurately, not less accurately, the reality of what is.

With this preamble, let us go on to consider what may practically and usefully be done to improve the structure and working methods of the United Nations.

UNIVERSALITY

A growing weakness of the United Nations is its lack of universality. At the San Francisco Conference, the countries represented had virtually all the effective power in the world. Therefore, an organization in which they were members could fairly be called a "world" organization, and it fairly mirrored the reality of power in the world.

Since San Francisco, that situation has greatly changed.

The ex-enemy states have grown in power since military defeat rendered them powerless. There are peace treaties with Italy, Hungary, Bulgaria, Rumania, and Finland. In Germany and Japan there are governments with growing power. Austria is reborn. There are new nations which are not members—the United States of Indonesia, Jordan and Ceylon, for example.

Several nations that were neutrals in the last war are not members—for example, Eire, Portugal, Switzerland, and Spain.

The United Nations is no longer a "world" organization, and its decisions cannot reflect reality if it excludes from membership a substantial part of the world community.

Admission of new members is a matter that has greatly agitated the United Nations.

Under present procedure, admission can only occur with the concurrence of both the General Assembly and the Security Council; and in the Security Council the veto power prevails.

The Soviet Union has prevented the admission of Italy, which was contemplated by the Italian Peace Treaty, and of other nations, such as Portugal, Eire, Jordan and Ceylon, because it judged that their admission would give more votes to the non-Communist bloc.

The United States and others have prevented the admission of such countries as Rumania, Bulgaria, and Hungary, although their admission also was contemplated by their peace treaties. The theory of the opposition was that these nations did not qualify under Article 4 of the Charter, which provides:

Membership in the United Nations is open to all other peace-loving states which accept the obligations contained in the present Charter and, in the judgment of the Organization, are able and willing to carry out these obligations.

Proof that Hungary, Bulgaria, and Rumania were not able and willing to carry out the Charter obligations is found in their violation of human rights. Further, Bulgaria' has participated in indirect aggression against Greece. An underlying objection has been that these countries were under the domination of the Soviet Union and had little real independence.

At various times, proposals have been made that candidates for membership approved by the United States, the United Kingdom, and France and candidates for membership approved by the Soviet Union should all be admitted as part of a "trade." The United States Delegation has so far been unwilling to make such a deal, and the World Court has given an advisory opinion to the effect that a member nation cannot properly condition its vote for one candidate on the acceptance of other candidates.

I have now come to believe that the United Nations will best serve the cause of peace if its Assembly is representative of what the world actually is, and not merely representative of the parts which we like. Therefore, we ought to be willing that all the nations should be members without attempting to appraise closely those which are "good" and those which are "bad." Already that distinction is obliterated by the present membership of the United Nations.

Some of the present member nations, and others that might become members, have governments that are not representative of the people. But if in fact they are "governments"—that is, if they "govern"—then they have a power which should be represented in any organization that purports to mirror world reality.

If the Communist government of China in fact proves its ability to govern China without serious domestic resistance, then it, too, should be admitted to the United Nations. However, a regime that claims to have become the government of a country through civil war should not be recognized until it has been tested over a reasonable period of time.

If the United Nations membership were made substantially universal, that might end a preponderant voting superiority of the United States and its friends which, while pleasant, is somewhat fictitious.

Communist governments today dominate more than 30 per cent of the population of the world. We may not like that fact;

indeed, we do not like it at all. But if we want to have a *world* organization, then it should be representative of the world as it is.

VOTING IN THE ASSEMBLY

If the membership of the United Nations is to be enlarged, and particularly if many more small states are to be admitted, there should be reconsideration of voting procedures in the Assembly.

The weight of Assembly action is lessened by the fact that each member nation, be it big or be it little, has one vote (except that the Soviet Union has three votes as the result of a Yalta decision). Thus, nations which represent a minority by any measure of population, productivity, or power can still muster a two-thirds majority in the Assembly.

The Latin American states and the Arab states, in combination, can often be a working balance of power within the Assembly, representing almost half of the total membership. They often have made an alliance for such purposes as the election of officers. On substantive matters the nations of Latin America and the United States have usually agreed, so that we have not been greatly disturbed by the voting procedure. However, it should be reconsidered if we want Assembly action to help peace by reflecting realities.

Immediately after the San Francisco Conference, I wrote in *Foreign Affairs* (October, 1945):

At San Francisco much was said about the inequity of a big power like the United States or Soviet Russia having a right of veto. Very little was said about Liberia and Luxembourg, for example, having equal voting power in the Assembly with the United States and Soviet Russia. The fact is, the small powers as well as the big ones are still tenacious of special privileges. So long as that is so, the Organization cannot be politically mature.

Assembly action cannot at the present stage of the world be made legally binding or more than a "weighty" recommendation. But the weight of its recommendations would be far greater if the votes reflected not merely numbers but also ability to con-

tribute to the maintenance of international peace and security—
a test, incidentally, which the Charter lays down for consideration in determining eligibility to membership in the Security
Council (Article 23, Section 1).

In the United States Congress we have two ways of voting.
In the Senate there are two votes per state, big and small. New
York, with nearly 15,000,000 people, and Nevada, with a popu-
lation of around 150,000, have an equal vote. In the House of
Representatives, in which the states are represented in propor-
tion to their populations, New York has 45 votes and Nevada 1.

I would not abolish, in the United Nations, an Assembly vote
which, like that of our Senate, reflects the sovereign equality of
all nations and gives them all an equal vote. But there might be
introduced, in addition, a system of "weighted" voting so that
the result would indicate, roughly, a verdict in terms also of ability to play a part in world affairs. Then it should be provided
that decisions on important matters would require a simple
majority, rather than two-thirds, under each of the two voting
procedures.

Any change to a dual voting system that includes "weighted"
voting should take account of the present privileged position of
the Soviet Union, which already has "weighted voting" in its
favor because two of its constituent states—the Ukraine and
Byelorussia—have one vote each, making, with the vote of the
Soviet Union itself, a total of three votes for that one nation.
The present method of giving the Soviet Union three votes is
awkward and cumbersome because it means not merely three
votes but three delegations, so that whenever a delegate of the
Soviet Union makes a speech a delegate from each of these two
states also has to make a speech.

One difficulty of General Assembly procedure is that Soviet
delegates believe that if a matter is important they must speak
about it lengthily. Also, if it is important, every other Communist
delegation represented must speak about it lengthily. Otherwise,
they reason, it might be inferred that there was not complete
harmony between the different Communist delegations. So, if Mr.
Vishinsky speaks about some important matter, he will usually

speak for two or three hours; then a delegate from the Ukraine will speak for two hours, and a delegate from Byelorussia will speak for two hours. Then delegates from Poland, Czechoslovakia, and usually Yugoslavia will also speak for two hours. This is deemed necessary to prove to the world how important the matter is, and how harmonious the Communist delegations are among themselves.

It would be much better to give the Soviet Union three or more votes—as might be determined under an arrangement also giving several votes to the United States, the United Kingdom, France, etc.—and to take away the right of component states of the Soviet Union to be independently represented for voting and speaking purposes.

If Assembly voting were a composite of "unit" voting and "weighted" voting, then that would permit further desirable changes.

It would make it reasonable to give the General Assembly exclusive responsibility for organizational matters such as the election of new members (Article 4, Section 2) and the appointment of the Secretary General (Article 97).

As the Charter now reads, the Assembly can act in these matters only "upon the recommendation of the Security Council." That provision was made at San Francisco so as to give the "great" powers, which predominate in the Security Council, an added weight in organizational matters.

There is good reason why, in these matters, there should be "weighted" voting. But there is no reason why it should be accomplished by the cumbersome method of dragging in the Security Council, where action is subject to the veto power of any "permanent" member.

There is no excuse for permitting a single vote in the Security Council to paralyze action on all organizational matters.

At the first meetings of the United Nations held in London in January–February, 1946, for organization, it seemed for a time that there might not be any organization at all because the Soviet Union, through the Security Council, asserted the right to veto the appointment of the Secretary General. Without a Secretary

General there could be no staff, and with no staff there could be no organization.

Many anxious days were spent. The Soviet Union refused to take any person suggested by the United States, the United Kingdom, France, or China. On its part, it at first proposed only persons who would obviously be merely stooges of the Soviet Union—persons who were members of the Communist Party and subject to its "iron discipline." Finally Trygve Lie was agreed upon; and he has served admirably and fairly. If, however, any misadventure made him no longer available and a new Secretary General had to be elected, it would be necessary, as things now stand, either to take whomever the Soviet Union demanded or to risk disruption of the organization.

That is an absurd situation which should not be tolerated. It can be ended if the justifiably greater concern of the larger nations, such as the United States, the Soviet Union, the United Kingdom, and France, is adequately reflected by "weighted" voting within the General Assembly. Then the illogical responsibility of the Security Council for organizational matters can be terminated.

VETO IN THE SECURITY COUNCIL

Whenever there is discussion in the United States about amending the United Nations Charter, it centers on the "veto." That is the blocking power given to the United States, the Soviet Union, the United Kingdom, France, and China as a result of the Charter provision that, except on "procedural matters," no action can be taken without the affirmative vote of each of them.

Up to January 1, 1950, the Soviet Union had used the veto 43 times. The United States has used it not at all. Therefore, the problem seems to us very simple. The veto has prevented the Security Council from doing what we wanted and what the Soviet Union did not want; therefore, the veto should be abolished.

However, it is really not quite that simple.

The Security Council is not a body that merely enforces agreed law. It is a law unto itself. If it considers any situation as a threat to the peace, it may decide what measures shall be taken. No principles of law are laid down to guide it; it can decide in accordance with what it thinks is expedient. It could be a tool enabling certain powers to advance their selfish interests at the expense of another power.

It has happened so far that a majority in the Security Council has been friendly to the United States, so that our veto has not been needed to protect our interests. But it may not always be so; and, if it should not be so, certainly the United States would want to have a veto power.

We have already seen that the United States insisted upon putting the Japanese mandated islands under "strategic" trusteeship so that we might be able, through veto power in the Security Council, to block any disposition of the islands which we thought was against the security of the United States. Would we consent, for example, to put ourselves in a position such that a majority vote in the Security Council could require us to turn those islands over to Russia for administration, or to surrender the Panama Canal as a measure which would be in the interest of peace?

So long as the Security Council is a law unto itself, capable of taking arbitrary action, no great power will consent to be bound in advance by whatever action may be taken against it. I feel confident that the United States would not consent to put itself in that position.

The veto is not merely a check on what could be arbitrary despotism. It also reflects, rather crudely, a basic reality. At the present stage of world development, the United Nations cannot be used to coerce any great power. Great powers may be subject to moral pressure; and, as we have seen, they are. The United Nations in this respect has achieved great successes by influencing the conduct of the Soviet Union in relation to Iran and Korea. It is always possible in the General Assembly to get a moral verdict or recommendation which cannot be blocked by anyone's veto. But there is not much point in getting a vote that is coercive against a great power. If the United Nations is to reflect the reality of world affairs, one reality is that great powers cannot be coerced except through defeat in war.

While there is thus some present justification for a veto power, the veto has been pushed to absurd lengths. The Charter provides that the veto shall not apply to "procedural matters"; but in fact it is applied to many matters that in essence are procedural and do not in any way touch the substantive rights of any nation.

We have already noted that, as the Charter is drawn, the Soviet Union (for example) can veto the admission of any new member and can veto the appointment of a Secretary General. Also, it can veto preliminary steps looking to the "pacific settlement of disputes" under Chapter VI of the Charter. There is really no reason for this; and on June 11, 1948, the United States Senate, in the "Vandenberg Resolution," expressed it as the sense of the Senate that our government should seek "voluntary agreement to remove the veto from all questions involving pacific settlements of international disputes and situations and from the admission of new members."

In the United Nations, the United States Delegation has tried hard to get voluntary agreement along the lines called for by this Senate resolution. However, it has not made any appreciable progress. The difficulty comes not only from the Soviet Union, but from the other permanent members: China, France, and the United Kingdom. The best we have been able to do is to get an agreement with the three mentioned to interpret "procedural" matters somewhat more broadly, and in that way slightly to reduce the scope of veto power. The Soviet Union has violently rejected any move whatever in this direction.

We should not, however, let the matter rest in this unsatisfactory state. The Security Council is badly and unnecessarily hobbled by the abuse of the veto in regard to what, in essence, are procedural and organizational matters. There ought to be an amendment of the Charter which will limit the use of the veto to matters of real substance.

ASSEMBLY PROCEDURES

If the United Nations General Assembly is to exert maximum authority, its sessions must continue to attract the leading statesmen of the world; today, sessions are so prolonged that they can hardly find the time to participate actively in the work of the Assembly and discharge their other duties.

The influence of the Assembly depends largely upon the world attention that it can attract, for only as it attracts attention can it have contact with world opinion, influence it, and be influenced by it. Thus, it is of the utmost importance that the delegations shall include both persons of international standing and prestige and those who have political authority in their own countries. Attendance by the foreign ministers of the great powers is particularly important.

If delegations to the United Nations were made up only of subordinate government officials, then, however capable they were, the influence of the General Assembly and indeed of the United Nations as a whole would be reduced almost to the vanishing point.

Today, processes of the Assembly are so cumbersome, speeches so long and so repetitive, that the regular sessions often last two months or more. In 1946, 1947, 1948, and 1949 there has also been a special session or second "part" of a regular session each year. Ministers of Foreign Affairs cannot serve as such and also attend throughout the meetings of the United Nations Assembly.

United States Secretaries of State have attended at least part of every regular Assembly session. Secretary Marshall was in Paris for nearly two months of the First Part of the 1948 Assembly. Most of the Foreign Ministers of the member nations were there, and Secretary Marshall's presence with them was vitally important from the standpoint of the prestige and influence of the United States at a time which was critical because of the Berlin blockade and the pending United States presidential election. But it involved an excessive drain upon the time of the Secretary of State

If the United Nations Assembly is to continue its present influence and add to this, ways must be found better to organize its business. More preliminary work should be done by the Interim Committee (the "Little Assembly") which has now been established. Perhaps the regular fall meetings of the Assembly could concentrate on the more important matters, leaving other items to a second session whenever necessary. Ways could be found to avoid repeating in the plenary meetings long speeches already made in committee.

In such ways, the leading statesmen of the world could meet together on major matters once a year.

New working rules are urgently required. If formulated, they would of themselves give new vitality and increased influence to the United Nations as the "Town Meeting of the World."

DEVELOPMENT OF INTERNATIONAL LAW

Some forms of United Nations growth have to wait on Charter amendments. Others can occur within the Charter as now written. That is true of collective security arrangements, and also of the development of international law.

It is generally agreed that a stable world order depends most of all upon the existence of an adequate body of international law which can be administered so as to secure justice. There is no such body of law today. Without it certain other steps cannot be taken. It is not safe to give coercive power to the Security Council or to any other international body unless that body is bound to administer agreed law. Without law, power is despotism. We ought not to try to impose international despotism upon others; neither should we consent to have it imposed upon ourselves.

There seems, however, to be no great zeal to develop international law as a foundation for world order. Governments and private groups often seem to want to create power before there is law to guide it.

At Dumbarton Oaks the Big Three did not make any provision whatever for developing international law. Neither did they so much as mention "justice." The concepts of "law" and "justice" were written into the Charter at San Francisco.

As it now stands, the United Nations Charter provides that one purpose of the United Nations is to settle international disputes "in conformity with the principles of justice and international law."

Article 13 of the Charter provides:

"The General Assembly shall initiate studies and make recommendations for the purpose of . . . encouraging the progressive development of international law and its codification."

Here is a task fundamental to world order, specifically assigned to the Assembly; and the Assembly can proceed free of Soviet or any other veto power.

These provisions give a great opportunity to all who want world government based on law.

The Assembly has set up a committee to study the codification of international law. It is composed of distinguished international lawyers, including Dr. Manley O. Hudson of the United States. The committee has made a beginning in attempting to define the basic rights and duties of states (nations).

It is good that this start has been made; but it is important not to think of international law as dealing only with states. States are artificial bodies. They are a kind of public corporation, and should not be a matter of primary or exclusive concern. The *individual* is the primary unit of value in any community, whether it be national or international. States are supposed to exist for the benefit of the individual, not the individual for the benefit of the state.

If international law is conceived of primarily as law to protect public corporations such as states and governments, and if this law is drawn up by the lawyers for the governments concerned, the result is almost sure to be an effort to preserve the *status quo.*

As we have remarked, holders of power usually conceive of "peace" as a condition where their power cannot be disturbed;

and they think of international law as a means for preserving corporate (state) power.

No government or state is entitled to be perpetuated as a matter of world law, without regard to the welfare of the individual human beings whom all states and governments are supposed to serve.

If the only domestic laws that we had were laws drawn up by corporation lawyers to protect the rights and privileges of corporations, we would not consider that a very happy condition of affairs.

There is, of course, need for international law dealing with the rights and duties of states as corporate bodies. But international law should also concern itself with the rights and duties of individuals. Fortunately, that, too, is dealt with by the United Nations.

One outstanding fact about the United Nations Charter is that it deals with peace, security, and justice not merely in terms of the corporate state but also in terms of individuals.

The Preamble to the Charter recites the determination of "the peoples of the United Nations" to "reaffirm faith in fundamental human rights, in the dignity and worth of the human person."

Article 1 of the Charter, defining the purposes of the United Nations, provides among other things that the purpose of the United Nations is "to achieve international cooperation . . . in promoting and encouraging respect for human rights and for fundamental freedoms for all without distinction as to race, sex, language, or religion."

Article 55 provides that "the United Nations shall promote . . . universal respect for, and observance of, human rights and fundamental freedoms for all without distinction as to race, sex, language, or religion."

Article 56 provides: "All Members pledge themselves to take joint and separate action in cooperation with the Organization for the achievement of the purposes set forth in Article 55."

The United Nations Commission on Human Rights and its Economic and Social Council have worked diligently on defining human rights and fundamental freedoms. Mrs. Roosevelt has given generously of her time and effort in this connection. A Universal Declaration of Human Rights was considered by the United Nations General Assembly in Paris in 1948, and it was adopted on December 10, 1948. At the time I was acting Chairman of the United States Delegation. Also, at the same time, a Genocide Convention was adopted for submission to the member states. It is designed to protect groups from injury because of their membership in some particular "national, ethnical, racial or religious group."

The Genocide Convention took the form of an international treaty that was to be submitted to the member nations for ratification. The Universal Declaration of Human Rights merely set up a standard toward which it was hoped the member nations would advance in their domestic legislation. An effort is now being made to draw up an International Convention on Human Rights which could be submitted to the member nations for ratification, and which in this way would translate at least part of the Universal Declaration of Human Rights into international law.

Thus there is some progress in making human rights a subject of international law.

One aspect of this matter deserves particular consideration in the United States: the question whether treaties which define the rights and duties of individuals will merely obligate national governments to seek appropriate legislation, or whether the treaties will themselves become the "law of the land" and automatically be enforceable by domestic courts just like national or state law.

The founders of our nation, who sought to make a union of the thirteen sovereign states, were emphatic that both federal laws and treaties should be the "laws of the land" and enforceable by and against individuals just like state laws. They felt that federal laws and treaties often would not work well if they only operated upon states and depended on intermediate state laws for enforcement. If the state did not pass the necessary laws, then there was no sanction except war. But if federal laws and treaties operated directly upon individuals, then it would be possible to enforce them through ordinary court procedures, and these might work when otherwise the treaties would be a dead letter or cause of war.

The authors of *The Federalist* discussed this proposition in no less than six of their papers (Numbers 15 to 20). Their basic thesis was expressed in a heavily capitalized sentence in the fifteenth paper, reading as follows:

The great and radical vice in the construction of the existing Confederation is in the principle of LEGISLATION for STATES or GOVERNMENTS, in their CORPORATE or COLLECTIVE CAPACITIES, and as contra-distinguished from the INDIVIDUALS of which they consist. . . . we must extend the authority of the Union to the persons of the citizens,—the only proper objects of government.

As a result of this thinking, they provided in Article VI of the Federal Constitution that the Constitution itself and all laws of the United States and "all treaties made, or which shall be made, under the authority of the United States shall be the supreme law of the land; and the judges in every State shall be bound thereby, anything in the Constitution or laws of any State to the contrary notwithstanding."

However, the United States is drifting away from that point of view. We do not seem to be willing to permit international law defining individual rights and duties to become the law of our land. The Genocide Convention was deliberately drawn so that it would not be "the law of the land," but would call only for subsequent domestic legislation. This seemed necessary in order to obtain ratification. The same problem will arise in connection with any convention on human rights.

Obviously, respect for and observance of human rights depends largely upon community sentiment; and it would be foolish to ignore the fact. But some basic rights are admitted by every civilized community and reflect the conscience of mankind. These rights are only rarely and spasmodically violated by community sentiment. Sustained and widespread violation comes only from those in power who seek by terrorism to preserve and extend their power.

Since that is so, international concern for such rights should take a form which cannot easily be nullified by national governments. If international law relating to human rights is no more than an appeal to national governments, that gives the whip hand to the totalitarian, police state governments which are the principal sources of abuse.

In the United Nations Assembly debates about the Universal Declaration of Human Rights Mr. Vishinsky made a long philosophical attack on the Declaration, on the ground that it implied that human rights existed other than by and through the consent of national governments. "The rights of human beings," he said (December 10, 1948), "cannot be considered outside the prerogatives of governments, and the very understanding of human rights is a governmental concept." Any other concept violated "sovereignty"; namely, "the right of a government to ensure for itself the development of its own people without any outside influence, to manifest its own will, to act within its own jurisdiction without any obstacles put forward by outside forces." He proposed an amendment to the effect that human rights and fundamental freedoms depended upon "national laws."

Those who operate a police state must always fight for the concept that there are no human rights except as governments choose to accord them. They cannot admit that human rights and fundamental freedoms exist irrespective of national laws or admit that international law should recognize those rights.

In the early days of the United States there was clear thinking and high purpose in these matters. There is again need for such qualities today.

We cannot effectively combat the police state unless we ourselves reject the police-state philosophy expounded by Mr. Vishinsky. Here is a challenge to all who believe that world order depends upon world law; to all who believe that the rights of human beings are superior to the corporate rights of states; to all who would have the United States stand in the world as the recognized champion of human liberty as against governmental despotism.

FUTURE OF COLLECTIVE SECURITY ASSOCIATIONS

The United States has taken a lead in organizing two collective security associations under Article 51 of the Charter: the Rio Pact of the Americas and the North Atlantic Pact. These two pacts have shown the flexibility of the framework of the United Nations. It is not a strait jacket. Much can be done *under* it that cannot be done *by* it.

Some do not appreciate this flexibility and seem to think that, to get the degree of collectivity they want, it is necessary to scrap the present organization and start afresh.

I have never seen any proposal made for collective security with "teeth" in it, or for "world government" or for "world federation," which could not be carried out either by the United Nations or under the United Nations Charter.

If the principal members of the United Nations, including the Soviet Union, are willing to take part in a proposed new world organization, then the United Nations itself could quickly be made into that organization.

If, as is the fact, the Soviet Union and others would not take part in the projected organization, then those who want to go ahead without them can form a collective security association under Article 51.

Nothing that is practical or desirable would be attained by destroying or undermining the United Nations or losing faith or hope in it. It is of the utmost importance to preserve an organization, almost any kind of organization, which has in its membership all the great powers and representation from both the Communist and the non-Communist bloc. The very fact that relations between these blocs are tense, that there are many points of conflict, and that war is possible makes it all the more important to have a place where the tensions can be openly discussed, and where the differences may be fought out with words rather than with bombs.

Events may lead to a separation of the Soviet Union and its

satellites from world organization. That, however, would be a grim event.

Germany, Italy, and Japan withdrew from the League of Nations shortly prior to their open acts of aggression. Stalin comments on that in the words: "In order to have their hands free, these three states withdrew from the League of Nations" (p. 624). This is recognition, from a significant source, of the fact that nations do not "have their hands free" so long as they are active participating members in a world organization for peace.

A scrapping of the United Nations to eliminate the Soviet Union is something that the United States ought to oppose if we want peace. It gives us no possibilities we do not now have, and would get us nowhere but backwards in our search for peace.

There are two collective security associations, in addition to the Rio and North Atlantic associations, which have been seriously discussed. One is a security association which would *not* have any *regional* aspect, but which would be open to all nations which would undertake automatically to go to war against any nation attacking one of the group. This proposal, which has been sponsored particularly by Hamilton Fish Armstrong, would involve a General Protocol, under Article 51 of the Charter, open to all member nations.

The other suggested form of collective security pact is regional and would bind the nations of the Asiatic-Pacific area by commitments like those of the Rio Pact and the North Atlantic Pact.

The General Protocol idea had much persuasiveness when it was first proposed, prior to the North Atlantic Treaty. There was much to commend it as an alternative to that treaty. It would have avoided one great disadvantage of our regional security pacts; namely, the appearance that the United States has drawn a line on the map of the world and has, in effect, said that we will fight anyone who steps across that line. As matters now stand, it might be inferred that we would not fight an aggressor who kept on the farther side of the line. If so, we should be offering immunity to aggression in the Pacific, Asia, and the Near and Middle East and impliedly offering to divide the world with Communism.

At the Senate Hearings on the North Atlantic Treaty official maps were in circulation which, pursuant to the Rio and North Atlantic pacts, traced the lines those pacts said could not be stepped across with impunity. I felt, and expressed, concern lest the result of drawing these lines should give encouragement to aggression, direct or indirect, on the other side of the lines.

Drawing precise lines has advantages, but also disadvantages. It might discourage the free peoples in the outer areas by giving them the impression that we abandon them and exclude them from our official concern. In sum, our regional action might speed up the encirclement that Soviet Communism plans for us. It might seem to leave us in the position of consolidating about one-fifth of the population of the world and acquiescing in the consolidation of the other four-fifths by hostile, despotic forces. That would be an awful blow to human liberty, and it would presage a final assault on us when conditions would have become very unequal, to our disadvantage.

However, now both the Pact of the Americas and the North Atlantic Pact are realities, and so it is not practical to substitute for them a General Protocol. In Asia, Soviet Communism has gained such victories that it is doubtful that either a General Protocol or a Pacific Pact would attract any substantial number of adherents.

The power of Soviet Communism in Asia has grown so rapidly and is now so menacing that the nations in that area, except perhaps those separated from the mainland, might now feel that to join the United States in a security pact would endanger them more than it would protect them.

If the free nations of Asia, particularly India and Pakistan, want some new security association with us, and take the initiative, then consideration may well be given to either a General Protocol or a Pacific Pact for collective security under Article 51. Unless, and until, that happens it would seem wiser for the United States to avoid any initiative.

It is, however, important to realize that the United Nations Charter, by Article 51, gives such flexibility that, when it is timely, the nations can have more and tighter systems of collective security. There is little doubt that there will be future occasions to take advantage of the immense possibilities of developing world order within the framework of the United Nations Charter.

A UNITED NATIONS GENERAL CONFERENCE

We have seen that the United Nations could be more influential for peace if these changes were made:

(1) Voting in the General Assembly to be altered so as to supplement the present "one vote per nation" provision with a provision also for "weighted" voting.

(2) Voting in the Security Council to be changed to limit the veto to substantive matters and eliminate it wholly in organizational matters and in the search for means of pacific settlement.

(3) Membership to be made universal.

(4) The working procedures of the General Assembly to be changed so that they will be less time-consuming and will assure the continuing participation of leading personalities.

These changes would make it much more likely that the United Nations will be a place where moral verdicts are rendered which will increasingly influence the conduct of all governments. They would make it more likely that the differences between nations will be fought out with words in the cockpit of the General Assembly rather than with bombs in the cockpit of death.

Further, and perhaps most important of all, the mere fact that the governments of the world now devoted effort to improving the United Nations would be heartening evidence of their faith in that organization as an ever growing power for peace and justice in the world.

The normal way to make these changes is to call a General Conference, under Article 109 of the Charter, "for the purpose of reviewing the present Charter." That would draw together the representatives of the nations of the world in a new great conference comparable to that of San Francisco. It would give the peoples of the world a new opportunity, as at San Francisco, to express their fears and hopes and to generate sentiments which no government would dare ignore.

The present is, by common consent, a time of crisis. The world is perilously poised on the brink of disaster. Under that circumstance there is no reason against, but every reason for, holding a world conference at which the concern of all peoples, particularly the "small" peoples, can be made manifest.

There is little to hope for, and much to fear, from a diplomatic conference between the leaders of a few of the great powers. The technical possibilities have been fully explored by competent technicians in the committees of the United Nations, such as the committees working on atomic energy and on "conventional" armaments. It is not likely that the heads of state themselves would invent technical solutions other than those which have already been developed, explored and found wanting. Furthermore, a diplomatic conference would almost surely produce either an appearance of agreement which would be dangerous and illusory, or else an appearance of disagreement which would be interpreted as marking the exhaustion of all possibilities short of war.

There is much to hope for, and little to fear, from another great world conference called primarily to modernize the United Nations in the light of its five years' experience, and to review broadly its basic objectives of peace, justice, human liberty, and regulation of armament.

This subject of armament has taken on new significance since the Charter was drawn. Article 11 gives the General Assembly power to consider "the principles governing disarmament and the regulation of armaments"; but it was drafted before any of the delegates at San Francisco knew that there was or could be such a thing as an "atomic" bomb. The bomb fell on Hiroshima on August 6, 1945, about six weeks after the San Francisco Conference was over. If it had been dropped during, instead of just after, the San Francisco Conference, Article 11 might have been drawn differently and more positively.

Whenever a General Conference to review the Charter is held, it should include this article as part of the review.

Dumbarton Oaks failed to implant in the United Nations the living spirit that was later found at San Francisco. So a conference now of the "Big Two," or "Big Three," or "Big Four," or

"Big Five" could not possibly produce moral and spiritual qualities such as made the San Francisco Conference the greatest international conference of all time—qualities which we need to recapture today.

The representatives of the smaller countries can make invaluable contributions. Men like Evatt of Australia, Spaak of Belgium, and Romulo of the Philippines—to mention only a few of many—brought to the San Francisco Conference and to the Assemblies of the United Nations points of view which could never have derived from the great powers themselves. We need more of that at the present critical juncture in world affairs.

Some of the changes in the United Nations which we have discussed could perhaps be accomplished without a Charter amendment.

Changes in working procedures of the General Assembly could be made under the existing Charter.

Admission of new members can and does occur under the Charter, although, if universality is really the goal, it would be better to amend the Charter to provide for it. Article 4, Section 1, makes a vote for the admission of a new member in effect a vote of confidence in the moral quality of the nation in question. It provides that new members must be "peace-loving states," and that it must be the judgment of the Organization that they are "able and willing to carry out" the obligations of the Charter. If the United Nations is to be a world organization, memberships ought frankly to depend upon whether there is a stable and effective national government. As between nations, diplomatic recognition involves no element of moral approval. It should be the same with admission to the United Nations.

Changes in voting procedures in the General Assembly and in the Security Council would require major Charter amendments.

There would be advantage in dealing at the same time with all four of the subjects I suggest. A shift to universal membership would relatively improve the position of the Soviet Union in the General Assembly and would make more palatable a reduction of Soviet veto power in the Security Council. Also, there is relationship between increased membership and voting and other procedures of the General Assembly.

Article 109 of the Charter provides:

A General Conference of the Members of the United Nations for the purpose of reviewing the present Charter may be held at a date and place to be fixed by a two-thirds vote of the members of the General Assembly and by a vote of any seven members of the Security Council.

So a General Conference can be called and held free of Soviet veto, although alterations in the Charter agreed to by the Conference would require Soviet ratification.

The Conference should be called soon, but should not be held until carefully prepared for by official studies and private discussions such as preceded San Francisco. As in the case of that Conference, there should also be full opportunity for public opinion to inform itself regarding the problems involved, and to express its views.

Important results might come from another General Conference of the representatives of all the peoples who would seek again, as at San Francisco, to find ways to express their determination "to save succeeding generations from the scourge of war, which twice in our lifetime has brought untold sorrow to mankind" and "to reaffirm faith in fundamental human rights, in the dignity and worth of the human person."

CHAPTER SEVENTEEN

WESTERN UNITY

The economic and military resources we can send abroad are limited. Because of that, we have dedicated them primarily to strengthening the West. That is good sense. To dissipate our goods aimlessly about the world is to waste them, and if a single area is to be picked, that will logically be the West. It is a vital area of which we are in many ways a part, and it is in great peril.

We have expended 90 per cent or more of our postwar external aid to upbuild the West; and, wisely, that aid has been tied into two distinctive programs: the economic program of the European Recovery Act and the military program of the North Atlantic Pact.

Both the European Recovery Act and the North Atlantic Pact have had a single basic purpose; that is, to promote a unity that will itself promote strength. That, too, was good sense. However, so far, the idea of unity of the West remains only an ideal. That is bad.

The European Recovery Plan has been a relief operation, so far. It has been, in essence, an oxygen tent put over the nations of Western Europe. It has kept them breathing, but it has not cured them. The symptoms of economic and monetary disintegration are still acute.

The defense program worked out under the North Atlantic Treaty and the Military Assistance Program has not created any genuine military unity. There is no unity of command because the source of command is always *political* authority, and, in the case of the members of the North Atlantic Pact, that authority is divided among many—twelve, in fact. Secretary of Defense Johnson said on January 30, 1950, that the North Atlantic Treaty "may well mean that *ultimately* our national defense will be so geared to the national defense of the other member nations that we will be forced to stand or fall collectively." However, that day is not now here. Today we can still fall separately.

What we have done has been worth doing because it gives us opportunity to do more. But what we have done will be a futility unless the opportunity we have gained is used to create in Western Europe a greater degree of unity than is now in prospect.

It is hard to think of a condition more illogical, more costly and more dangerous than the continuing disunity of the West.

The countries participating in the Marshall Plan have a total population of more than 200,000,000, and there is a high level of education and culture. That population is greater than the entire population of the Soviet Union or of the United States.

The people have much the same beliefs, traditions, and practices. The Western peoples may, to themselves, seem to be made up of many differences. But the rest of the world gives their area, with that of the United States, a single name: "The West." It gives the inhabitants, collectively, a single name: "Europeans." To others, at least, it seems that we are so alike that they do not bother to learn the different names by which we artificially differentiate ourselves. One word fits us all.

There is nothing in the differences of the European peoples that prevents their getting along together. Big and even little businesses throughout Western Europe are tied together by trade associations like our former N.R.A. In that way the businessmen of the different countries work together in as much harmony as the national politicians permit. Workers, through their labor unions, have always cooperated closely. Here in the United States, we have demonstrated that the different nationalities of Europe can live happily in the same cities and even on the same streets.

These 200,000,000 and more people have, in Europe and in their African colonial possessions, a great part of the world's natural resources. Coal, iron, copper, gold, potash, phosphate, uranium, are only a few of the many mineral resources found in greatest richness within this Western-controlled area, a natural wealth that cannot be matched either in the Soviet Union or in the United States.

The people are inventive and resourceful. In England, the Industrial Revolution had its birth; and many of the greatest inventions of industrial and medical science have come from the brains and laboratories of Western Europe.

Why should an area that possesses such tremendous resources, human and material, be a poorhouse where the people live in a state of weakness which is frightening to them and their friends and a source of delight to their foes?

There is only one reason. All the great qualities and assets possessed *collectively* must be discounted because they are not possessed *unitedly*. Disunity alone prevents Western Europe from being a great—perhaps the greatest—distinctive area of spiritual, intellectual, economic, and military power.

This diagnosis of the case of Europe is nothing novel. It has been long accepted by all. Today, the leaders of Europe repeat the same refrain. Attlee says—or until recently said—"Europe must federate or perish." Churchill leads a movement for European unity. President Auriol of France said:

"Europe must unite herself if she wishes to recover and live, and if she does not want American assistance to be a gesture without future or a humiliating charity."

De Gasperi of Italy, Spaak of Belgium, and Adenauer of Germany say the same. General William J. Donovan, chairman of the American Committee on United Europe, made public on February 20, 1950, expressions by more than twenty-five leading statesmen of fourteen European democracies, giving their governments' support for some form of economic and political integration of their countries, and treating such a development as a practical necessity within the near future.

All the words make a chorus with scarcely a discordant note.

Since disunity is so perilous and unity so precious, and since this is recognized by all concerned, why, may we ask, does integration not happen?

It does not happen because the tradition of complete national independence has become so deeply rooted that many politicians, officeholders, businessmen, and beneficiaries of state aid feel that the least change would involve risks for them. The *status quo* is always supported by vested interests, and in Europe these vested interests have always been powerful enough to prevent peaceful change to unity.

Recurrent efforts have been made to unite Europe by violence. Napoleon tried it; so did the Kaiser; so did Hitler; so, now, does Stalin.

Such violent efforts are bound to be recurrent and, sooner or later, to succeed unless peaceful efforts first succeed. Western Europe itself is not strong enough to defend the *status quo* of disunity, and the task for others becomes ever harder.

Preservation of this disunity—sometimes called "independence"—of the nations of the Continent of Europe has for one hundred and fifty years been dependent upon outside aid. England, then primarily an overseas country, made it her policy to keep the Continent divided so that she could be the balance of power. She thwarted Napoleon's efforts to unite Europe by force. She was a principal obstacle to the forcible unification efforts of the Kaiser and Hitler. Now the United States, with economic and military aid, is supporting a divided West as against the efforts of Soviet Communism to unite Europe under its domination.

A divided Europe offers temptations that, it seems, ambitious despots do not resist.

We should ask ourselves this question:

Should an area whose population and resources entitle it to be a great source of strength continue to exist as a source of weakness merely because the shift-over to unity frightens, without reason, a few powerful vested interests?

As we have already observed, the luxury of "independence" is growing ever more costly because the separate nations of Western Europe are less self-sufficient than ever with the loss of their foreign investments, their Eastern colonies, and their East-West European trade.

The United States now has the opportunity to bring about peacefully what every Western leader, without regard to nation or party, recognizes ought to be done, but what will not be done unless there is friendly but firm outside pressure.

The United States can and should take that opportunity and exert that pressure.

We have the right to do that because, at Europe's request, we have made a tremendous investment in Western Europe.

In 1917, when it seemed that Europe might fall under the militaristic rule of the German Kaiser, we joined the battle and, through a great outpouring of man power and economic resources, helped to turn back the despotic threat. Again in 1940, when much of Europe had been overrun by the armies of Nazi Germany, the United States, even before declaration of war, threw its weight into the scale and again played a major part in rolling back that new threat of despotism. Now again we have undertaken a gigantic economic and military effort in aid of Europe.

Those three efforts, within a single generation, have cost us something. There is scarcely a village in the United States that cannot display a roll of honor listing the names of their young men who died fighting in defense of Western civilization. Our national debt has grown from about $3,000,000,000 in 1917 to $257,000,000,000 at the end of 1949. The greater part of that represents the economic cost of those three efforts, and the third is not yet completed.

This investment of blood and treasure gives us a certain right and need to speak. Also, we have unique qualifications to speak. Most of our American people derive from Europe. Our ancestors were largely English or Irish or German or Italian or Polish or French, or of some other nationality that had roots in Europe before it took root also in America. There is a blood relationship between our people and the peoples of Europe. We know the racial differences that are involved, for they are part of the very lifeblood of our own nation.

Furthermore, we know by our own experience what can and should be done when danger looms that only unity can avert. We invented our federal system when we were in a condition like that of Europe today, faced with a like danger. Our thirteen independent sovereign States were threatened by the despotic rulers of the then great empires of Britain, France, and Spain. Those citizens who were farsighted saw plainly that the States, divided, were subject to strife among themselves and weak in the face of danger. They knew that, as put by Alexander Hamilton in words that have become classic:

To look for a continuation of harmony between a number of independent, unconnected sovereignties in the same neighborhood would be to disregard the uniform course of human events and to set at defiance the accumulated experience of ages.[1]

So, to end disharmony that would be catastrophic in the face of external peril, the American States created a central authority which could deal with those few matters which were deemed to be of serious common concern. The States were not willing, as the nations of Europe surely would not be willing, to make a total surrender of sovereignty. Each State insisted upon retaining the right to deal singly, and in its own distinctive way, with all matters that did not urgently affect the common welfare and, above all, the common defense.

The system thus invented is one of great flexibility. Under it, we have developed a degree of unity that would have been utterly unacceptable to us at the beginning, and which it would be quite impracticable to duplicate in Europe today. We have learned and shown how light and flexible, yet how strong, can be the bonds of federal unity.

Finally, whatever some would say, all know that if we sought the unity of Western Europe, that would not be part of any "imperialist" design. It is pretended by Communist propaganda that we desire to make Western Europe into a United States colony. Actually, our goal is a Europe which, through unity, will gain so much strength that neither the United States nor the Soviet Union nor any other power whatsoever will ever be able to use Europe for purposes alien to the free development of Europe itself. We want Europe to have so much economic strength that it will be prosperous in its own right, and not dependent on economic grants from others. We want a Europe that has so much

[1] *The Federalist*, No. 6.

moral and intellectual dynamism that, in the tradition of the Magna Charta and the Declaration of the Rights of Man, it will continue to arouse men to strike off any shackles that curtail their self-development. We want a Europe capable of inventing a new industrial revolution that will continue to multiply the productivity of human labor. We want a Europe that will again produce great literature, music, and art, and such religious movements as have in the past inspired and enriched the world.

What we do, we do as a matter of enlightened self-interest; but it is a self-interest that coincides with the welfare and well-being of the peoples concerned as defined by their own leading statesmen.

We have not only the moral right, we have not only the experience, we have not only the worthy motive, but also the responsibility.

Today we are helping to finance the reconstruction of Western Europe. We cannot avoid responsibility for the result. The prewar structure was a structure that repeatedly had burst out into flames. The human and material losses over the years have been colossal and irreparable. After each past conflagration, the structure has been rebuilt substantially as before. Shall we make ourselves responsible for repeating that folly?

If a banker were asked to lend the money for rebuilding a tenement house which had proved a ghastly fire hazard, and which had burned down several times with terrible loss of life, he would, I think, refuse unless modern fire preventives were introduced. He would be morally condemned if he put up the money to finance rebuilding a proven firetrap. That is what the United States will be doing unless we incorporate in our present program of aid to Western Europe features which will induce the Western European peoples to rebuild in a form that will realize their vast potentiality for peace and welfare.

The present administration has been careful to avoid seeming to press for unity within the nations of Western Europe. It has felt that this might appear to be unwarranted interference in the internal affairs of friendly nations. Also, it has felt that pressure from the United States might be resented, and so react against the result we wanted. Neither the President nor any one of his recent Secretaries of State has come out strongly and clearly on the subject of integration.

On November 18, 1948, when I was a delegate to the United Nations Assembly, I made a speech before the American Club of Paris in which I said rather outspokenly much of what I have set down here and which I had already said at Senate hearings on the European Recovery Plan. My speech had been read in advance by Secretary of State Marshall, and its delivery was given weight by his presence. It was widely broadcast in Europe, despite difficulties created in France by the Communist members of the union that handled radio transmission. That speech, made under those conditions, was the closest to an authoritative and strong United States expression on the subject that had been made up to that time, or perhaps since, although in recent months Paul Hoffman, the Administrator of the European Recovery Act, and Averell Harriman, the Special Ambassador under that Act, have been seriously concerned about the subject and have put on pressure, particularly for a clearing union to finance the movement of European trade. But the full weight of the Administration's influence has never been brought into play.

There may have been justification in trying a hands-off policy for a time, in the hope that unity would come about of itself. However, it now seems clear that Western European unity will not have any early reality unless strong pressure is exerted by us. The hands-off policy has not succeeded, and we face a choice between exerting pressure to get done what needs to be done and acquiescing in a continuing disunity which makes impossible, so far as can be foreseen, any real solution of the problem of Western Europe, and particularly the problem of Germany.

Under the European Recovery Plan there has been established in Paris the Office of European Economic Cooperation (O.E.E.C.), and committees have been set up to work out programs for increased economic unity. There are various proposals and agreements to create customs unions between different countries of Europe. There has also been established the Council of Europe with its Committee of Ministers and its European Consultative Assembly—bodies which, it is hoped, will promote political unity. There are many private agencies and volunteer bodies seeking to promote European unity.

The fact that all these organizations have come into being shows how intense and widespread is the feeling that something needs to be done. But so far there have been no decisive acts, and only a short time remains according to the international time-table.

That timetable is determined by three factors. One is the running out of the period (1948-1952) of the European Recovery Plan; another is the growth, in Europe, of planned national economies, and the third is the revival of Germany.

It is difficult to see how any degree of economic unity can be achieved in Europe unless it is done while there are still large sums freely available from the United States to cushion the shocks which are inevitably part of an economic adjustment. Economic unity provides a bigger market and increases the ability to produce cheaply by spreading costs over larger volume. That means mass production, and a shifting of capital and labor into larger units.

It is not going to be easy for the European governments concerned to provide the subsidies needed to cushion that transition period. Also, they could not readily agree upon how the burden should be divided. The "counterpart" funds resulting from European Recovery aid are ideally designed to provide the necessary financial cushion.

The counterpart funds are the local currency equivalent of dollars given by the United States to pay for imports from the "dollar area." The pounds sterling, francs, lire, and guilders that accumulate could be used as shock absorbers.

So far, the counterpart funds have not been used in that way. They have been used for national purposes. In a couple of years there may be no more flow of dollars to create counterpart funds; and, if economic unity has not assumed some reality before that day arrives, then it is not likely that it will ever come about peacefully—unless the United States undertakes a second European Recovery Plan to accomplish what the first program should have done.

The second factor which bears on our time schedule is the increase in Europe of the economic planning which destroys adaptability.

Socialization and "planning" demand insulation. The movement in that direction has not yet gone so far that it prohibits a beginning of unity. However, the trend is one which, as it goes on, makes it more and more difficult for governments to take part in a larger, freer society.

The longer people live in hothouse conditions, the more reluctant they are to open the windows. They seal the windows until, some day, someone outside smashes them or inside pressures blow them out. We do not want to delay until that has to happen.

The third place where time is running out is Germany.

There is no good solution of the problem of Germany unless Germany, or at least as much of it as is free, is brought into the framework of the West as an integral part of the West.

There cannot be that integration unless the West itself is integrated. You cannot place a picture in a frame unless there is a frame.

Age-old disputes between France and Germany, such as the one over the Saar, cannot be permanently solved in terms of a choice between French nationalism and German nationalism.

We have already seen that a revived nationalistic Germany would have ominous bargaining power between East and West; that the defense of Europe requires a defense of Germany, and that it is difficult to conceive of a successful defense of Germany that does not involve participation by German man power.

These problems can be solved if Western Europe draws together, politically and economically, so as to give birth to hopes and aspirations that are larger than any single nation, and if the Germans are a part of them.

If there were a real political unity of Western Europe for common defense, then Germans, individually, could be part of that defense. We cannot risk a German national army. We might risk having Germans individually part of a European army, along with French and Belgians, under non-German command and stationed anywhere in Western Europe, preferably not in Germany.

It is possible to foresee, in this way, the creation of a military force in Western Europe strong enough to hold off a military invasion from Russia.

I have not heard anyone suggest any other practical solution; and this solution must await the coming into being of a political entity in Western Europe which has authority and can attract loyalty on a basis broader than that of any single nation or coalition of nations.

So far as German economy is concerned, there is imperative need for a large market.

In Germany, the density of population is greater than ever before because of the presence of about 10,000,000 people expelled by the Poles and Czechs. Germany is smaller than before the war because of loss of territory to surrounding states. So, although smaller in area, Germany holds a larger population than before the war—a population now estimated at almost 70,000,-000. West Germany alone has a population of more than 45,-000,000; it has little agricultural land, and if the people are to survive they must industrialize. Only by manufacturing can they produce the goods with which to buy the food and raw materials they need. This in turn requires markets.

If there is not to be a recurrence of the vast misery and unemployment which enabled Hitler to come to power in 1933 and make Germany into a war arsenal, then the Germans must manufacture large amounts of consumer goods and dispose of them. Either the West must find that possibility for the Germans or they will turn to Soviet Communism, which seems to offer it to them.

Any program for integrating Germany into Western Europe must make the non-German West strong enough to hold its own against German dominance, which might result if the unity of the non-German West were confined to France, Benelux, and Italy. Great Britain is needed as part of Western Europe. Perhaps the United States also should become more fully identified with

Western Europe. It may be that the North Atlantic Treaty should be tightened into a North Atlantic Union for common defense in order to give the Western European nations sufficient courage to make Germany part of the more complete unity that Western Europe should be.

The physical recovery of Germany is proceeding with a rapidity which is frightening to many.

I was in Berlin a few months after V-E Day, and the destruction I saw defies description. The scene was one of inexpressible horror, with the shell-shocked inhabitants existing without heat or light in the damp rubble. I thought of Toynbee's *Study of History* and his thesis of challenge and response. I said to myself that if the German people responded to the challenge represented by the awful destruction visited on them by World War II, then indeed they would be formidable. That is happening, and now only a short time remains within which to deflect into European fellowship a spirit which otherwise will take the form of malignant nationalism.

I have talked about this problem of unity to the leading governmental figures of Western Europe. Almost without exception they have said to me, "The United States must push us." Probably if we did push them they would publicly protest and try to shift to us responsibility for what may seem politically difficult. Some seem to be in a political position in which they can do what they know ought to be done only if they seem to be pressed from without. If this is so, it is not the first time that politicians protest publicly against what they advocate privately. While from our standpoint it would be better if the European politicians acted of their own accord, we cannot at this grave juncture stand on ceremony.

Our postwar effort in the West is not an effort to win a popularity contest. Popularity, even if we could buy it, is not worth $20,000,000,000. Also, we are not popular now. We are trying to do a constructive and creative task which needs to be done if Western civilization is to be saved, and if it is to be the magnet which will attract Eastern Europe to the West.

Also, I believe, we want to do a complete job so that we can leave it and turn our attention and our material aid to the pressing situations elsewhere, notably in the Pacific and the Far East.

We are engaged in a global struggle, as in World War II. We cannot expect success if we so scatter our efforts that we are ineffectual everywhere. We have made the recovery of Western Europe our major initial goal, but it must not be our sole concern. As quickly as possible, we need to turn elsewhere. To do that safely requires increased unity in Europe.

There is only a short time left for doing this constructive job. Indeed, it is touch-and-go whether the timetable set by the exhaustion of Marshall Plan funds, the growth of "hothouse" economies, and Germany's rapid revival can still be met.

The Administration has adequate authority from the Congress, which has always seen the need more clearly than the Administration. The Congress wrote into the Economic Cooperation Act of 1948 the policy provisions which set up as a target the creation in Europe of "a large domestic market with no internal trade barriers," and which stated that the continuity of our assistance should at all times "be dependent upon continuity of cooperation among countries participating in the program." The Congress, the next year, added to this policy declaration the further declaration that it is "the policy of the people of the United States to encourage the unification of Europe." The Congress wrote into the Mutual Defense Assistance Act of 1949 the condition that military aid should be used only to promote "an *integrated* defense" of the North Atlantic area, as planned by the Council and Defense Committee under the North Atlantic Treaty.

The Congress has made perfectly clear that it believed that our economic and military aid to Western Europe should be more than a relief operation, and should create a genuine unity which could turn present weakness into the strength that the free societies need desperately at this critical juncture in world affairs.

The situation is ripe for great achievement. There is occasion for supreme effort lest that possibility should slip away, perhaps forever, with fateful consequences to all concerned.

CHAPTER EIGHTEEN

POLICIES IN ASIA

In Asia and in the Pacific there is no strong bulwark against the Soviet Communist offensive. The Western powers have, in general, followed the policy of promoting colonial evolution to independence, and there are many new nations as a result. That, as we saw, was a good start. But it will not of itself frustrate Soviet Communism's diabolically clever tactics which combine fraudulent propaganda with terrorist infiltration. Most of the new governments face grave problems, and they and their peoples are inexperienced in self-government.

In the past, the United States policy in the East rested on the foundation of friendly relations with China. Our people, through government, missionaries, doctors, and educators, have shared and built Chinese friendship for more than a century. Out of it have come such political doctrines as the Hay Doctrine of the "Open Door" in China, the Hughes Doctrine of "territorial integrity" for China, and the Stimson Doctrine of "nonrecognition of the fruits of aggression." Out of it have also come the Boxer Fund scholarships, Christian colleges in China, and medical centers, including a great Rockefeller Foundation development at Peking.

I was with Generalissimo Chiang Kai-shek in Hankow in the spring of 1938. Japan had then been fighting China openly and actively for a year; the capital, Nanking, had fallen, and the seat of government had been moved to Hankow. That city was already under heavy air attack; and, shortly after, it was captured, forcing the Chinese capital west to Chungking.

The Generalissimo was at the time under strong pressure to make a compromise with Japan. He discussed it with me. Terms had been offered which would have been very advantageous for him and his government. He decided, however, to base his policy on the historic friendship of the United States toward China. He had reached the conclusion that, sooner or later, the United States would come into the war against Japan; and he decided that China should resist, even if it meant standing alone, until that day should come. The day came three and a half years later, but only after China had been subjected to a terrible ordeal.

The United States on its side increasingly sought the survival of a free and friendly China, and in our negotiations with Japan we willingly faced the possibility of war rather than agree to the replacement of the Chinese National Government with a Japanese puppet regime.

On November 26, 1941, in one of the final prewar documents, our Government asked Japan to agree that

The Government of the United States and the Government of Japan will not support—militarily, politically, economically—any government or regime in China other than the National Government of the Republic of China with capital temporarily at Chungking.

War was the reply, and, indeed, the reply which our government anticipated.

Throughout the ensuing war the United States government assumed that peace would give what we risked war for; namely, a friendly Chinese government free from domination by an alien, unfriendly despotism. Such a China, it was thought, would welcome partnership with us in our policy of promoting political independence in neighboring lands. A friendly China could help everywhere in Asia and the Pacific.

With that in mind, President Roosevelt did much to build up the prestige and world influence of China. He met with Generalissimo Chiang Kai-shek and Mr. Churchill at Cairo in November, 1943. He insisted upon giving China great-power status. He gave the Chinese National Government at least a face-saving part in the proceedings at Dumbarton Oaks, and arranged that China should be one of the five Permanent Members of the United Nations Security Council, with veto power.

After the war, that policy collapsed, and China has become the spearhead of Soviet Communist policy in Asia and the Pacific. All that the United States did to enhance the prestige of China and to give it a leading position in the United Nations and in the world may now be turned against us.

There are many causes for the Communist success in China. Basically, the eight years of war with Japan and large-scale Japanese occupation left the Chinese nation bankrupt and in chaos; and in those circumstances Communism always has a great appeal. Also, as we have seen, the Russian Communists had been working in China more than twenty years, preparing for such an eventuality.

The United States itself is not, however, without fault. When the Japanese surrendered on September 2, 1945 (V-J Day), the Chinese National Government shared the prestige of victory, and it had considerable military power. It was a time—perhaps the only time—when the situation might have been saved. But the United States government in December, 1945, decided that the National Government should come to terms with the revolutionary Communist elements in China, and "that a China disunited and torn by civil strife could not be considered realistically as a proper place for American assistance" (Presidential instructions of December 15, 1945, to General Marshall).

General Marshall was sent to China as a special representative of the President to effect a coalition of the National Government and the Chinese Communists. As required by that policy, he pressed the Generalissimo to make that coalition, and he sought to deal "impartially" with both the Nationalists and the Communists (State Department Chinese White Paper, pp. 134, 631).

Subsequently, the United States learned what Chiang Kai-shek had already learned as to the futility of "cooperation" with Communists. As Secretary of State, General Marshall completely reversed the 1945 policy. In December, 1945, our government had taken the position that the United States would not give assistance to a Chinese government *unless* it came to terms with the

Communist regime. On August 12, 1948, Secretary Marshall advised our Embassy in China that "the United States Government must not directly or indirectly give any implication of support, encouragement or acceptability of coalition government in China with Communist participation." On December 30, 1948, the official position of the State Department, confirmed by the President, was that, "should a government come into power which comes to terms with the Chinese Communists, all aid should cease" (State Department Chinese White Paper, p. 402).

If in December, 1945, our government had taken the position which it took three years later, then the National Government of Chiang Kai-shek *might* have provided a nucleus which, with United States advice and help, would have developed into a liberal and progressive government of China. In 1945 the Generalissimo would probably have accepted United States advice—military, political, and economic—if he had trusted the motives of the United States. Our misguided policy of December, 1945, was pressed upon the Generalissimo only a few months after the June 15, 1945, disclosure to him by Ambassador Hurley of the Yalta Agreement whereby the United States had promised to obtain for the Soviet Union great gains at the expense of China, subject to the concurrence of Generalissimo Chiang Kai-shek. Also that Yalta Agreement went on to provide: "The President will take measures in order to obtain this concurrence on advice from Marshal Stalin."

It could not reasonably have been expected that, in the circumstances, the Generalissimo would have trustingly accepted our advice to come to terms with the Communists—advice which he knew was wrong, and which we ourselves, belatedly, recognized as such. Also, he must have distrusted General Marshall's advice to him not to attack the Communists in Manchuria.

We must build a totally new policy towards Asia, and it is necessary to build under conditions when the historic friendship between the United States and China is supplanted by the enmity of those who now rule most of China. The Communist regime in China can exert a powerful hostile influence throughout Asia and the Pacific.

Secretary Acheson has inherited a task of exceeding difficulty and delicacy. There is no quick or easy solution. Our motives are suspect because of our close association with England, France, and Holland, the great colonial powers in Asia and the Pacific. Our prestige is low because Chiang Kai-shek staked his national policy on friendship with the United States and suffered grave reverses.

We have to proceed with wisdom and with care. But also we need to proceed, because during the four years that followed the collapse of our ill conceived China policy of December, 1945, we have seemed to be without policy, purpose, or resolution.

Certain general considerations should be borne in mind.

Any policies regarding Asia and the Pacific must be a logical development of the policy of peaceful evolution to national independence. They should reenforce, not undermine, the independence of the new nations. That independence has been newly achieved, and while the Western colonial powers may feel that they acted promptly and generously, those who have won political freedom feel that the action came only grudgingly and under pressure. Those peoples are, and for some time will be, suspicious of the motives of any Western power, including the United States. It will be feared that the West is using the threat of Communism as an excuse to regain political mastery over the liberated peoples. Any Western pressure is bound to react in favor of the Communist effort to arouse violent revolt against the present governments. Already, as we have seen, these governments are labeled "lackeys" of the West. We should give help where we can and where it is wanted, but we must not seek to impose it under unwelcome conditions.

It may be recalled, for example, that the European Recovery Program developed through easy and natural stages. Secretary Marshall in June, 1947, at Harvard merely put forward an "idea," not a "plan." Indeed, the idea was so general in terms that at the time it attracted hardly any attention in the United States.

It was the warm reception of the Marshall idea by the foreign ministers of England and France that caused it to be developed into a Plan. Even so, the United States has been vociferously attacked in France and Italy on the theory that its aid was turning these countries into United States dependencies. On December 8, 1947, when I was in France, *L'Humanité,* the official paper of the French Communist Party, came out with a screaming headline:

"NO! FRANCE DOES NOT WANT
TO BE A COLONY, MR. DULLES!"

If the Communist parties in Western Europe feel that they can make political capital by charging the United States with intent to turn these countries into colonies, it is clear that we must be scrupulously careful in our relations with countries which, within the last five years, have in fact been colonial possessions of the West.

Another general consideration is that any policies for Asia and the Pacific must recognize the distinctive religions and cultures of Asia. It is relatively easy for the United States to work with the peoples of Europe because we belong to the same "Western" civilization. Our religion, culture, political institutions, education, and ways of life are much the same; and, in consequence, we think much alike and can understand one another. But when we work with the peoples of Asia it is a different matter. Christianity has a foothold there, and Chinese Christians have had an important influence; but that is now largely lost. In the main, our association will be with habits of mind, ideas, and attitudes very different from our own.

The religions of the East are deeply rooted and have many precious values. Their spiritual beliefs cannot be reconciled with Communist atheism and materialism. That creates a common bond between us, and our task is to find it and develop it.

In the United States different religious groups have worked together to seek the common goal of world order. Protestants, Catholics, and Jews have found it possible to cooperate despite differences of religious belief. We need to develop a like relationship with the peoples of Asia and the Pacific in organizing protection of the spiritual values which we all cherish.

If we adhere loyally to the two principles above indicated, then we shall be qualified to help establish a permanent Association of the Free Nations of Asia and the Pacific. It would not, at least in the beginning, be an essentially *military* alliance, as the North Atlantic Treaty turned out to be. That military alliance was the culmination of much that went before, and without the prelude the alliance would have meant little. An Association for Asia and the Pacific would best start as a consultative council of those who have a common concern for national independence and human freedom and want to do something about it.

In this, as in any other Far Eastern matter outside the scope of the Japanese Peace Treaty, it is important that the responsibility should be equally shared by the governments of the free countries of Asia and the Pacific. The United States should participate, not because it is a "great" power, but because it has responsibilities for Japan and for its own Pacific islands (Guam, Hawaii, etc.) and for former Japanese mandated islands that it now administers in trust. We must not forget that we are only one nation among sovereign equals.

Already the United States has special responsibilities towards certain Eastern countries which it must make good. In doing so, it can set an example which will be influential throughout Asia and the Pacific, and can recapture some of its lost prestige.

Our particular opportunity and responsibility in that respect is Japan. We can, if we will, help Japan to be an exhibit in Asia of what a free society can develop in spiritual and intellectual richness and material well-being. It is not an easy task, for in Japan there is dense population, a lack of fertile land, and a need for industrial production and overseas markets. There is need for spiritual regeneration and political education. If we can help the Japanese to satisfy their needs, material and spiritual, that of itself will exert an influence throughout Asia and the Pacific. "Conduct and example" are more effective, in the long run, than either propaganda or force.

In China, the Communist rulers will not be able to solve the economic and social problems of the country or to realize the hopes which their propaganda has aroused. There will be great discontent because of economic failures and because of the coercion and terrorism of a police-state government. Our task will be to keep hope alive and to show, wherever we have the opportunity, the advantages of a free society. Japan, because of its geographical closeness to China, gives us this opportunity to an exceptional degree. Just as our position in Western Germany and West Berlin gives us an opportunity to demonstrate advantages of a free society that will attract the captive peoples in Central and Eastern Europe now under Communist domination, so our position in Japan can be used to exert a similar attraction. To get that result we shall need in Japan, as in Germany, to avoid the appearance of developing military power for use against the victims of former Axis aggressions.

In Viet Nam the United States recognized the government of Bao Dai on February 7, 1950, after the Soviet Union on January 30th had recognized the rival regime of Ho Chi Minh. The stage is thus set for a test of influence. The chance for the success of a non-Communist government would have been improved if the French had moved more rapidly to grant real independence. As it is, there is a civil war in which we have, for better or worse, involved our prestige. Since that is so, we must help the government we back. Its defeat, coming after the reverses suffered by the National Government of China, would have further serious repercussions on the whole situation in Asia and the Pacific. It would make even more people in the East feel that friendship with the United States is a liability rather than an asset.

In South Korea we have responsibilities due to the fact that we were in occupation of that area and primarily sponsored its transition to independence. We were remiss in the early years in not encouraging the local authorities to develop a loyal and disciplined security force. That omission is now being made good. But there is continuing need of economic support and of some military aid, if this young nation which we helped bring into the world is to survive.

To the Philippine Republic we have, of course, moral responsibilities which have been reflected in many ways. The final independence which we proclaimed in 1946 would be a mockery if it were merely the prelude to the servitude of Soviet Communism.

Yet in the Philippines Communist-led guerrillas have been fighting for several years, and the government has not been able to suppress them.

In Indonesia we also have a certain duty to help maintain political and economic stability. The United States took the lead in the United Nations Security Council in fostering the transition from Dutch administration to complete independence. The new government of this populous and naturally rich area faces great problems, and the United States should stand ready to extend sympathy, advice, and even material aid.

In the areas that we have mentioned—Japan, South Korea, the Philippines, and Indonesia—the United States has taken action which in the eyes of the entire Asiatic world has implications for the future. That is a fact. If we attempt to ignore the implications, we shall be bereft of influence and friends in that part of the world. It is regrettable that the Eastern situation has developed to its present critical stage at a time when we have heavy tasks in Western Europe which are not yet completed. But Soviet Communism is carrying on the "cold" war on two fronts, and we cannot safely disregard the Eastern one.

Little can be accomplished without bipartisanship with respect to Far Eastern policies. So far there has been none, and none has been sought. The Administration has kept its own counsel as regards this part of the world, and although the Japanese surrendered in 1945 the public still has no inkling as to what may be contemplated with respect to a Japanese peace treaty.

Stalin, twenty-five years ago, saw and said that China and the colonial areas could serve as the "road to victory" over the West. Soviet Communism has been moving along that road, and the end, I fear, is not yet. The peril is so great that the people of the United States and their leaders, without regard to party, should know more than they now know; and the Administration should seek to bring responsible Republicans into its confidence in this matter. What we have said about the need for bipartisanship in foreign policy applies with special force to Asia and the Pacific, where postwar bipartisanship has never yet been practiced, and where grave peril looms.

CHAPTER NINETEEN

THE ROLE OF THE MILITARY

When the world thermometer registers, "Not war, not peace," it is hard to decide whether to follow military judgments or political judgments.

In any case there is need for a strong and modern military establishment. After the First World War we virtually disarmed ourselves, and hoped that our example would promote peace. Instead, it encouraged aggressors to arm and to start grabbing.

After the Second World War we again started to scrap our military establishment, and we quickly went far in that direction. But the Soviet attitude was so truculent that we woke up to the danger and reversed our course. We shall need to be a strong military power until there can be limitation of armament that dependably applies to everyone.

A militarily strong United States is not just a selfish program for the United States. All the free nations of the world want the United States to be strong. They have said that again and again at the meetings of the United Nations Assembly. They feel that United States military strength is the only shield they have against Russian terrorism.

The fact that we are committed to a strong military establishment does not, however, mean that military considerations ought to dominate our foreign policy. Military advice is professional advice, given by those whose job it is to assure us a military advantage if war comes. Naturally and properly, they advise *full* insurance. But to follow that advice in every particular may mean loss of the "cold" war and the loss of peace.

The military profession can produce great statesmen. General Eisenhower and General Marshall are two of our time. But when military people function in their military capacity, they are specialists. They do not purport to be judges of economics or of world opinion. They do not attempt to take account of possibilities that reside in moral forces. They do not claim to understand the working of organizations like the United Nations, and the intangible but powerful influences that radiate from them. It is not their business to measure the resources of diplomacy and conciliation. In the United States, at least, they assume that final decision will be made by the national government after expert judgments on all relevant factors have been assembled and weighed.

This is what the American people have always wanted, and it has resulted in what General Eisenhower calls "the necessary and wise subordination of the military to civil power."

That "subordination" means that the American people have faith that war is not inevitable; that our policies should seek peace, and that we should take some risks for peace, just as in war we take risks for victory. It implies that the civilians in our government who make final policy decisions must be willing to accept the responsibility of overriding at times the purely military judgment.

The leaders of the Soviet Union are civilians whose judgment is controlling as against military judgment. That does not mean that they ignore military power. It means quite the contrary. Stalin on May Day, 1946, said that military force was to be guarded as "the apple of one's eye." But it is the civilian, not the military, leaders who dominate the policy making and are going to decide how to prepare for the risk of war, whether to move to war and, if so, how rapidly and when. Also, it means that the Soviet leaders are squeezing all the gain they can out of their "peace" offensives.

The Communist Party leaders who run the Soviet government have always made the military a subordinate department. They have been afraid that the Army, made up of Russian people rather than Party members, might spearhead an anti-Communist revolution. So, except when there is actual war, the Party puts the generals into a secondary position. The Kremlin staged no great triumphal parades for its generals when the war was over. Most of them were retired to genteel living in remote villas.

During the five years that began with the San Francisco Conference of 1945, I have attended ten major international conferences averaging about two months in duration. Throughout the conferences I have sat across the table from leading Soviet personalities such as Molotov, Vishinsky, and Gromyko. I have never felt that they were overawed by military advice, or that their strategy or tactics were dominated by military considerations.

That does not mean that the Communist Party leaders are peace-loving. We know that they preach violence—at least the violence of class war. I assume that they have been getting and using military advice, and, conceivably, they may be planning another Pearl Harbor; but, if so, it will not be merely because the military want it, but because the Politburo decides on it after considering all factors, especially the imponderables upon which Soviet Communism depends so much to conquer the peoples of the world.

In our own case, the military have been more obvious partners in postwar policy making.

During the war military considerations naturally and properly had priority. Words spoken by the Joint Chiefs of Staff were the last words, subject only to the President himself.

That was the set-up when our nation made the transition from war to what we hoped would be peace. But it has not been real peace. For this reason, and since there are with us no antagonisms and suspicions between the civilians and the military, the wartime set-up has, to a large extent, carried over. The Joint Chiefs of Staff continue to have a large part in making our foreign policy, and the National Security Council is now a top policy-making body. It has been interposed between the State Department and the President. Until it was created the State Department was the President's "right hand" in conducting foreign policy. Now the State Department is in many respects subordinated to the National Security Council in the field of foreign policy.

The National Security Council during most of the period under review has been predominantly military in character. Its composition was altered on August 10, 1949, to reduce the preponderance of military influence. Previously, in addition to the President, there were six members: the Secretary of State, the chairman of the National Security Resources Board, the Secretary of Defense, the Secretary of the Army, the Secretary of the Navy, and the Secretary of the Air Force. Now the three last mentioned are not members unless specifically appointed by the President and confirmed by the Senate.

During the past five years the military viewpoint has predominated, for better or worse, in a good many instances. Here are a few illustrations:

GERMANY

The United States maintained military government in Germany until the summer of 1949. Each of the other three occupying powers—the United Kingdom, France, and the Soviet Union—had put its authorities in Germany under the civilian direction of its Ministry of Foreign Affairs at least two years earlier.

The military attitude toward the Germans did not always coincide with the State Department attitude.

The soldiers of our country and of other countries have always appraised the Germans highly because of their military prowess. Some of our military advisers seemed to feel that, because the Germans had defeated the French, our postwar policy should be based primarily upon Germany rather than France. They did not see, and indeed were not situated where they could fully see, the disastrous political repercussions of that in the non-German countries of Western Europe.

THE JAPANESE MANDATED ISLANDS

The military were insistent that we should have complete strategic control of these islands, and their attitude embarrassed our preparations for the San Francisco Conference and embarrassed us in advancing at the United Nations the program of colonial evolution in Asia as against the Soviet program for violent revolution there.

The military were scarcely in a position to appraise the importance of our colonial policy as an offset to Stalin's program of violent revolution.

LATIN AMERICA

Our relations with Latin America have occasionally been strained by the efforts of our government to meet the views of the National Security Council and Joint Chiefs of Staff on bases in Latin America.

The base in Panama got considerable public attention. The Panama government was not willing to commit itself to as long a lease as our military people thought necessary in order to justify a big expenditure there.

That was no doubt a sound military judgment; but it did not attempt to appraise the element of good will in our relations with Panama and other Latin American countries, whose views in such matters tend toward solidarity. In the end, we suspended the project for the base.

ITALIAN COLONIES

The solution of this problem was complicated and delayed by the views of the military regarding bases for the British in Libya, North Africa. Because of the close relations between the British and American defense establishments, the two governments were disposed to work together in the matter. In the end our positions had to be altered somewhat in order to reconcile them with the opinions that predominated in the United Nations Assembly and to make possible a solution there. Again, the military were unable to appraise, and did not attempt to appraise, the many intangibles in the situation.

NORTH ATLANTIC TREATY

The parties to this treaty were, as we have seen, more numerous than had been originally contemplated. The treaty was originally sponsored by Canada, the United Kingdom, France, the three Benelux countries, and the United States. These countries had very close association in peace and in two world wars, and had similar political institutions. When the treaty was conceived, many felt that it could be of greatest service by solidifying a political unity that would, in turn, give reality to military unity and common defense. However, the military people felt that it would be more advantageous to enlarge the membership in order to get certain strategic advantages—notably, bases in Greenland, Iceland, and the Azores, and Alpine passes. Thus, the North Atlantic Treaty assumed a pattern that was essentially strategic, and political values were lost which the military did not, and could not, appraise.

Here are five illustrations—there could be more—from Europe, Africa, Latin America, and the Far East which show how difficult it is to strike a proper balance between military and political factors.

I suppose that most of the American people feel that our foreign policy should try to give the military whatever they think will help them defend the United States most effectively in case of war. Probably public opinion would, on the whole, have backed the military in the situations that I have indicated. Each reader might imagine himself in the position of the United States government and ask himself whether he would have said "Yes" or "No" to the military viewpoint in each of the five situations which I have described. My guess is that the "yeses" would have the great majority. No doubt that is why the government answers were largely "Yes." In this country the government necessarily and properly pays a great deal of attention to public opinion.

It is, however, dangerous to let military factors determine foreign policy.

It is always tempting to accede to military requests because they take a tangible, concrete form. You can see guns, battleships, airplanes, bases. They are material things that can be measured. On the other side are intangibles, things not seen. In reality, these are vitally important. To get an air base at the price of good will may be a very bad bargain.

Soviet leaders, in their program of world conquest, have successfully kept military factors in the background of their foreign policy. We have kept them so far in the foreground that when Communist propaganda talks loudly and persistently about our far-flung bases, the peoples of the world—whether they live in North Europe or in the Mediterranean, in Latin America or in the Pacific—know of their own knowledge what Communist propaganda is talking about.

This has greatly helped Soviet Communism to win victories and has helped Communists in other lands to exert more influence and increase their following.

It is, I think, a fair question to ask: Who has been helped most by seeming to give our foreign policy a militaristic pattern—the United States or the Soviet Union? We have, perhaps, gained some military advantage. But we have paid a high price in moral and psychological disadvantages. Just how high that price is, we can only guess, for only a small part of the cost has been revealed.

If you have answered the five questions which it was suggested you put to yourselves, ask yourselves now this further question:

Do the foreign bases we have acquired have, all together, a military value greater than the knowledge of atomic and hydrogen bombs that has been betrayed to the Soviet Union by those of pacifist tendencies who, like Mr. Fuchs, "had complete confidence in Russian policy"?

We are engaged in an armament race. The race is very exciting, and it is easy for the followers to be carried away by their excitement and lose their sense of proportion.

We are, as a nation, working intensively to make atom and hydrogen bombs and jet bombers, and we feel we need to have everywhere good places from which to launch them. We feel our government should get for us bombs and bases, and get as many of both as possible. We have not stopped to count the cost in political and moral disadvantages. Public sentiment in this matter is strong and makes it hard for civilian officials who themselves see that safety is not to be found merely in the modern equivalent of horses and chariots.

We shall not qualify for survival if we become a nation of materialists, and if we give the impression of growing hard and inhuman, and deaf to the cry of mankind that a way be found to save them from the death, the misery, the starvation of body and soul that make up the human cost of recurrent wars, particularly modern "total" wars.

Military needs are important, and a strong military establishment is a necessity. But we shall fail in our search for peace, security, and justice unless our policies, in reality and also in appearance, give priority to the hopes and aspirations for peace of the peoples of the world. Let us remember these facts:

The Kaiser followed implicitly the dictates of military expediency.

It was the same with Mussolini and Hitler in the 1930's.

It was the same with the Emperor of Japan.

Each of these governments had, at the beginning of war, great military advantages. Each was defeated.

The peoples of the world have long looked on the United States as a peace-loving nation. Because of that we have had good will everywhere and, when war came, we were able to organize great alliances that marshaled most of the man power and resources of the world against those who were deemed to be militaristic. Our moral authority, in time, overcame initial military disadvantages.

Let us not trade that moral birthright for a mess of pottage. As a result of excessive zeal to give the military whatever they professionally suggest, we have let it appear that we have gone militaristic. The Soviet Union, which has perhaps the greatest military force in the world, whose leaders preach the necessity of violence, appears as the advocate of peace. Even in the United States there are important groups, such as that headed by Henry Wallace, which accept that view, and Mr. Wallace goes about the world preaching it.

It is imperative that our government should get good military advice. I have no doubt that we are getting it, for American officers are the most competent and most patriotic of any in the world. But that advice should be weighed by those who believe that war is not inevitable, that we can and must have peace, and that it may be necessary to take some chances for peace. Indeed, history suggests that only those who are willing to take some chances for peace have a good chance of winning total war.

CHAPTER TWENTY

NEW TECHNIQUES

A basic weakness of the free societies is inability to maintain contact with the captive peoples in the Communist police-state system.

Dictatorships usually present a formidable exterior. They seem, on the outside, to be hard, glittering, and irresistible. Within, they are full of rottenness. They "are like unto whited sepulchres, which indeed appear beautiful outward, but are within full of dead men's bones, and of all uncleanness." We saw that in Germany, and how, because of it, dictatorships can be shaken from within.

In the First World War, President Wilson sensed the discontent of the German people with their dictatorial, militaristic rulers. Even before the days of radio, he was able to make an appeal which reached the German people and shook their determination to carry on the war.

In the Second World War, the Nazis fought bitterly to the end, and victory was a far longer and more costly operation. That was because we did not capitalize upon the inner weakness and rottenness of Hitlerism. The slogan of "unconditional surrender" helped Hitler keep the Germans fighting until the very last.

We can see now that the war could have been won more quickly by appealing to the German people and offering them some hope if they threw the Nazi gangsters out. The private records and diaries of the Nazi leaders in Germany show that the situation was rotten to the core. The Nazi leaders hated and distrusted one another. Only by the greatest of good luck did Hitler himself escape the several well planned attempts to assassinate him.

One of our embarrassments in World War II was, of course, the fact that it was awkward to hold out hope of freedoms which our ally, Soviet Russia, denied its own people and wished to deny to others.

There is, however, no reason now why we should not use the most effective peacetime method we can devise to carry hope and truth and the prospect of liberty to the peoples who are the prisoners of Soviet Communism.

There is widespread discontent even within the Soviet Union itself. The Russian people are, on the whole, a religious people. They cannot be happy at the constraints placed upon their Russian Orthodox Church. They have never had much political liberty; but they have had considerable personal liberty, and do not like a system that leaves them no life of their own.

The inhabitants of the Ukraine eagerly greeted the Germans as liberators when they first appeared. There was a large-scale revolutionary movement on foot at the time, and it would have provided a powerful force against the Communistic despotism, had the Ukrainians not been alienated by German brutality.

The very fact that the Soviet government operates as a police state is evidence of continuing tension between the government and the people. It shows that the government feels it has to spy upon the people and terrorize them. Credible testimony adduced before the United Nations indicates a concentration-camp population of about 15,000,000. High officials of the Soviet Union whom I have known personally have mysteriously disappeared into what the French delicately call "oubliettes"—places where men are forgotten. The methods used within Russia are methods against which human beings have always rebelled, and there is no reason to think that human nature has changed even in Russia.

Still more unhappy are the peoples in the overrun countries. In Central Europe religion has long been a more dynamic force than in Russia. In many places, the strongly anti-Communist Roman Catholic influence is predominant. Also, in these areas there is a love of country which is powerful and makes the people resent the domination of Russia.

The patriotism of the Polish people has survived many territorial dismemberments, and we can be confident that it survives today.

In Czechoslovakia, it is so difficult for the Soviet government to find dependable persons to carry out the horrid tasks of the Communist police state that it sends Russians to do it, either openly or surreptitiously.

In Yugoslavia, where the government was, and is, passionately Communist, there has developed an open revolt against Stalin's brand of Communism, which imposed a pattern of life made in Moscow that grated against the traditional practices and loyalties of the people.

In Germany, there is a steady flight of Germans from the Soviet Zone into Western Germany. They seek to escape the terror to which the people are subjected by their Soviet rulers.

Many prominent officials and sports heroes of the overrun countries, who have been allowed to travel abroad, refuse to return home, and many more have wished to remain abroad but have feared the consequences to their relatives at home.

At meetings of the United Nations, I have often talked secretly and intimately with official representatives from the overrun countries of Central Europe. They tell reliable and circumstantial stories of the rottenness within their countries, of the mounting terror, and of the suspicion and mistrust which exist among the Communist officials as each anticipates the inevitability of recurrent purges and wonders whether he or his opposite number will survive.

There is, of course, another side of the picture. Soviet Communism does provide certain things for certain people, and it would be a misjudgment to assume that everything is evil and that no one is satisfied. Soviet leaders seek to provide for the "masses," like herds of domesticated animals. They take care of them as such. They drive them to a field for pasture. They drive them back to a shelter. They milk them. They provide veterinarians and indoctrination. They give "security" in the same sense that an intelligent dairy farmer gives security to his docile cows.

But there is ample evidence that, in Europe, millions and millions of people are profoundly dissatisfied with the despotic rule of Soviet Communism.

If we turn to China, we find long-standing conditions, aggravated by war, which will make it very difficult for a Communist government to establish a stable order.

The Chinese through their religious and traditional habits of thought have become an individualistic people. The family has been the highest unit of value, and individual loyalty has been to ancestors and descendants. There has been only a little of the broader loyalty to fellow man or to some social or class group or to nation.

The population is in excess of what the resources and distribution facilities can support.

For a great many years now, China has been a land of unrest. It has been infested with local "armies," both those that were official and those that made up the followers of bandits and war lords. Even government armies in China have seldom represented any disciplined group standing for loyalty to country. There is little patriotism in China, and armies have been a means whereby some of the people obtained a better chance of survival than they had as civilians. A soldier seldom got much pay, because most of the pay was taken by the generals; but he did get a uniform and a rifle and a certain license to live off the land.

This background assures that Communism will have a hard time regimenting the Chinese people. Its armies in China have had some success in arousing a sense of social responsibility and in imposing discipline on its supporters. But it would be a miracle if Communism were quickly able to master the underlying sense of separateness; to impose a pattern of conformity upon a people that is individualistic; to produce and distribute the food necessary to allay unrest; and to maintain order where disorder has been chronic.

This will be the more difficult for the Chinese Communist regime because its ally and backer is a country—the Soviet Union—which *takes from* its associates rather than a country like the United States which *gives to* its associates.

The Soviet-Chinese Agreement of February 14, 1950, stipulates, to be sure, that the Soviet Union will, over a five-year period, provide China with goods worth $300,000,000, or $60,000,000 a year. This, however, is insignificant compared to the value of the booty the Soviet Union has taken from the northern areas, particularly Manchuria, which the Soviet Union has looted of its industrial equipment, and the value of Manchurian raw material now subject to Soviet control.

It may be that the Chinese Communists can function with a higher degree of discipline than the Nationalist Government. But the Chinese people will not like or willingly accept the process of being forcibly conformed to the collectivist brand of society that Moscow dictates.

Wherever we look within the areas of Communist conquest, whether we look to the West or to the East—even if we look into the Soviet Union itself—we find conditions of unrest.

It could not be otherwise, given the methods which Soviet Communism employs. It wins its way with extravagant propaganda, so much so that when Communists first take over a government they are often greeted as liberators and as providing the people with new hope. But then it demonstrates the incapacity of despotism to be creative and constructive in new and alien environments.

Dictatorships are arbitrary and inflexible. There is very little delegation of responsibility. When there is any such delegation, the agents are usually too fearful to use it. They know that if they make a mistake they will have to pay a heavy penalty. The disposition is to act only under absolute, written directives from the immediate superior. That gives protection.

I have known two top Soviet diplomats who disappeared into outer, or rather inner, darkness because they exercised a slight discretion and permitted themselves some flexibility. Such occurrences have a paralyzing effect when it comes to building creatively and constructively in a foreign land, where good results depend on resourcefulness and inventiveness and willingness to take a chance.

Three years ago, when talking with a leading diplomat from a Communist country, I remarked that even an idiot could throw a monkey wrench into a complex mechanism. I said that Soviet Communism deserved no medal for demonstrating the ability to wreck the complicated machine that is our modern industrial world. The real test would come when, having destroyed that machine in various countries, Communism tried to construct a machine to take the place of what it had destroyed. That, I forecast, they would find extremely difficult to do. What is happening now shows the reality of such difficulties.

Even today the Communist structure is overextended, over-rigid, and ill founded. It could be shaken if the difficulties that are latent were activated.

"Activation" does not mean armed revolt. The people have no arms, and violent revolt would be futile. Indeed, it would be worse than futile, for it would precipitate massacre. We do not want to do to the captive peoples what the Soviet Union did to the Polish patriots in Warsaw under General Bor. They were incited by the Russians to revolt against the Germans, and the Soviet army stood near by, content to watch their extermination by the Germans, feeling that, in the process, both Nazi Germany and free Poland were being weakened. We have no desire to weaken the Soviet Union at the cost of the lives of those who are our primary concern.

There is, however, a duty to prevent whole peoples from being broken in mind and spirit, which is what Soviet Communism seeks. It is trying to break them, just as it breaks the individual defendants who figure in its purge and spy trials.

We can picture these haggard persons; for example, Cardinal Mindszenty and Robert A. Vogeler in Hungary; the Protestant pastors and Michael T. Shipkov in Bulgaria. We have read the words by which they abjectly confessed to what they could not have done. We see what can happen to minds and spirits when individuals are cut off from all normal contacts, terrorized and exposed to the insistent repetition of falsehood. As Shipkov said, the purpose and the result is "to break you down completely and deprive you of any will power or private thought or self-esteem."

That is what Soviet Communism is trying to do to the captive peoples, *en masse*. It is isolating them from normal contact with what is going on in the world; it terrorizes them and it constantly pounds falsehoods into their consciousness.

The free peoples must try to frustrate this gruesome process. We must, if we can, bring to the captive peoples some ray of hope, some knowledge of the truth. We must, if we can, keep alive in them love of God and of country, faith in human fellowship and belief in the dignity and worth of human personality.

We live in dread of weapons of mass destruction. We should not be concerned only about the mass destruction of bodies. We should equally be concerned about the mass destructions of minds and spirits.

Soviet Communism cannot consolidate its position or extend its sway except as it can monopolize the physical means of access to men's minds and hearts. To break that monopoly is to break the most potent weapon of that despotism.

The task of communication with peoples enslaved by Soviet despotism has become one of tremendous difficulty. The Iron Curtain of Soviet Communism is policed with a thoroughness that shows how weak the Communists feel their internal position to be.

During World War II the militarily advantageous "shuttle" bombing of Germany was discontinued at the request of the Soviet Union, primarily because American fliers brought with them information about the outer world, and magazines that pictured it.

The Soviet Union prevented states such as Poland and Czechoslovakia from sharing in the free grants we were prepared to make under the Marshall Plan because these would have breached the Iron Curtain.

The break with Tito has occurred in part because Tito did not observe strictly the injunction of nonintercourse with the "enemy" West.

Today the satellite countries of Europe and Communist China are deliberately seeking to bring the United States to reduce its diplomatic and consular staffs, and even to break relations, as has happened in Bulgaria, because of Communist fear of even that tiny penetration behind the Iron Curtain.

If the United States is to carry any ideas, any information, any message of good hope, to the subject peoples, it will be necessary to develop specific techniques.

Soviet Communism, as we have seen, has developed both organization and techniques. It has its schools for agitators; it has its radios; it has its influence, open and secret, in the press, radio, and movies of the free world; it has its trained agents and its spies.

We on our side have few ways of getting ideas or information behind the Iron Curtain or finding out what goes on there. We have spent many billions of dollars during the last five years getting ready for a possible war of bombs, planes, and guns; but we have spent little on the war of ideas in which we are deeply engaged and are suffering reverses that cannot be canceled out by any amount of military power.

We are just beginning to wake up to the need. We have the Voice of America. Senator McMahon, on February 2, 1950, said that it should be called the "Whisper of America." It has, however, after a fumbling start, begun to have some influence behind the Iron Curtain—enough to demonstrate the enormous possibilities that exist in getting facts and ideas to people who will otherwise be beaten into a pliant mass by the incessant repetition of Communist propaganda. A new relay station near Salonika, Greece, opened in March, 1950, will extend the possibilities of communication. That is a good development.

In many of our labor unions patriotic leaders have done a magnificent job in eradicating communist elements. They have joined with trade unionists abroad to create the International Confederation of Free Trade Unions and have thus provided an alternative and a challenge to the communist-dominated World Federation of Trade Unions (WFTU).

There is a private organization called the National Committee for Free Europe. It was formed in June, 1949, with the "hearty endorsement" of the State Department to give aid and asylum to leading political exiles from Central Europe. In order to help them maintain contact with their friends at home and keep the flame of freedom burning in the hearts of their compatriots, it is establishing its own broadcasting facilities, "Radio Free Europe."

This organization has been violently denounced by Communist press and radio. They call it "Project X" and attribute it to a plea which I made in a speech in May, 1948.

I hope that the organization will quickly become as formidable, though not as wicked, as Communist propaganda portrays it.

Despite these favorable developments, the United States does not yet have any adequate means of carrying any message to the captive peoples of Europe; and the East is wholly neglected.

No governmental department has adequate authority or resources to fight a world battle to liberate the souls and minds of men. The United States also lacks the needed skills and techniques. This is probably a field where private effort is most effective; but in one way or another ways for enlarged and more incisive action must be found.

The planning of such activities ought to be centered in a high-ranking authority. The military have this in their Joint Chiefs of Staff. Our government's Economic Assistance program is under an administrator (Paul Hoffman) of Cabinet rank. It is just as important to give high authority and strategic direction to the efforts to frustrate the fraudulent propaganda by which Soviet Communism softens up its intended victim, and the terrorism and false propaganda by which it consolidates its hold.

Efforts in the military and economic fields can never achieve full success if we ignore the "cold-war" campaign and permit one country after another to fall to Communist propaganda and terrorism and be consolidated for Communism by those methods. That extension and consolidation is proceeding at a rapid pace, largely made possible by our apathy and our inability to engage effectively in this phase of world struggle to which Soviet Communism gives priority even over considerations of military advantage.

Some may suggest that, if we took even a moral offensive in the "cold war," we should precipitate a shooting war. I believe, on the contrary, that peace depends upon the growing internal difficulties of Soviet Communism and its inability to consolidate its present and prospective areas of conquest.

If war is not now imminent—and available evidence points to that—it is primarily because Soviet leaders have not yet consolidated their present position, have not yet broken the spirit of the captive peoples, have not yet exhausted the possibilities of their "cold-war" offensive, particularly in Asia, and do not yet feel industrially equipped to wage a major war against the United States.

The great danger of war would come if and when Soviet leaders successfully combined Eastern Europe and Asia into a vast political, industrial, and military unity and completed the "encirclement" phase of their strategy. They would then be so strong that they might well plan to finish their conquest by war.

Also, war might come if encirclement of the West proceeded so fast and so uninterruptedly that our people became panicky and felt that they must precipitate a shooting war as the only means of breaking the ever tightening noose. When people begin to feel desperate they are inclined to seize upon any tools lying ready at hand. If we wish to avoid the utter disaster of war, we had better have at hand some good tools for waging a non-shooting war.

Communist encirclement and consolidation need not happen. We need not become so panicky that we look on war as an acceptable solution. Soviet Communism is not irresistible, and it can be checked peacefully if only we create the means of doing so.

In Moscow in 1947, I met all but two of the members of the Politburo at a dinner given by Marshal Stalin at the Kremlin. As I sat and looked upon their faces, I got an impression of tremendous controlled power. They showed the toughness of men who had lived dangerously, and who had survived because, so far, they had killed before being killed. They showed the fanaticism of men who sense that they have a new formula which identifies the general welfare of the world with their own despotic power. They showed the quality of cold calculation which has made the Russians the world's greatest chess players. They showed a sense of unhurriedness which goes with belief that their task is not one of a year, not one of their own lifetime, but, as Stalin put it, one of "an entire historical era," and that "tactics of retreat" are as important as "tactics of advance."

All that is very formidable. But the despotism of Soviet Communism has great weaknesses, such as always go with despotisms. Two observable weaknesses are the underlying distrust and suspicion within the top leadership, and the lack of mobility which comes when there is little delegation of authority, so that no significant decision can be taken until after debate within the Politburo. These are major weaknesses; but they are weaknesses that are fatal only under pressure. If there is no pressure, purges can occur, organizational wounds can be healed at leisure, and the despotism can go on. If there is no pressure, then there is time for the reference back to the Politburo and its deliberation.

The despotism of Soviet Communism needs to be subjected to the pressures which would come if we spread everywhere truth and hope and the conviction that the American people are uncompromisingly dedicated to the cause of human liberty and will not be willing to sacrifice that cause in an effort to make a self-serving "deal" with the despotic masters of the captive peoples.

Under the pressure of faith and hope and peaceful works, the rigid, top-heavy and overextended structure of Communist rule could readily come into a state of collapse.

CHAPTER TWENTY-ONE

OUR SPIRITUAL NEED

Something has gone wrong with our nation, or we should not be in our present plight and mood. It is not like us to be on the defensive and to be fearful. That is new in our history.

The trouble is not material. We are establishing an all-time world record in the production of material things. What we lack is a righteous and dynamic faith. Without it, all else avails us little. The lack cannot be compensated for by politicians, however able; or by diplomats, however astute; or by scientists, however inventive; or by bombs, however powerful.

Once a people comes to feel dependent on material things, unfortunate consequences are inevitable.

At home, our institutions do not attract the spiritual loyalties needed for their defense. There is confusion in men's minds and a corrosion of their souls. That makes our nation vulnerable to such hostile penetration as is illustrated by the spy activities so far revealed. No F.B.I., however efficient, can protect us under those circumstances.

Abroad, our foreign policies can be implemented only by money and goods. These are limited; and because they are limited our policies are limited. Limited policies inevitably are defensive policies, and defensive policies inevitably are losing policies.

Today our military leaders define what they conceive to be strategic areas for military defense—perhaps the "North Atlantic Area" as set forth in the North Atlantic Treaty. We draw a line which, like the Maginot Line, we then fortify as our defense.

Economists and budgetary experts, department heads and the Congress calculate how much we can afford to give away in economic subsidies. The result may be, for example, $5,000,000,000. Then we study to see where it can be spent to the best advantage. and, generally speaking, we spend it within the strategic area which the military have defined.

The result of this planning in military and economic terms is the staking out of a citadel, which we try to fortify and to provision. We have no affirmative policies beyond, for we cannot go further with material things. Already we are straining our material resources to the limit, and we cannot greatly expand the scope of our policies if that means expanding our material expenditures. Regional policies as expressed in the Rio Pact, the North Atlantic Pact, and the Truman Doctrine for Greece and Turkey, suggest that the Americas, Western Europe, and the Mediterranean mark the limits of our concern, because they mark the limits of our immediate military and economic interests. We seem to have lost the spirit which animated Lincoln when he said of our Declaration of Independence that it gave "liberty, not alone to the people of this country, but hope for the world for all future time. It was that which gave promise that in due time the weights should be lifted from the shoulders of all men."

Up to the present, the American people have always had those qualities of the spirit that can be projected far beyond the limited reach of our material grasp. Those are the qualities that have made us great.

Our nation was founded as an experiment in human liberty. Its institutions reflected the belief of our founders that men had their origin and destiny in God; that they were endowed by Him with inalienable rights and had duties prescribed by moral law, and that human institutions ought primarily to help men develop their God-given possibilities. We believed that if we built on that spiritual foundation we should be showing men everywhere the way to a better and more abundant life.

We realized that vision. There developed here an area of spiritual, intellectual, and economic vigor the like of which the world had never seen. It was no exclusive preserve; indeed, world mission was a central theme. Millions were welcomed from other lands, to share equally the opportunities of the founders and their heirs. We put our experiment on public exhibition so that all might see and follow if they would. Through missionary activities and the establishment of schools and colleges, American ideals were carried throughout the world. We gave aid and comfort to those elsewhere who sought to follow in our way and to develop societies of greater human freedom.

That made it easy to conduct the foreign policy of the United States. In those days influence and opportunity abroad and security at home came naturally as by-products of what our people stood for in the world. Americans were welcomed everywhere because, it was judged, they were working in a common human cause. Our economic opportunities were not circumscribed by fears and jealousies such as penned in many others. We were the least militarized of any Western nation, yet, for a century, we were not endangered. No foreign ruler could have brought his people to try to destroy the "great American experiment" which they admired and the spiritual fruits of which they shared.

These conditions prevailed for one hundred years and more. Then, as our material power waxed, our spiritual power seemed to wane. We appeared to be less concerned with conducting a great experiment for the benefit of mankind and to be more concerned with piling up for ourselves material advantages. Our vision seemed to contract, and our sense of mission to lessen. Others began to think of us more as a possible source of money and material things and less as a source of inspiration and of guidance.

We have had to meet the severest test that can come to a people, the test of prosperity.

It was said by Jesus that material things will be added unto those who seek first the Kingdom of God and His righteousness. But when that happens, then comes the great trial. For, as Jesus warned, those material things can readily become the rust that corrodes men's souls.

Thus there is a familiar pattern. Men who feel a sense of duty to some higher Being strive here to do His will. Because of their

faith, they have power and virtue and simple wisdom. They build
not only for the day, but for the morrow; not merely for themselves, but for mankind. A society so founded will, when nature
favors, produce wealth and luxury for many. When those by-
products come, they seem so good that they become promoted to
be the all-sufficient end. Men are drawn away from long-range
creative effort. They struggle to get and to hold material things.

With that change comes ever growing danger. Americans had
security in the only way in which security can be assured, namely,
as a by-product of great endeavor. When our endeavor lagged and
we began to seek security as an end in itself, it more and more
eluded us. It will always be that way. However rich we are,
security cannot be bought at any money price. Five billions, or
fifty billions, is not enough. Security and peace are not purchas-
able commodities. The Roman emperors in their declining days
tried to buy peace, and the effort only whetted the appetites of
those who sought to destroy them.

While our influence and security have been declining, those of
Soviet Communism have been rising. That is not primarily due
to the fact that Russia as a nation has great power, although the
Red Army is a background threat. It is rather due to the fact
that Soviet Communism has a creed, a creed of world-wide im-
port. It is a creed in which the hard core of Party members believe fanatically, and which they are spreading with missionary
zeal throughout the world.

There is no nook or cranny in all the world into which Communist influence does not penetrate. When the Politburo is making policies it does not say that there is no use having a policy for
Guatemala or the Union of South Africa or the United States of
Indonesia because they are too far away and cannot be reached
either by the Red Army or by economic subsidy. Neither of these
devices is the primary reliance of Soviet Communists in policy-
making. They can and do implement policies with the portrayal
of a "great Soviet Communist experiment" with which, during
this century, they are catching the imagination of the people of
the world, just as we did in the nineteenth century with our "great
American experiment."

We know that that Communistic portrayal is a fraud and a delusion. We know that Soviet Communists will not open their experiment at home to the test of free and impartial inspection. We know that those who are finally caught by the false lure of that portrayal quickly learn how different is the reality. The spider spins a beautiful web which shimmers in the sunlight, and he invites the fly into his parlor. Communist propaganda, like the spider's web, does attract. Once it has caught the people, despotism sucks them spiritually dry. But, as a prospect, Communism does have an appeal to the "masses" everywhere in Asia, in the islands of the Pacific, in South America, in Africa, and even in Western Europe.

The prestige of Soviet Communism in the world has been greatly increased by the fact that even in the West the governments have adopted what, at first glance, seem to be basic parts of Soviet Communist doctrine.

Stalin said, "The strength and vitality of Marxism-Leninism lies in the fact that it does base its practical activity on the needs of the development of the material life of society" (p. 602).

Many non-Communist countries of the world, including indeed many "Christian" nations of the West, now seem to put primary emphasis upon developing "the material life of society" and to subordinate the spiritual development of the individual. The Communists cite that to prove that even the Western societies have had to adopt the materialistic thesis of Communism. The leaders in the West do not make any convincing denials, and the prestige of Soviet Communism in the world is greatly increased.

The difficulty is that we, ourselves, are unclear as to our faith and the relationship of that faith to our practices.

We can talk eloquently about liberty and freedom, and about human rights and fundamental freedoms, and about the dignity and worth of the human personality; but most of our vocabulary derives from a period when our own society was individualistic. Consequently, it has little meaning to those who live under conditions where individualism means premature death.

Also, we can talk eloquently about the material successes we have achieved, about the marvels of mass production, and about the number of automobiles, radios, and telephones owned by our people. That materialistic emphasis makes some feel that we are spiritually bankrupt. It makes others envious and more disposed to accept Communist glorification of "mass" effort to "develop the material life of society."

We are in a dilemma, and it is a grave dilemma. Because we have not resolved it, our spiritual influence in the world has waned, and we are tied down to the area that we can reach and influence by material things—guns and goods. That is why it is possible for our encirclement to proceed apace.

We cannot successfully combat Soviet Communism in the world and frustrate its methods of fraud, terrorism, and violence unless we have a faith with spiritual appeal that translates itself into practices which, in our modern, complex society, get rid of the sordid, degrading conditions of life in which the spirit cannot grow.

We are still unsure in our own minds where to look for solid ground between individualism and materialism. Our faith lacks the power and clear definition that would make it contagious in the world.

The religious faith of our founders emphasized individualism because the original environment called for personal resourcefulness and pioneering. Individual effort was the best way to get the satisfaction which comes from a sense of being creative. Also, individual creativeness was usually the means whereby society as a whole was most enriched.

But extreme individualism is no integral part of our religious heritage. The Jewish and Christian faiths have at all times emphasized the duty of man to his fellows; and that duty is fundamental in our religious faith. The moral law, the law of the Prophets, is sublimely compressed into the two injunctions "Thou shalt love the Lord thy God," and "Thou shalt love thy neighbor as thyself."

There is an essential difference between a spiritual society and a materialistic society. The difference is not that the spiritual society is purely individualistic while the materialistic society is purely collectivist. It is not that the free society ignores material welfare while the materialistic society makes material welfare primary. The difference is that the spiritual society seeks material welfare by relying on and developing the individual's sense of duty to his fellow man and his willingness to exercise self-control and self-restraint in the discharge of that duty. The materialistic, irreligious society, which denies the existence of God or of a moral law, cannot depend upon love of God and love of neighbor. It must depend on governmental compulsion rather than on voluntary controls.

We have failed lamentably to see that we can get social justice without practising atheism and materialism. It depends upon the willingness of the individual voluntarily to accept and discharge social obligations to his fellow man.

Because we have not seen that, many of our people have lost faith in a society of freedom. As a nation, although still religious, we have lost the connection between our religious faith and our practices. We keep religion and practices in separate compartments. We no longer see that our faith is relevant to modern conditions.

Once the connection between faith and works is broken, we can no longer generate a spiritual power that will flow throughout the world. The "conduct and example" of which our founders wrote are no longer a beacon light to those who live in the deep shadows cast by a mighty despotism. We have no message to send to the captive peoples to keep their hope and faith alive.

We must change all that. We can, and must, reject totally the Marxian thesis that material things are primary and spiritual things only secondary. Slavery and despotism, even if they seem expedient, can never be right. We must not be afraid to recapture faith in the primacy of human liberty and freedom, and to hold to the religious view that man is destined by God to be more than a material producer, and that his chief end is something more than physical security. We must believe that men everywhere ought to be released from the spiritual, intellectual, economic, and political strait jackets into which they are increasingly being put on the theory that this will improve the material welfare of the social group to which they belong.

Equally, we must clearly see that a society of freedom is not a society of uncoordinated self-seeking individuals. It is a society that is coordinated. But the bonds are primarily the bonds of fellowship which derive from belief that men are destined to be brothers through the Fatherhood of God, that each man is his brother's keeper, and that we should love our neighbors as ourselves.

That belief translates itself into a society of individuals who love God and their fellow man, and who fear only God and not any man; who work hard as a matter of duty and self-satisfaction, not compulsion; who gain personal and family security primarily through ability and willingness voluntarily to earn and save; who are self-reliant, resourceful, and adaptable to changing conditions, and for whom life is not merely physical growth and enjoyment, but intellectual and spiritual development. It also translates itself into public organizations, through which men willingly cooperate, at national and local levels, to do what they cannot well do otherwise.

But governmental authority at all times and places is limited by the principle that governmental action expresses, but does not replace, voluntary acceptance of social responsibility. Government action must stop short of seeming to shift social responsibility from the individual to the government.

That limitation on governmental power makes some imperfections inevitable. The existence of imperfections does not prove that the system is wrong, and it need not make us feel ashamed or defeated. In a sense, the existence of flaws proves that the system is right. Human nature at best is imperfect, and any system which is based on human nature is bound to have defects. The only system that is theoretically flawless is one of absolute despotism, "unlimited power, based on force and not on law" (Stalin, p. 129). Then, in theory, all disharmonies, all imperfections can be removed, all grit can quickly be cleaned out, and perfect mechanical harmony can result. However, the attempt to do that creates moral enormities. That is always the case when men indulge in the conceit that they can do better than God.

Our greatest need is to regain confidence in our spiritual heritage. Religious belief in the moral nature and possibilities of man is, and must be, relevant to every kind of society, throughout the ages past and those to come. It is relevant to the complex conditions of modern society. We need to see that, if we are to combat successfully the methods and practices of a materialistic belief.

There is no use having more and louder Voices of America unless we have something to say that is more persuasive than anything yet said.

To find that message is, above all, a task for the spiritual leaders of our nation. In finding it they can contribute, and contribute decisively, to the peaceful frustration of the evil methods and designs of Soviet Communism.

Many preachers and educators bemoan the fact that scientific knowledge has greatly advanced man's capacity to do harm. We must not believe that new knowledge is, of itself, something to be shunned. Great material power is dangerous in an age of materialism. It is not dangerous in an age of spiritualism. New scientific knowledge is dangerous today because it comes at a time when spiritual leadership has failed to make clear the connection between belief and practice. It is more important to advance the spiritual clock than to try to stop or set back the scientific clock.

President Wilson, in an article written a few weeks before he died, reviewed the threat of the revolutionary doctrines and practices of Communism. He concluded:

The sum of the whole matter is this, that our civilization cannot survive materially unless it be redeemed spiritually. . . . Here is the final challenge to our churches, to our political organizations, and to our capitalists—to everyone who fears God or loves his country.

CHAPTER TWENTY-TWO

CONCLUSION

The world has never known sustained peace, and certainly there is no place now for easy optimism. Also, there is no place now for a panicky assumption that war has become inevitable. There is good reason to believe that peace can be preserved if the American people, in fellowship with other free peoples, make positive and well directed efforts to frustrate Soviet Communist methods of fraud, terrorism, and violence. To say that is not to whistle in the dark. We possess, today, assets for peace which no generation has ever had before. All the efforts, all the sufferings, of past generations have not gone for nought. They place us nearer to the goal of peace.

(1) There is a world-wide moral condemnation of war such as never existed before. Today it seems almost unbelievable that only thirty years ago, after the First World War, there developed a world-wide sentiment that war was wrong, and that it ought not to be used as an instrument of national policy. Throughout the centuries that preceded, war had always been looked upon as a lawful international process. Even the Hague Peace Conferences of 1899 and 1907 did not attempt to end war. Rather, they were designed to make war less cruel and more tolerable.

Now, after World War II, the moral condemnation of war has become so well-nigh universal and so intense that it has to be reckoned with as never before.

There is no longer any glorification of war, and the religious conception of a "just war" is undergoing modification now that wars carry with them mass and indiscriminate destruction of non-belligerents.

When the leaders of the great powers speak at the Town Meeting of the World, each tries to persuade the immediate audience and the world that he is more peace-loving than the others. Soviet leaders conduct "peace offensives" in the United Nations and peace propaganda throughout the world. They advocate class war; but, at least publicly, they decry national war.

In the United States there is a public sentiment which, if maintained, will be a fierce obstacle against any temptation to launch a so-called "preventive war" or deliberately to prod or trick potential enemies into acts which could plausibly be made a pretext for war. Some may feel that our nation is better equipped to win a shooting national war than to win a class war. Even so, public opinion exercises a powerful and, we can believe, a conclusive restraint against any who might feel that the choices are all so bad that war may be relatively tolerable.

We belong to a generation that has already subjected countless human beings to incredible horror, and we know that millions were sustained in their agony by the thought that the very intensity of their suffering would make a total of suffering so immense as to compel those who survived to find a way to live in peace. We may not yet have found that way in any mechanical sense; but at least we and others are moved as never before to reject war as a means for achieving good ends.

(2) We have, in the United Nations, a world organization for mobilizing the moral judgment of the world, and for focusing that judgment upon any potential aggressor. We cannot foresee with certainty the future of the United Nations; but we can know that, even as it is, if it does not shrink in stature, it is a powerful instrument for peace.

It is much more powerful than the League of Nations that collapsed prior to World War II. Today every nation that has a substantial military establishment is a member of the United Nations. The United States was never a member of the League of Nations. The Soviet Union and Germany were members only briefly; and by the end of 1939 the United States, the Soviet Union, Germany, Japan, and Italy, all were outside it. There is now an organization for peace, which, inadequate though it is, is far more potent than any that has heretofore existed.

(3) There is fear of war as never before. Fear is a bad emotion if it paralyzes creative action. Also, it is bad if it leads to panic. When people on a boat rush in panic first to one side, then the other, they overturn the boat. We do not want that kind of fear. There is, however, a fear that is salutary. We can profitably stand in awe of the mysterious forces of nature God has given for our good, which war would misuse for unfathomable evil.

(4) There is greater recognition than ever before that peace is not a static and stagnant condition of the world, but can be, and should be, a condition of selective change. In the past, war was partly a consequence of the fact that change was inevitable, and that, internationally, there were no means of change except war. That is why, for so long, war was a lawful form of national action.

Since the fighting stopped at the end of World War II, many momentous changes have occurred peacefully. We have recorded some of them. In the face of this record, no nation can fairly claim that only by war can it get a greater and deserved opportunity in the world. Never in history has there been so clear a recognition of the fact that the possibility of peaceful change is a fundamental prerequisite to peace.

(5) We see the danger as never before. Usually in the past, great wars came with surprising quickness which caught people unawares. We now see the danger, and we have been seeing it for some time. It is not pleasant to see danger. Some people would prefer to shut their eyes to it, even at the cost of being taken unawares. That, however, is not conducive to peace.

There always has been danger of war, and probably for the next generation at least there will continue to be danger of war. If at any time in the near future it seems that the danger of war has passed, that will be a period of greatest peril. Then we may be tempted to relax and get careless and disarm, materially and morally. By so doing, we should expose ourselves to a sudden attack, which is most likely to come at such a time.

If we are to live in peril, it is far safer, although not pleasant, to see the peril. Then there is a better chance that it will be avoided.

(6) The American people now see, as never before, their responsibility in the world. That is important, because events press leadership into our hands.

After World War I the American people, who even then possessed preponderant power in the world, turned soft, sentimental, and undisciplined. We abandoned what George Washington called "a respectable defensive posture," not as a matter of principle or considered policy but because we found that posture uncomfortable. We adopted an attitude of illusory aloofness. We refused to join the League of Nations, and we sought to enclose our economy and be an oasis of prosperity in a world of misery. We were without vision, and did not see that the revolutionary theories of Marx had found powerful embodiment in Russia, and that misery and despair in Germany were breeding Nazism. Many were fascinated by the beautiful prospect that could be painted with words, such as those in the Kellogg-Briand Pact, and thought that great results could be accomplished quickly, without hard work.

The American people have behaved differently since World War II. We have not relapsed into a state of supineness. We are maintaining a powerful military establishment, even though that involves substantial sacrifices. We have achieved a new level of peacetime productivity and have shown a willingness to share it with others. Since hostilities ended, we have made available to other countries about $30,000,000,000, through grants or loans, and have thereby provided many nations with the economic margin for the survival of their people. In the ten years up to 1950, private voluntary contributions to those abroad amounted to more than $1,100,000,000.

The United States has taken leadership in creating a world organization, and has played an active part in that organization. We have joined in two major collective security organizations within the framework of the United Nations Charter, and in each we have made some surrender of our sovereignty in the interest of collective self-defense.

All in all, the American people have gone far to correct deficiencies that contributed to World War II. Our national leadership has shared in making some major policies for peace, and the American people have backed them courageously and at personal sacrifice. These policies are inadequate. They should be supplemented and developed; but what is needed is well within the capacity of those who have already done so much.

There may come a time in the life of a people when their work of creation ends. That hour has not struck for us. We are still vital and capable of great endeavor. Our youth are spirited, not soft or fearful. Our religious heritage and our national tradition are not forgotten.

If our efforts are still inadequate, it is because we have not seen clearly the challenge and its nature. As that is more clearly revealed, we shall surely respond. And as we act under the guidance of a righteous faith, that faith will grow until it brings us into the world-wide fellowship of all men everywhere who are embarked on the great adventure of building peacefully a world of human liberty and justice.

INDEX

INDEX